Exploring Megalithic Europe

Exploring Megalithic Europe

Amazing Sites to See for Yourself

Julian Heath

ROWMAN & LITTLEFIELD
Lanham · Boulder · New York · London

Published by Rowman & Littlefield
An imprint of The Rowman & Littlefield Publishing Group, Inc.
4501 Forbes Boulevard, Suite 200, Lanham, Maryland 20706
www.rowman.com

6 Tinworth Street, London SE11 5AL, United Kingdom

British Library Cataloguing in Publication Information Available

Library of Congress Cataloging-in-Publication Data

Names: Heath, Julian, 1969– author.
Title: Exploring megalithic Europe : amazing sites to see for yourself /
  Julian Heath.
Description: Lanham : Rowman & Littlefield, 2019. | Includes
  bibliographical references and index. | Summary: "From the Mediterranean
  to the colder climes of Scandinavia, this book takes readers on a
  journey through Europe, examining its diverse range of megalithic
  monuments, also looking at what insights these remarkable structures may
  provide into the ancient communities who were responsible for their
  construction"— Provided by publisher.
Identifiers: LCCN 2019013551 (print) | LCCN 2019980823 (ebook) | ISBN
  9781538120910 (cloth) | ISBN 9781538120927 (ebook)
Subjects: LCSH: Megalithic monuments—Europe—Guidebooks. |
  Europe—Antiquities—Guidebooks. | Europe—Description and travel.
Classification: LCC GN803 .H376 2019 (print) | LCC GN803 (ebook) | DDC
  936—dc23
LC record available at https://lccn.loc.gov/2019013551
LC ebook record available at https://lccn.loc.gov/2019980823

♾™ The paper used in this publication meets the minimum requirements of American
National Standard for Information Sciences—Permanence of Paper for Printed Library
Materials, ANSI/NISO Z39.48-1992.

For my fellow "Renegades"—Jim, Kev and Tom
(beware of Sergeant Reeves!), and Rachel (you had to wait
a long time, but you can stop drumming your fingers now).

7.3   Standing stones in the Outer Circle, Avebury   98

7.4   The enigmatic Silbury Hill   101

7.5   Stonehenge   106

7.6   Bluestone outcrops on Carn Menyn   108

7.7   Bedd Arthur bluestone oval, with Carn Menyn seen in the distance   110

7.8   Bluestone pillar and Carn Menyn (the bluestone was brought down from Carn Menyn by an RAF Chinook helicopter)   112

8.1   The "false" entrance at Belas Knap   116

8.2   The megalithic facade at West Kennet   117

8.3   Entrance at Wayland's Smithy   120

8.4   Kit's Coty House   123

8.5   Entrance at La Hogue Bie   125

8.6   Interior of Le Dèhus   127

8.7   A face from the past: "Le Gardien de Tombeau"   127

8.8   The Câtel statue menhir   129

9.1   The author and "Oscar" at Carreg Coetan Arthur portal dolmen, Pembrokeshire   132

9.2   The Dyffryn Ardudwy burial chambers and cairn   133

9.3   Pentre Ifan, with Carn Ingli seen on the horizon   134

9.4   Bach Wen portal dolmen, with Gyrn Goch rising dramatically behind the monument   134

9.5   Entrance at Bryn Celli Ddu   140

9.6   The Bryn Celli Ddu "pattern" stone   142

9.7   Decorated megalithic upright at Barclodiad y Gawres   144

10.1   The spectacular but controversial mound of Newgrange   148

10.2   Early 1900s photograph of the entrance and decorated curbstone at Newgrange   149

10.3   Sketch of plan and cross section of Newgrange from *Wakeman's Handbook of Irish Antiquities*, 1903   150

10.4   Aerial view of Knowth and its "satellite" tombs   153

10.5   Passage tomb at Loughcrew   154

10.6   Miosgán Meabha (Maeve's Heap) on the summit of Knocknarea   156

10.7   The Altar wedge tomb and the Milky Way   160

10.8   Sunset at Poulnabrone portal dolmen   162

11.1   Maeshowe in winter   166

11.2   Cross sections of Maeshowe's passage and chamber   167

11.3   Interior of Midhowe stalled cairn   171

11.4   Camster Long cairn and entrances   172

11.5   The megalithic facade at Cairnholy I   174

11.6   Cairnholy II   175

11.7   The northeastern passage grave at Balnuaran of Clava   179

12.1   The Gollenstein menhir   182

12.2   The Spellenstein menhir   183

12.3   The Hüven *hünengrab*   185

12.4   The Visbek "Bridegroom"   186

12.5   The Züschen *Steinkiste*   187

12.6   *Hunebed* D18 at Rolde, with *hunebed* D17 visible in the background   188

12.7   The Schimmer Es *hunebed*   189

12.8   Aerial view of the Borger *hunebed*   190

13.1   The Poskær Stenhus round dolmen   192

13.2   The Hulbjerg passage grave   193

13.3   Klekkende Høj passage grave   194

13.4   The larger of the Tustrup passage graves   195

13.5   The remains of "Ragnvald's Grave"   197

13.6   Ales Stenar   198

Preface

*W*hile I was an undergraduate at the University of Liverpool (rather a long time ago now!), I had the great privilege of being involved in excavating one of the most impressive megalithic monuments in Europe: the Prissé-la-Charrière long mound in western France. It was a truly memorable experience being able to work on this huge prehistoric tomb (100 meters long, about 17 meters wide, and 4 meters high), with its megalithic burial chambers containing the bones of people who died some six thousand years ago during the Neolithic or "New Stone Age." Working on the excavation of the Prissé-la-Charrière long mound sparked my enduring fascination with Europe's megalithic monuments and the shadowy prehistoric people who constructed these compelling structures.

Exploring Megalithic Europe is aimed at an interested general readership and sets out to explore the "megalithic" monuments built in many parts of Europe by a diverse range of prehistoric communities over a period lasting several thousand years ("megalithic" comes from the ancient Greek *megas*, "great," and *lithos*, "stone"). The following pages will examine the architectural and archaeological evidence found at these remarkable ancient structures to see what light it may shed on the long-dead prehistoric communities responsible for their construction.

Anyone setting out to write an accessible account of the European megalithic phenomenon faces the fact that huge numbers of megaliths survive in the diverse landscapes of Europe, and he or she must therefore be selective about which monuments to include and which to exclude, as it would be well-nigh impossible to cover all of them (in any case, a comprehensive account of Europe's megaliths, even if it could even be achieved, would run the risk of becoming rather tiresome and causing "megalithic fatigue" in readers). In *Exploring Megalithic Europe*, then, we are going to investigate not only the more famous and spectacular megaliths found in many parts of Europe but also some examples that have been rather overlooked in favor of megalithic heavyweights such as the world-famous Stonehenge or the equally renowned monuments of Brittany.

After an introduction to Europe's megalithic monuments, we move on to the region that many scholars believe was the birthplace of the European megalithic phenomenon—Brittany, in northwestern France. Brittany contains an abundant and amazing collection of megaliths that are unrivaled elsewhere in any other part of Europe, and it would be an excellent first port of call for anyone wishing to experience these monuments face-to-face. Chapter 3 examines notable megalithic tombs found in other parts of France, also looking at tombs and other megaliths in Switzerland and mainland Italy. Chapter 4 takes us to the Iberian Peninsula; as will be seen, both Portugal and Spain are richly endowed with megalithic monuments, with some truly outstanding examples found in both countries. Some archaeologists are also of the opinion that it was in Portugal, not Brittany, that megalith building in Europe was born. In chapter 5, we head to the central Mediterranean and the Maltese archipelago to explore the magnificent megalithic temple complexes found on the islands of Malta and Gozo. The lesser-known but still impressive monuments that were built by the prehistoric communities on the Mediterranean islands of Sardinia, Menorca, and Corsica will also be investigated in this chapter. Chapter 6 is concerned with the stone circles of Britain and Ireland, with these rings of stone perhaps the most enigmatic of all Europe's megalithic monuments. Next, we travel to the county of Wiltshire in southern England to investigate two of the finest monuments of Europe's megalith builders: Stonehenge and Avebury. In chapters 8–11, the famous megalithic tombs of England, Wales, Ireland, and Scotland are examined along with some that are not so well known. In the concluding two chapters, we head north to Germany, Holland, and Scandinavia, which are also home to some superb tombs and other fine megalithic monuments. *Exploring Megalithic Europe* concludes with a list of websites that are worth investigating by those readers who want to delve more deeply into the world of Europe's megalith builders.

Finally, it is hoped that readers will be inspired to visit some of the megalithic monuments of Europe. If so, there are, of course, megalithic "celebrities," such as the iconic Stonehenge, the remarkable stone rows of Carnac in Brittany, and the mighty megalithic tomb of Newgrange in southern Ireland, which are a prerequisite for the budding megalith explorer. However, readers will also come across many other superb megaliths in the following pages. Like their more famous counterparts, these monuments have allowed us to catch brief glimpses of the lives and beliefs of their builders and provide a deeply fascinating link to Europe's prehistoric past.

Acknowledgments

*F*irst, I would like thanks Charles Harmon, my editor at Rowman & Littlefield, who provided guidance and much-needed encouragement, helping me to finish what was not an easy book to write; thanks also go the rest of the team at Rowman & Littlefield who worked on the preparation and publication of *Exploring Megalithic Europe*. In addition, I would like to thank the many individuals who have kindly provided me with, or allowed me to use, photographs of various megalithic monuments. They are too numerous to mention, but your contributions are greatly appreciated. Finally, thanks and love to Pamela "Monkey Trousers" Norman for her support and for putting up with my frequent disappearances into the office while I was writing this book.

An Introduction to Megalithic Europe

> Of all prehistoric remains yet discovered, none seem to fascinate people more than the spectacular megalithic remains of Western Europe. These huge, rough-hewn stone monuments of the past loom like gray icebergs out of the ground and incite passionate discussions about why they were erected and what they could possibly mean.
>
> —Brian Hayden, *Shamans, Sorcerers, and Saints: A Prehistory of Religion*, 219

It is hardly surprising that the megalithic monuments found in their thousands across the diverse landscapes of Europe, from Mediterranean islands to Scandinavia, are a great source of fascination, as they are enigmatic, dramatic, and awe-inspiring structures. Exciting academic and popular imaginations alike, the megaliths are probably the most studied and debated aspect of European prehistory. Although these impressive structures continue to be a source of much debate among archaeologists, it is generally agreed that they were ritual and ceremonial monuments that played a key role in the religious lives of the widespread prehistoric communities that constructed them.

The evidence found at megalithic monuments often speaks of a cult of the dead or of "ancestors" among the megalith builders and indicates that the sun and moon were worshipped as major deities, with the landscape also viewed as an "otherworld" inhabited by supernatural forces. This evidence also suggests that certain bright stars were objects of religious veneration for at least some of Europe's megalith builders. Numerous ethnographic accounts of nonstate, or "primitive," tribal cultures, whose ways of life were like those of Europe's megalith builders, have documented religious beliefs such as these, with these accounts also hinting at the complexity of the "megalithic pantheon."

For example, the Chumash of California had a ranked hierarchy of sky beings, with the sun coming first and "believed to be an aged widower living in a quartz crystal house, who carried a blazing torch on his daily journey across the sky."[1] After the sun came the moon, a female deity "who controlled human health and the menstrual cycle of women."[2] The Chumash also viewed many stars as important sky beings; for instance, the evening star was a feared deity who reigned as chief of the underworld. In regard to how nonstate societies viewed the landscape around them, it has been noted that "many groups of native North Americans . . . view mountains as highly symbolic and sacred locales; they are part of creation myths and stories and are key places in the ceremonial use of the landscape."[3] Groups such as the Lakota, Cheyenne, and Arapaho, for instance, have long considered the Black Hills mountain range of South Dakota, Wyoming, and Montana sacred, with peaks such as Bear Butte and the famous Devil's Tower associated with human and animal spirits, as well as mythical heroes such as Falling Star, a man who was half human and half star. In the mythology of the Aboriginal peoples of Arnhem Land, the landscape was formed by ancestral beings such as the Rainbow Serpent or Gulinji, the flying-fox man.

Studies of nonstate or "traditional" societies also indicate that it was not just hills and mountains that were viewed as important mythological and sacred places by Europe's megalith builders. Franz Boas (one of the founding fathers of American anthropology) remarked that for the Tsimshian people of America's northwest coast, "all nature, the heavenly bodies, rocks and islands, waterfalls, animals, and plants are beings of supernatural power whom a man can approach with prayer, whose help he can ask, and to whom he may express his thanks."[4] Similarly, it has been remarked that "pre-modern societies do not accept the sharp differences between matter and soul but see the whole world as an orchestra of living entities. Sky, clouds, landscapes, rivers, rocks and trees are experienced as animate entities, equipped with mental capacities which are more or less similar to those of humans and ghosts."[5]

Archaeologists have also realized that even though convenient building material lay nearby, Europe's megalithic builders would often quarry stone from sources that were miles from the structures into which it was incorporated. This decision shows that practical considerations did not always determine the choice of building materials for many megalithic monuments, suggesting that stone was quarried from sacred parts of the landscape believed to be inhabited by spirits and deities. By taking stone from these places, the megalith builders may have believed that they were appropriating some of the supernatural power associated with them.

Figure 1.1.   The Kerloas menhir, Brittany, France (image courtesy of Gerald Haubold, CC BY-SA 3.0).

THE MEGALITH BUILDERS AND THEIR MONUMENTS

The megalithic monuments of Europe broadly date from ca. 5000 to 1000 BCE, a lengthy time span that encompasses three hugely important periods in European prehistory: the Neolithic and the succeeding Copper and Bronze Ages. The Neolithic is surely the most significant of these three periods, as it was during this time that a truly profound change took place in prehistoric Europe, with farming replacing the hunter-gatherer lifestyle that people had been following for many thousands of years in the preceding Mesolithic (Middle Stone Age) and Paleolithic (Old Stone Age). Instead of seeking out food resources in the wild, and often following a semi-nomadic existence as a result, people now began settling down in permanent farming settlements, with life revolving around domesticated crops and animals. Many novel types of material culture also emerged during the Neolithic, although it is the polished stone axes and pottery made by Europe's first farming communities that are often seen as the defining objects of this time. The great significance of the marked shift in prehistoric lifestyle, which took place during the Neolithic, or New Stone Age, cannot be underestimated: "The Neolithic was a period of momentous change in which can be seen the birth of our modern world. It marks the moment when humans took control of the planet (not necessarily for the good), rather than simply existing upon it."[6] Ultimately, the Neolithic gave rise to the incredibly complex and technologically sophisticated societies in which many of us live today, societies that are socially stratified, overpopulated, and not infrequently violent.[7]

The Copper Age (also known as the "Chalcolithic") marks the time when prehistoric communities in Europe discovered the secrets of metalworking, learning how to extract and turn copper ore into objects such as simple, axes, daggers, and personal ornaments.[8] It seems likely that the first metalsmiths must have been viewed as individuals with "magical" powers by those people who had knowledge of the technological processes involved in the extraction of metal ore and its subsequent transformation into actual objects.

In the Bronze Age, prehistoric smiths realized that by alloying tin with copper, they could produce objects that were made from a much more durable material: bronze. Scholars often view the Bronze Age as the time when the first "arms race" took place, and, indeed, huge amounts of weaponry (e.g., swords and spearheads) have been recovered from various sites across Europe.

Megalithic Monument Types

Although countless megalithic monuments have undoubtedly been destroyed in Europe by unscrupulous landowners or overzealous Christians intent on demolishing pagan sites, it has been estimated that approximately five hun-

Figure 1.2.   Pentre Ifan portal dolmen, Pembrokeshire, Wales (image, author).

dred thousand examples still survive. At first sight, the variety of megalithic monument types in Europe is rather bewildering, but there are basically five main types: single standing stones, or "menhirs" ("long stones"); stone circles/enclosures; megalithic tombs featuring one or more burial chambers; stone rows or alignments; and megalithic "temples." Rock-cut tombs are also seen as a part of the wider megalithic phenomenon in Europe, with these generally found in the Mediterranean regions and often used for collective burial like their counterparts above ground.

Many of the megalithic tombs in Europe have burial chambers that are accessed by passages of varying length under covering mounds and are therefore unsurprisingly known as passage tombs or graves. The passages at these fascinating monuments "may have been as much for the comings and goings of the spirits who inhabited these constructions as for human suppliants."[9] Often the catch-all term "dolmen" ("stone table") is also used for megalithic tombs, which can be a little confusing, as dolmens are a distinctive and early type of Neolithic megalithic tomb consisting of a single burial chamber with or without a covering mound.

Although often containing human remains and often representing the collective burial of hundreds of people over several generations, these tombs would have been much more than just simply places where the dead were interred:

Figure 1.3. Hulehøj passage grave, Island of Bøgo, Denmark (image courtesy of Sand-piper, CC public domain).

"These monuments were at the center of complex ritual practices including the ritual deposition of both human remains and other artifacts and were almost certainly involved in the [establishment] of complex relationships between living individuals and groups, spiritual beings, ancestors and the world or cosmos."[10]

Indeed, many archaeologists now question the idea that the primary purpose of megalithic tombs was burial. However, "tomb" remains a convenient label for these monuments, given that the dead were often placed in them. The smaller megalithic tombs can probably be seen in a similar light to the rural parish churches of medieval Europe, with the larger and more spectacular examples functioning as megalithic "cathedrals" that served a wider area and group of people.

We might also like to think that the builders of Europe's megalithic monuments lived in egalitarian societies with little or no social ranking, but this arrangement seems unlikely. As American anthropologist Brian Hayden has said, "It seems fairly evident that megalithic society was organized in hierarchical fashion with major power vested in big men or chiefs and their supporting elites. The sheer size of the megalithic constructions and all that they imply concerning control over labor attests to this."[11]

This argument could not be applied to all of Europe's megalithic monuments, as some are relatively modest in size. However, some of the examples included in this book do strongly suggest that there were powerful leaders and tribes who were able to command and control the hundreds, if not thousands, of people that must have been required for their construction.

Ethnographic evidence lends support to the idea that many of Europe's megalithic monuments were probably built for elite or "special" members of society. For example, in the Torajan highlands of the island of Sulawesi (eastern Indonesia), standing stones are still erected to commemorate the dead; the larger the standing stone, the greater the wealth and power of the family that erected it. Likewise, in the Kodi district on the island of Sumba (also in eastern Indonesia), there is a living tradition of constructing elaborate megalithic tombs. These tombs "provide the most enduring and impressive symbols of individual importance and renown [representing] both the height of personal achievement and the ability to summon a vast amount of communal labor."[12]

Until the mid-twentieth century, standing stones were also erected in remote parts of the Borneo highlands, as recorded by intrepid anthropologists Tom Harrisson and Stanley O'Connor: "As the stones were collected from a different place, those bringing the stones were likely to meet with all sorts of enemies. Headhunting at that time was frequent. To erect a stone would therefore need a strong force. A great gang of people was needed to meet these dangers and to transport the stone to the erecting spot. Only the big stones were used by powerful families."[13]

Anthropological studies have also shown that the standing stones erected by more recent nonstate societies were often viewed as the dwelling places of the

Figure 1.4.   Boscawen-un stone circle, Cornwall, England (image courtesy of Roger Driscoll).

spirits of the ancestral dead and were also often seen as being able to influence the life, health, and prosperity of the communities that erected them. Standing stones such as these were revered, and it was taboo to move or destroy them. Those foolish enough to do so, it was believed, would bring bad luck and harm on themselves. It seems likely that the standing stones of Europe were seen in similar light by the various prehistoric communities that erected them.

MEGALITHIC ORIGINS

Why, around seven thousand years ago, many communities in Europe suddenly decided to start erecting great stone monuments in the landscape is a major issue of late European prehistory that continues to cause much debate among archaeologists. However, it has long been known that the first megalithic monuments emerged along Europe's Atlantic facade, more specifically, in Portugal and Brittany, which contained dense populations of indigenous Late Mesolithic (Middle Stone Age) hunter-gatherers. The distinguished British archaeologist Colin Renfrew famously proposed that the earliest megaliths in Europe were megalithic tombs built as territorial markers by early farming groups, who needed to stake their claim to good agricultural land, which was becoming scarcer because of a rising population. Renfrew's territorial model is still influential today, as it does seem likely that at least some megalithic tombs (and other megaliths) were used by different groups or tribes to signal ownership of land that they considered rightfully theirs. However, many archaeologists now view the emergence of the European megalithic tradition as representing some type of response by native hunter-gatherers to the novel Neolithic lifestyle of the immigrant farming groups settling near or within their traditional territories.

Traditionally, Brittany rather than Portugal is "understood as the birthplace of European megalithic monumentality,"[14] although the megalithic tradition may possibly have emerged simultaneously on a "broad front among communities intricately linked by the sea."[15] Whatever the case, the early megalith builders of Brittany and Portugal appear to have been in contact with each other, as indicated by the megalithic enclosures, or "cromlechs,"[16] that were built in both regions. These typically horseshoe-shaped monuments have their open ends facing east. Furthermore, some menhirs in both Portugal and Brittany feature a distinctive carved motif resembling the curved end of a shepherd's crook as well as motifs that look like crescent moons. The "crook" motifs perhaps symbolize the conversion to the Neolithic lifestyle and the importance of domesticated livestock to Europe's earliest farming communities. Alternatively, rather than symbolizing shepherd's crooks, these motifs could perhaps depict throwing sticks that were used by Late Mesolithic hunters.

Figure 1.5. Vales do Meio cromlech, Évora District, Portugal (image courtesy of Ángel Felicísmo, CC BY-SA 2.0).

Many archaeologists now believe that the megalithic enclosures and standing stones of Brittany and Portugal mark the earliest manifestations of the megalithic phenomenon in Europe; at the least, they were erected alongside the first chambered tombs. The fact that standing stones were "recycled" into the architecture of some Early Neolithic tombs in both Brittany and Portugal lends support to the idea that they are the oldest aspect of the megalithic phenomenon in Europe. Whether Late Mesolithic groups erected these standing stones can perhaps never be known for sure. However, "it is certainly possible . . . that it was these populations, or some elements of them, who in a process of profound cultural and economic change became the first megalith-builders."[17]

It is perhaps also worth mentioning that evidence has been found to suggest that menhirs were not totally unknown in earlier Mesolithic Europe. In 2012, what appears to be a 12-meter-long standing stone was discovered submerged beneath the Mediterranean Sea on an underwater shelf (the Adventure Plateau) off the coast of Sicily. This intriguing stone, dated to around 8000 BCE, features what seem to be three man-made holes; it "is made from stone other than those which constitute all the neighboring [underwater] outcrops, and is quite isolated with respect to them."[18]

It could be that the origins of Europe's first megalithic tombs lie in the shell-midden burials of Brittany and Portugal's final Mesolithic coastal communities. In some cases, large numbers of individuals were interred below these mounds, which were largely formed from the discarded shells of edible marine mollusks such as mussels and clams. The most famous of these Late Mesolithic shell-midden cemeteries are Téviec and Hoedic (dated to ca. 5300–4800 BCE).[19]

Located about 19 miles apart on two small islands in the Bay of Quiberon, Brittany, these burial sites would originally have been located on the mainland near the coast. At Téviec a total of twenty-three people had been successively buried under large shell middens in ten graves lined and covered with large stone slabs that formed boxlike "cist" graves, with small cairns placed on top of the cists after the last burials were put into them. These structures are thus viewed by several scholars as "proto-megalithic" tombs and the forerunners of the first ones built by Brittany's earliest Neolithic communities. Nine similar graves containing a total of thirteen people were discovered at Hoedic, and menhir-like slabs (nearly 1 meter high) were also found at the head of two of the graves.

ANTIQUARIANS AND ARTISTS AT THE MEGALITHS

The beginning of the great fascination with Europe's megaliths can be traced back to the sixteenth century, when early "antiquarians" or "antiquaries" such as William Camden visited many megalithic monuments in Britain and Ireland, which he recorded in his famous work, *Britannia* (1586). It was not until the eighteenth century, however, that a significant number of antiquarians began to turn a serious gaze toward Europe's megaliths, with English, French, and Scandinavian scholars particularly active in this early megalithic research.

One of the most notable of these scholars was William Stukeley (1687–1765), a Lincolnshire doctor who gave up medicine to become a clergyman in the Church of England, of whom it has been said, "The first explosion of megalithomania was set off by . . . William Stukeley. The genius of this man has never been justly acknowledged."[20] Genius or not, there can be little doubt that Stukeley's delightful drawings of megalithic monuments remain a valuable source of information for modern archaeologists, as many of the sites he recorded have since been altered or destroyed. Somewhat bizarrely, Stukeley believed that megalithic sites in Britain were built by ancient Celtic druids of the Iron Age, whose religion centered on a serpent cult that was most significantly represented in the layout of the famous Avebury megalithic complex. To be fair to Stukeley, however, he was a man of his time, and the light that scientific archaeology was to shed on the purpose and dating of megalithic monuments was still many years in the future. In Europe in general, Stukeley had a great influence on the popular but erroneous idea that megaliths were the work of the druids, with megalithic tombs often viewed as places where gruesome human sacrifices were made. This druidic association with megalithic monuments persisted until the later nineteenth century, when it was seriously challenged, subsequently being discarded as antiquarians began to realize that the megaliths were far older than the druids of Iron Age Europe.

Across the channel, the remarkable megalithic monuments of Brittany were attracting the attention of Christophe-Paul de Robien (1698–1756), a lawyer and president of Brittany's parliament, with his valuable notes and drawings preserved in an unpublished but important manuscript held at the Bibliothéque municipale in Rennes. It has been noted that de Robien "can be considered the founder of Breton Archaeology."[21] An important figure in the development of Scandinavian archaeology is C. G. G. Hilfeling (1740–1823), who traveled widely in both Denmark and Sweden, carefully surveying and drawing megalithic monuments, some of which he also excavated. Hilfeling is seen by many of his modern counterparts in Denmark and Sweden as the first professional archaeologist in Scandinavia.

In the nineteenth century, excavating ancient sites became even more of a fashionable pursuit for "gentlemen scholars" not only in Europe but also in America,[22] and this "vogue for excavations initiated a propitious era for the study of megaliths."[23] In truth, most of these nineteenth-century "archaeologists" were often little more than treasure hunters and did considerable damage, recklessly digging into megalithic monuments with their picks, spades, and shovels. Nevertheless, several important works containing accurate plans and fine drawings of Europe's megalithic monuments were produced during this time.[24] Huge numbers of artifacts and human remains were also discovered by the nineteenth-century megalith explorers. These ancient objects began to provide previously unknown insights into the shadowy megalith builders, even if little or no attention was paid to the archaeological contexts they came from.

Artists at the Megaliths

The megalithic monuments of Europe have also been a source of inspiration to many artists. For example, the Romantic painters of the nineteenth century, strongly drawn to their brooding mystery and beauty, produced some wonderfully evocative works, such as *Megalithic Grave near Vordingborg in Winter* by Johan Christian Dahl (1788–1857) and *A Walk at Dusk* by Caspar David Friedrich (1774–1840).

It is hardly surprising that Stonehenge, one of the most spectacular megalithic monuments of Europe and an icon of prehistory known around the world, has also inspired many artists. The most notable of these are the famous English landscape painters John Constable (1776–1837) and J. M. W. Turner (1775–1851), who both produced wonderful paintings of Stonehenge. In the twentieth century, Stonehenge provided the well-known sculptor Henry Moore with the inspiration for some of his sculptures, and the famous Avebury monument inspired the artist Paul Nash, who is better known for his iconic paintings of World War I battlefields, to produce works such as *Landscape of the Megaliths* (1934). One of the earliest surviving paintings of a European megalithic monument

Figure 1.6.   *A Walk at Dusk*, by Caspar David Friedrich, ca. 1840 (CC public domain).

Figure 1.7.   John Constable's dramatic portrayal of Stonehenge, 1835 (CC public domain).

is found in the church of Saint-Merri in Paris. Dating to the sixteenth century, this romantic artwork depicts Saint Geneviève (ca. 422–502 CE), patron saint of Paris, as a shepherdess who sits with her flock within a small but fine circle of around thirty-seven stones; the circle "is painted with such conviction that it becomes the most realistic feature of the whole composition."[25] Saint Geneviève was born near the town of Nanterre, just west of Paris, and, interestingly, French researchers in the early twentieth century discovered that a stone circle resembling the one in the painting had formerly stood near Nanterre but was destroyed in the mid-eighteenth century.

THE FOLKLORE OF THE MEGALITHS

The megalithic monuments of Europe are steeped in folklore, and unsurprisingly, given the huge size of many of the stones used in the architecture of the megaliths, people often attributed them to the work of long-lost races of giants. Another common element of megalithic folklore is the association of tombs with fairies, elves, and similar magical beings. A famous example of this is provided by the superb La Roche-aux-Fées (Fairies' Rock) monument at Essé, Brittany, which was said to have been built by fairies who carried its huge stones in their aprons from a rock outcrop some 3 miles away. The prehistoric flint arrowheads made by many of the megalith builders, which people came across by chance in medieval and later times, were also often referred to as elf darts, elf shot, or fairy arrows. It is possible that the ancestral spirits, which were probably believed to live within the dark burial chambers of the megalithic tombs by their builders, were preserved in folk memory but gradually transformed over time and "became less ghostlike and more fairylike."[26] It may be more likely, however, that this common theme of megalithic folklore originated in medieval times.

Darker supernatural forces were also linked to Europe's megaliths, with many examples seen as the haunts of witches, demons, and even the devil himself, which seems to have led to "black magic" being performed at some monuments. For example, the Le Trepied passage grave on Guernsey in the English Channel Islands "figured largely in the witchcraft trials of the post-Reformation period. According to the confessions extracted under torture from some of the accused, the devil in the shape of a black goat . . . sat on the central capstone of the dolmen whilst his adherents danced around in ritual worship, chanting his praises."[27] There is also the account of one of the accomplices of the infamous Baron Gille de Rais, a medieval serial killer and occultist of the fifteenth century who murdered an unknown, but very large, number of children. During the trial of de Rais, this accomplice testified that the baron "had gone to a field of large standing stones to invoke a demon who had a great treasure in his control."[28]

Another common aspect of megalithic folklore is that standing stones represent human beings who were turned to stone by God for some wrongdoing, with dancing or playing games on the Sabbath popular reasons. It was not always having fun on a Sunday, however, that led God to turn people to stone. For example, an unusual Neolithic rectangular enclosure of standing stones known as the Jardin aux Moines (Garden of the Monks), which is situated in the picturesque forest of Broceliande, Brittany, was said to be a group of debauched monks who violently turned on Saint Méen after he had tried to dissuade them from taking part in an orgy. God was angered by the monks, and his retribution was swift. Better known is the legend of the famous megalithic stone rows of Carnac, also in Brittany, which in local folklore represent the remains of pagan Roman soldiers who were punished by God for pursuing Saint Cornelius. On the island of Anglesey, North Wales, an area rich in both megalithic remains and folklore, the Carreg Lleidr standing stone was said to be a man who had been petrified for stealing a Bible from a nearby church.

Many standing stones or menhirs were also seen as being able to promote fertility and healing. For instance, there is the well-known and curious Mên-an-Tol stone in Cornwall, southwest England. This round, upright slab measures about 1 meter high by 1 meter wide; a hole about 0.5 meters in diameter through its middle was probably deliberately hollowed out of the stone, although it could perhaps be a natural geological feature. Either way, in local folklore, it was said that if a woman passed through the hole in the stone backward seven times on the night of a full moon, then she would become pregnant. Children with rickets were also passed through the hole in the hope that they would be cured, and farmers hoped that by passing through the hole, they would be ensured a bountiful harvest. In Brittany, at the famous Kerloas menhir, both men and women would rub their naked bellies on the surfaces of this huge monument (approximately 9 meters in height) in the hope that their offspring would be healthy and beautiful. Women seeking a husband would climb to the top of the well-known leaning menhir of La Tremblais (also in Brittany) and slide down it, hoping that doing so would help them find a spouse.

Many standing stones were also said to be able to magically turn around or travel to nearby rivers and streams, where they would drink or bathe, often after hearing the clock strike midnight or the cock crow at the break of day. One of the earliest surviving accounts (if not the earliest) of this aspect of megalithic folklore was recorded in the late twelfth century by the archdeacon of Brecon cathedral, the famous Gerald of Wales, or Geraldus Cambrensis. He tells us of a magical menhir on the island of Anglesey: "There is, for example, a stone almost in the shape of a human thigh-bone, which has this extraordinary property, so often proved true by the local inhabitants, that however far away it is carried, it returns of its own accord the following night."[29] In France, local folklore had it that anyone daring to question or mock the magical movement of standing

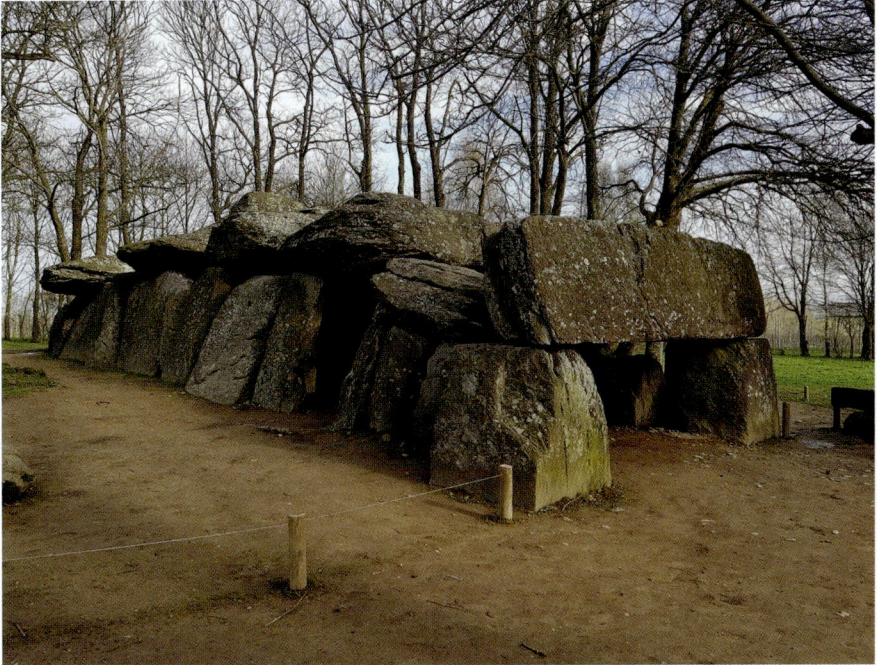

Figure 1.8.　La Roche-aux-Fées gallery grave, Brittany, France (image courtesy of Elliot Capper).

stones would be hexed or cursed, as "the stones were felt to contain living beings, unseen but real, genial yet easily offended";[30] similar beliefs were held in many other parts of Europe.

These are just a few examples from the widespread and voluminous megalithic folklore of Europe, which was developed by largely illiterate, rural communities with little or no notion of the age and purpose of these great stone monuments or of the people who built them. However, at least in some cases, this folklore may provide us with faint echoes of the rituals and beliefs of the various prehistoric peoples of Europe who constructed megalithic monuments and left them as remarkable stone testaments to their long-lost lives and beliefs.

· 2 ·

The Heartland of Megalithic Europe

*I*t seems fitting to begin our exploration of megalithic Europe in the place that many scholars consider the birthplace of megalith building: Brittany.[1] This beautiful coastal region of northwestern France takes its name from the Celtic Iron Age tribes who migrated here from Britain at the end of the first millennium BCE. This ancient British connection is revealed by the similarities seen between the native Celtic language of Brittany and that spoken in Wales and Cornwall. Brittany is best known, however, for its remarkable collection of superb megaliths, which are unparalleled elsewhere in Europe and make this compact French peninsula a "megalithic wonderland."[2]

THE CARNAC ALIGNMENTS

Undoubtedly the most famous of Brittany's numerous megalithic monuments are the Carnac alignments. These enormous multiple rows of standing stones run for miles, like giant petrified snakes, across the Breton countryside near the town of Carnac in the southern *département* of Morbihan, which boasts one of the highest concentrations of European megaliths, with many of them superb monuments.

The three major Carnac alignments are Kerzerho, Le Ménec, and Kermario, which each contain more than a thousand standing stones of varying sizes, with the largest about 4 meters high and the smallest standing 50 centimeters. The Kerzerho alignment is the longest of the three, and its stone rows run for almost 1.5 miles across the landscape, with Le Ménec and Kermario both measuring more than half a mile long. To the east of Le Ménec is the fourth-largest Carnac alignment, Kerlescan, which measures just under half a mile long and

17

Figure 2.1.   The Kermario alignment (image courtesy of Martin Cigler, CC BY-SA 3.0).

comprises around 550 standing stones. Although the chronology of the Carnac alignments is uncertain, their origins are thought to lie in the Early Neolithic ca. 4500 BCE, with standing stones being progressively added to the rows by prehistoric communities for at least the next thousand years or so. It is also worth noting that long after the Neolithic communities who erected the stone rows were gone, local people had a tradition of adding new stones to the rows, every year, with this custom continuing until at least as late as the early nineteenth century.

The remains of megalithic enclosures, or cromlechs, can also be seen at the end of some of the Carnac stone rows, with the largest and best preserved of these attached to the western end of Le Ménec. This huge stone ring measures 91 by 71 meters (making it the largest megalithic enclosure in Brittany) and even has modern houses built inside its closely set standing stones. A large enclosure is also located at the western end of Kerlescan; it is, unusually, square shaped in plan and open to the north, although the enclosure is partially blocked along this side by the huge 90-meter mound of the Le Manio *tertre* (an Early Neolithic long mound containing a small burial chamber). The standing stones at the eastern end of Kermario actually run over the mound of the *tertre* known as Le Manio 2. This long mound was built around an earlier standing stone, on the base of which five snakelike carvings came to light when Le Manio 2 was excavated in the early 1920s. Intriguingly, four polished stone axes were also found buried at the base of the stone, and a fifth one was found lying about 1 meter away. What these carvings represent is anyone's guess, but snakes were often associated with the underworld in ancient mythology and feature in many of the creation myths of various nonstate cultures around the world.

Scottish engineer Professor Alexander Thom, who surveyed and recorded hundreds of megalithic sites (mostly British stone circles) with his son Archie, proposed that the Carnac alignments were part of a vast lunar observatory that also included nearby menhirs. The Thoms also believed that the Carnac alignments were set out with mathematical precision by their builders, who used a standardized unit of measurement, which Alexander Thom labeled the "megalithic yard."[3] Few archaeologists today would agree with the lunar observatory theory, but the fact that the Le Ménec, Kermario, Kerzerho, and Kerlescan stone rows are "aligned roughly west-south-west/east-north-east may indicate an interest in summer sunrise or winter sunset."[4] The most popular interpretation of the Carnac stone rows is that they were processional avenues along which large gatherings of Neolithic people passed to perform religious rituals and ceremonies at the large enclosures that lay at their ends. Alternate suggestions are that the Carnac stones were set up to honor the ancestors, with the alignments being "spirit avenues" along which the dead walked, or perhaps the stone rows were symbolic barriers marking off special parts of the landscape.

There are several other megalithic enclosures in Morbihan, such as the two notable examples on the tiny island of Er Lannic, which lies on the coast near the famous Gavrinis passage grave. These two large, horseshoe-shaped cromlechs were once located on dry land, but rising sea levels have since encroached on the monuments, and the southern one can now only be seen at low tide, with the same being said for many of the stones that make up the northern enclosure. These two monuments probably date to the second half of the fifth millennium BCE, and the archaeological evidence found at them suggests Er Lannic was an important ceremonial site connected with the production of polished stone axes. Axe motif carvings were also found on a couple of the stones used in the enclosures. They were excavated in 1930 by the famous Breton archaeologist Zachaire Le Rouzic,[5] who uncovered various Neolithic artifacts, including numerous sherds from around five hundred ceramic "vase supports." The traces of burning frequently seen on these small, finely decorated, dish-like objects reveal they were used as "incense" burners, as traces of birch-bark tar have been identified on them, although it has also been suggested that they were used for burning narcotics. Le Rouzic also found the remains of several hearths, many stone axe fragments, and nearly forty stone axes made from a type of rock known as fibrolite. Some of the axes were "rough-outs" and had not been ground and polished to their finished state, with these unfinished axes probably brought to Er Lannic from nearby Port Navalo.

THE TUMULUS DE SAINT-MICHEL

Lying on the outskirts of Carnac is the massive Tumulus de Saint-Michel (Saint Michael's Mound), the largest of the so-called Carnac mounds (which roughly date to ca. 4500–4200 BCE) and one of the largest prehistoric burial mounds in the whole of Europe. In fact, this famous monument is so large that it has a seventeenth-century chapel built on its summit and measures 125 meters long, 60 meters wide, and 10 meters high.

It was not until 1862 that the first serious attempt was made to uncover the Neolithic secrets of the Tumulus de Saint-Michel, when Réne Galles, the military subintendant of Morbihan—or, more specifically, his workmen—dug a vertical 8-meter shaft through the center of the mound, which was made from layers of rubble and a claylike marine sediment gathered from some distance away. At the bottom of the shaft, a small burial chamber with a large broken capstone was discovered. No self-respecting archaeologist of today would sink a shaft through a prehistoric burial mound, and a good deal of sensitive and valuable archaeological information was probably lost as a result of Galles's "excavation technique." However, to be fair, he was just following in the footsteps of most nineteenth-century antiquarians, who were not exactly scientific in their approach when it came to investigating megalithic and other prehistoric monuments. In the burial chamber, Galles found thirty-nine superb stone axes (eleven of which were made from Alpine jadeite) and around one hundred perforated beads and nine pendants of Iberian variscite (a green gem-like stone). Interestingly, the axes had been deliberately placed vertically, like miniature standing stones, in the deposit of black "dust" that covered the chamber floor, with their cutting edges pointing skyward. Fragments of cremated human bone and charcoal were found between the rough slabs that had been used to pave the chamber floor and in the deposit that covered them. Two years later, Galles returned to the Tumulus de Saint-Michel, determined to find the much larger—and thus more richly furnished—burial chamber that he believed must exist in such an impressive burial mound. Unfortunately, the tunnel that he had driven through the western end of the mound at ground level, at considerable expense to himself, turned out to be a waste of time and money, as nothing new was discovered as a result.

Unluckily for Galles, he had simply started his tunnel from the wrong end of the Tumulus de Saint-Michel. In 1900, Zacharie Le Rouzic's engineers began digging a tunnel in its eastern end and almost straightaway discovered a passage grave. As the tunnel progressed toward the center of the mound over the next couple of years, a small stone circle and three cist graves built from narrow stone slabs were also discovered along its axis. In July 1902, the tunnel finally arrived at the central burial chamber found by Galles in 1862, and over the course of

Figure 2.2.   The Tumulus de Saint-Michel (image courtesy of Yolan, CC BY-SA 2.0).

the next two years, Le Rouzic found a total of twenty-one stone cists clustered around its uprights. Many of these were more like small stone boxes and seem to have been used as containers for ritual deposits, with numerous variscite beads, flint tools, and pottery recovered from them; one slightly larger example contained the bones of a sheep or cow. A second burial chamber was also discovered to the south of the main central one, and the two chambers and stone cists were covered by a large, dome-like cairn.

The Tumulus de Saint-Michel was also used as the location for a long-standing annual Breton custom, which was recorded in T. C. Worsfold's *The French Stonehenge* (1901):

> A curious custom obtains at the period of the summer solstice every year in connection with this tumulus, for on the top of it a huge bonfire is lighted at eventide, which is the signal for others to be kindled on similar prominent eminences in the district for a distance of twenty or thirty miles; and at the same time fires are also lighted in the farmyards. . . . These fires are called in the Breton patois "Tan Heol" = "the Fire of the sun"—and also, but obviously by a later introduction, "Tan Sant Jan" = "the Fire of St. John."[6]

Could it be that this custom had deep roots, representing a folk memory of one carried out by the Neolithic communities of the Carnac region more than six thousand years ago?

Seven other Carnac mounds survive within a thirteen-mile radius of the town of Carnac, all of which have huge covering mounds, with beautiful ceremonial stone axes like those from the Tumulus de Saint-Michel and other lavish grave goods recovered from within their burial chambers. More than one hundred of these axes were found during an antiquarian investigation of the Mané-er-Hröek Carnac mound in 1863, with most of them recovered from a cavity that had been dug below the stone-paved floor of the burial chamber. A superb jadeite axe was also found lying on the chamber floor, with its narrower pointed end resting on a perforated jadeite ring "as if penetrating the latter in an arrangement that has been held to have sexual connotations."[7] The massive size of the Carnac mounds and the high-quality grave goods found within their chambers speak of the existence of high-status groups in the Carnac region in the Early Neolithic.

BRETON PASSAGE TOMBS:
LE PETIT MONT, GAVRINIS, AND BARNENEZ

Many fine passage graves survive in Brittany, and in local folklore these monuments represent entrances to a supernatural realm, their passages and chambers haunted by a race of tiny beings known as the Corrigans, which are like the fairies or pixies of Britain and Ireland. It is also interesting to note that a study of the Breton passage graves suggests that many have their entrances aligned with either the rising or the setting sun, as is the case with many other passage tombs in Europe. This can hardly be a coincidence of construction and points to a belief in a solar deity, although it is strongly suspected that some passage graves were aligned not on the sun but on the moon, indicating that a lunar god or goddess was also worshipped by their builders.

Le Petit Mont

Representing one of the best known and largest of Brittany's numerous passage graves, Le Petit Mont ("the little mountain") is located on the very end of the Rhuys Peninsula in the Gulf of Morbihan, providing visitors with fine views over the lovely Quiberon Bay. Le Petit Mont is a multiphase monument that began life in the Early Neolithic in 4600 BCE; it basically comprises a small, single-chambered passage grave that was superseded by a huge circular, stepped cairn (about 50 meters in diameter), covering two passage graves. The massive granite slab (4.3 meters long by 3.4 meters wide) that forms the floor of Passage Grave II was originally a freestanding menhir from somewhere else that had been carefully worked to represent an anthropomorphic human figure with curved shoulders and a round head.

Unfortunately, Le Petit Mont was severely damaged when, in 1942, German soldiers built a large bunker and flak gun emplacement into the southeast corner of the cairn, destroying one of the burial chambers and causing the collapse of the other (which has since been restored). This bunker now houses a small museum. The megalithic "trilithon" setting of two megalithic uprights and a lintel stone at the entrance to Le Petit Mont is thought to be a much later addition from the later Iron Age or Gallo-Roman period.

Gavrinis

Constructed some six thousand years ago, Gavrinis, also in the Gulf of Morbihan, is one of the finest passage graves in Europe and stands in splendid isolation on the small island from which it takes its name. The sea-swamped stones of the Er Lannic megalithic enclosures lie opposite, across the narrow strait of water that separates them from Gavrinis. This famous monument is of a similar size to Le Petit Mont, comprising a stepped stone cairn measuring some 50 meters in diameter and 7 meters high. Below the cairn, an 11-meter-long passage leads to a square burial chamber of about 5 by 5 meters, with around eighty megalithic slabs used in the construction of the passage and chamber.

As impressive as the megalithic architecture of Gavrinis is, it is the megalithic "art" covering most of the stones used in its construction that makes this Breton passage tomb so special. No other Neolithic tomb in Europe is so richly decorated with megalithic art, which mainly comprises highly enigmatic swirling and zigzag-like carved motifs. Excavations carried out at Gavrinis from 1979 to 1984 by Brittany's director of antiquities, Charles-Tanguy Le Roux, uncovered new examples of this megalithic art on the outside faces of some of the slabs used

Figure 2.3.   Replica of the passage at Gavrinis, Bougon Museum (image courtesy of Ismoon, CC BY-SA 3.0).

in the passage. This art must therefore have been carved into the slabs before they were covered by the huge cairn.

However, "the main surprise was come to from the chamber's capstone, laid bare in the course of restoration work."[8] Le Roux realized that this had once been part of a massive decorated menhir, which had been broken into fragments, and that another part of this standing stone had also been used as the capstone in the burial chamber of the La Table des Marchand passage grave, some 2 miles from Gavrinis: "This block's dimensions and form, the pattern of the break, and the grain of the granite indicate that it joins up with the Gavrinis capstone, if one turns one of them over. The mutilated figures would then come face to face."[9] When reconstructed, the decoration depicts two animals with long curving horns, probably representing wild or domesticated cattle (although it is possible that one of the animals is a horned goat/sheep), as well as what looks very much like a stone axe, perhaps in a sheath, and a *hache-charrue*, or "axe plow." The meaning of the curiously shaped axe-plow motif has long baffled archaeologists, but a recent theory is that it represents a sperm whale rather than a rudimentary farming implement.

Le Roux's discovery that the capstones of the Gavrinis and La Table des Marchand passage came from a massive broken menhir that had subsequently been "recycled" into the architecture of these two passage graves was a famous one, providing striking proof that at least some of Brittany's decorated menhirs dated to earlier than its passage graves. Le Roux also suggested that the capstone used for the roof of the burial chamber in the nearby Carnac mound of Er Grah/ Er Vingle was a third broken fragment from this menhir. If so, this standing stone would, when complete, have been a magnificent megalith measuring approximately 14 meters high, 4 meters wide, and 1 meter thick. It is also possible that the decorated backstone of the La Table des Marchand's burial chamber represents a recycled menhir that had once stood somewhere else. This stone has rows of "crook" motifs carved into its surface, and some archaeologists have suggested that these symbolize a field of domesticated wheat or barley rather than shepherd's crooks or hunter's throwing sticks.

Barnenez

Located on the coast of the beautiful Kernéléhen Peninsula and overlooking the Bay of Morlaix, in the *département* of Finistère, the Barnenez passage tomb somewhat dwarfs Gavrinis, its trapezoidal stepped cairn measuring approximately 75 meters and reaching a maximum height of around 8 meters. This fantastic monument would probably have been destroyed by an unscrupulous local road builder, who took a large chunk out of its northwestern end in 1954 before being halted by the authorities, who had been alerted to his illegal quarrying by the French archaeologist Pierre-Roland Giot. Sadly, this individual had already

Figure 2.4. The decorated capstone and backstone in La Table des Marchand's burial chamber (image courtesy of Myrabella CC BY-SA 3.0).

destroyed another passage tomb that lay nearby on the headland, but, happily, he was heavily fined and ordered to pay for the restoration work that needed to be carried out at Barnenez because of the damage he had caused.

Barnenez contains not one but eleven small passage tombs, which lie alongside each other below its massive stone mound. Five of these were probably built ca. 4500 BCE (or perhaps even a couple of hundred years earlier), with the other six added around three hundred years later, when the Barnenez cairn was enlarged. Some of the burial chambers also have corbelled roofs formed from slabs of stone that were progressively overlapped by their builders to create dome-like vaults above the floors of the chamber.

The Barnenez passage tombs were excavated from 1954 to 1968 by Pierre-Roland Giot, who uncovered fragments of human bone and artifacts such as flint arrowheads and pottery, four stone axes, and a copper knife and "bell beaker," revealing later ritual use of the monument by the famous Beaker culture.[10] Giot also found that some of the stones used in the construction of the tombs had been decorated with megalithic art, among which were stone-axe and snake motifs, as well as a "buckler," or *écusson*, motif, that had been carved into a capstone of one of the tombs (suggesting that this slab was a recycled menhir). These enigmatic motifs have been noted both in megalithic tombs and on menhirs in Brittany, and a popular idea is that they symbolize a female deity or goddess who watched over and protected the dead.

BRETON GALLERY GRAVES

Also found in the Breton landscape are several "gallery graves," or *allées couvertes* (covered alleys), as they are known in France, a distinctive type of megalithic tomb found in several parts of Europe. Although there are variations to be found in the architecture of gallery graves, they essentially consist of two parallel rows of upright megalithic slabs and capstones, which together form rectangular or square, boxlike megalithic chambers or "galleries"; circular "porthole" entrances were also carved in their front slabs. Included among the Breton *allées couvertes* are the Dolmens Angevin, so called because there is a large group of these monuments near the city of Angers in the Pays de Loire region to the east of Brittany, which are set apart from other gallery graves by their low but massive "trilithon" entrances of two uprights and a lintel stone. Included among the Breton Dolmens Angevin is the famous La Roche-aux-Fées (Fairies' Rock [figure 1.8]) in the Ille-et-Villaine *département*. One of the finest megalithic tombs in France, it measures some 20 meters long by 5 meters wide, with the weight of its thirty-two massive uprights and nine capstones estimated to be about 500 tons. It is thought that the huge stones used in the construction of La Roche-aux-Fées

Figure 2.5. The massive Barnenez cairn, with the blocked-up entrances of its passage graves visible at the base (image courtesy of Gerald Haubold, CC BY-SA 3.0).

were quarried from a rock outcrop in the forest of Theil-de-Bretagne some 2.5 miles away and that its entrance is aligned with the midwinter sunrise.

Representing another variant of the gallery grave tradition are the *arc boutée* monuments, and these are only found in Brittany. Only eight examples of these unique megalithic structures remain in the Breton landscape, and they were probably always rather rare, even in the later Neolithic when they were built. Instead of having megalithic uprights and capstones forming rectangular or square chambers or galleries, the side stones of the *arc boutée* lean inward at a forty-five-degree angle to meet their counterparts on the other side, with the chambers thus shaped like an inverted *V*. Therefore, these striking megalithic monuments look rather like long tents, albeit ones made from massive stones.

BRETON MENHIRS

Brittany abounds with menhirs, or prehistoric standing stones, with more than a thousand examples known, although the three western *départements* of Morbihan, Finistère, and Côtes d'Armor lay claim to the densest concentrations of these enigmatic megaliths. Many of these standing stones are thought to have been erected in the first half of the fifth millennium BCE, with the first ones perhaps even erected by Brittany's final Mesolithic hunter-gatherer communities.

Some of the Breton menhirs are more famous than others on account of their great size. For example, on the crest of a pretty, wooded hill overlooking the Kerlescan alignment is the impressive 6.5-meter-high menhir known as the Géant du Manio. Even taller, though, is the superb Kerloas menhir (figure 1.1). Measuring 9.5 meters high, this mighty slab of granite stands in the Breton countryside about 2 miles from the village of Plouarzel in the *département* of Finistère and can be seen from many miles away. In fact, the Kerloas menhir was once about 2 meters taller, but some two hundred years ago a lightning strike blasted off its top, part of which is said to have sailed through the air to land on the roof of a nearby farmhouse. The smooth surfaces and the shallow facets that

Figure 2.6. The Champ Dolent menhir (image courtesy of Espirat, CC BY-SA 4.0).

can be seen on the narrower sides of the stone show how it was carefully shaped and dressed before it was hauled into the air. As noted, the "Kerloas menhir is testimony to the organization and commitment of the Neolithic communities who erected it; the closest possible source of the material is 2 km down slope."[11] Another renowned menhir is the Menhir de Champ Dolent, which stands just outside the town of Dol-de-Bretagne in the Ille-et-Villaine *département*. The Champ Dolent equals the Kerloas menhir in height and bulk, although it has been carefully worked into a more oval shape than the former.

This towering menhir is thought to weigh about 100 tons and to have been sourced from a massif some 2.5 miles away, again representing considerable effort and organization on the part of the people who raised it from the ground (this can be said for many of Europe's megalithic monuments). An interesting piece of folklore attached to Champ Dolent has it that every time somebody dies, the stone sinks further into the ground, and when it has completely disappeared, this will signal doomsday and the end of the world.

Europe's Greatest Standing Stone: Le Grand Menhir Brisé

No other menhirs still standing in Europe are as tall as the Kerloas and Champ Dolent monuments. However, both would be easily dwarfed by the remarkable Le Grand Menhir Brisé, Brittany's most famous standing stone, which now lies shattered on the ground, broken into four colossal fragments, on the outskirts of the village of Locmariaquer in the Gulf of Morbihan. Before it came crashing down, with what must have been an almighty thud heard by people miles away, this menhir stood around 20 meters high, measuring about 4 meters wide. It has also been estimated that when complete, the Grand Menhir would have weighed between 270 and 330 tons. Remarkably, geological studies have revealed that the nearest source of the granite-like orthogneiss rock of which the Grand Menhir is made is the Rhuys Peninsula, which lies some 5 miles away. Radiocarbon dates obtained on charcoal found at its base revealed that it was erected in the first half of the fifth millennium BCE.

Excavations carried out in the vicinity of the Grand Menhir have revealed that it originally stood at the end of an alignment measuring about 60 meters in length, which comprised nineteen or twenty standing stones in total. Only the pits and sockets of these missing stones were found, but the decorated capstones in the chambers at the nearby La Table des Marchand and Gavrinis passage graves, mentioned above, probably came from a huge, broken standing stone that had originally stood in this alignment. The decorated backstone at Gavrinis, featuring the crook motifs, may also have originally stood in this alignment. It has also been argued that the Grand Menhir broke in half during its erection because of a natural geological flaw and that only the bottom fragment of the stone was raised in this alignment: "There is no reliable evidence that the menhir was ever raised intact. It could be the case that an accident during the erection of the *Grand Menhir* prevented the successful completion of the monument."[12]

Most scholars, however, are of the opinion that the Grand Menhir was successfully raised intact. Since the eighteenth century at least, scholars have speculated about what caused this behemoth of a standing stone to fall. One theory, for example, is that it was struck by a bolt of lightning. More plausible is the idea that the Grand Menhir and other toppled standing stones in the region were felled by a violent earthquake that rocked the Gulf of Morbihan around 4300 BCE. Alternatively, it could have been deliberately destroyed, in an act of Neolithic iconoclasm, by a new elite during a time of social and religious upheaval in Brittany. If so, this would have been no mean feat, but it would still have been a whole lot easier to "knock down" the Grand Menhir than to "put it up."

THE MEANING OF THE MENHIRS

Of all Europe's many megalithic monuments, menhirs are the most mysterious. Some plausible suggestions, however, have been made about the possible symbolism of Brittany's standing stones. For example, it may be that monuments such as Kerloas, Champ Dolent, and the Grand Menhir were carefully worked and shaped to represent giant, polished stone axeheads set in the ground. Whether or

Figure 2.7. The shattered remains of Le Grand Menhir Brisé (image courtesy of Louis Carlier, CC BY-SA 3.0).

not this was the case, stone axes played a special part in the religious rituals and ceremonies of Brittany's Neolithic communities, as revealed by the deposits of beautifully made stone axeheads found in many of the region's megalithic tombs and by the axe motifs found carved into the stones used in the construction of these tombs and also on some standing stones. Hoards of stone axeheads buried in the ground have also been found in Brittany, such as the remarkable one discovered at Arzon in 1894. This collection comprised seventeen axeheads of fibrolite and jadeite that had been inserted into the ground and arranged in a tight circle, with their blades pointing upward, looking like a stone circle in miniature. There are other possibilities, and some see the menhirs as having phallic connotations, with the unique circular bosses carved in relief on the base of Kerloas menhir perhaps providing support for this idea. Another plausible theory is that some menhirs represented ancestral figures or "guardian spirits" who watched over both the dead and the living. The truth is that we can only ever make informed guesses as to the meaning of Brittany's standing stones, but examples such as the Grand Menhir certainly "bear witness to the determination and organisation of a society that was responsible for such impressive monuments."[13]

• 3 •

Megaliths of France, Switzerland, and Italy

$\mathcal{A}$lthough Brittany has the "monopoly" on megalithic tombs in France (and French megaliths in general), many other examples can be found scattered throughout the various French *départements*. Perhaps the best known are those of the Bougon necropolis in the Deux-Sèvres *département* in western France. These famous monuments were discovered in April 1840 by French antiquarians, who have left us with an evocative account of their entry into one of the tombs (Tumulus A) of the Bougon necropolis: "The second day, after slowly alternating hopes and fears, the workers penetrated a layer of piled-up rubble in which we perceived an enormous, long, thick stone. Suddenly, the ground caved in; we searched, we dug again; an opening was made, we slid inside. Everywhere were bones, bodies, and pots, some broken, others intact; there were upright pillars, overturned pillars, dry-stone walls, some crumbling, ruined by weather and time; underfoot, human clay, above our heads, an enormous block of stone. Gigantic structure! How many centuries have flowed over her!"[1]

The five somewhat unusual tombs found in the Bougon necropolis differ from each other in their architectural details but are all basically passage graves, some of which have corbelled roofs. All the tombs are of a substantial size, although Tumuli A, F, and C represent the three largest examples, also yielding some fascinating finds. The former (which dates to ca. 4000 BCE) comprises a circular stepped cairn measuring about 42 meters in diameter and 5 meters in height, with an off-center passage leading from the entrance to a large but low rectangular burial chamber (about 7 meters by 4 meters and some 2 meters high). The capstone of the chamber is thought to weigh around 90 tons, and the antiquarian excavation conducted here in 1840 uncovered the skeletons of around two hundred people who had been interred with artifacts such as round-bottomed pottery vessels, beads, stone tools, and necklaces made from seashells. Perhaps the most interesting discovery was the male skull found at the base of

31

the megalithic slab used to block the passage, which displayed not one but three "trepanations," revealing evidence of what was essentially Stone Age surgery, as these trepanations would have involved the removal of circular discs of bone from the skull with a flint tool of some sort. Many other instances of trepanation have been discovered on Neolithic skulls from sites across Europe and may have been carried out on people who were suffering from neurologically related health problems such as migraines and epilepsy and even on people with mental health disorders (in Neolithic times, such people may perhaps have been believed to be possessed by dangerous or evil spirits). It is also possible that Neolithic trepanning helped to remove fractured bones and clean up dangerous pools of blood that had gathered just below the surfaces of the skulls of people who had received serious head wounds, either in violent assaults or in episodes of warfare.

Tumulus F consists of two corbelled burial chambers located at either end of a huge, stepped trapezoidal cairn measuring nearly 80 meters long, 12–16 meters wide, and some 3 meters high. Excavations here in 1977 brought to light the skeletons of around ten people, both adults and children, in one of the burial chambers, with the remains divided between two separate horizontal stone slabs. Six radiocarbon dates recovered from the bones in both the 1970s and the 1990s indicated two separate episodes of burial within the chamber: the first around 4700 BCE and the second about seven hundred years later. The earliest date, which relates to the lower burial deposit, is one of the earliest yet obtained from any megalithic tomb in Europe.

Tumulus C is roughly circular in form, measuring a substantial 60 or so meters in diameter and 4 meters high, with antiquarian investigation of its small burial chamber in 1845 discovering four skeletons and flint tools and pottery. The skeletons were reputedly found in an upright, seated position along one of the walls of the burial chamber and were said to have been attached to stone "hooks" that protruded from one of the megalithic uprights in the chamber.

Figure 3.1.   Tumulus A at the Bougon necropolis (image courtesy of Liberliger, CC BY-SA 3.0).

PRISSÉ-LA-CHARRIÈRE

This enormous, chambered long mound is also located in the Deux-Sèvres *département* of western France, not far from the city of Niort, with archaeologists Chris Scarre, Roger Joussaume, and Luc Laporte jointly directing excavations here between 1995 and 2013. The archaeological investigation of this rather remarkable prehistoric monument revealed that it was a complex and somewhat bewildering (at least at first sight) multiphase structure dating to ca. 4400–4200 BCE. Essentially, the excavations revealed three megalithic tombs incorporated into a massive stone cairn (100 meters long, 15–19 meters wide, and 3.5 meters high), which consisted of a complicated arrangement of interconnecting dry-stone walls and terraces. The earliest of these tombs was a megalithic chamber in a small circular cairn (a "rotunda" grave) that had subsequently been closed and covered beneath a "short" long cairn measuring 23 meters long by 8 meters wide, which in turn was buried and incorporated into the western end of the later massive cairn. The other two tombs were passage graves located alongside each other in the long northern side of Prissé-la-Charrière. The archaeologists realized that the westernmost of the two passage graves was built as an integral feature of the later cairn and that the other one was an earlier freestanding

Figure 3.2.   Prissé-la-Charrière (image courtesy of Professor Chris Scarre).

monument that had later been incorporated into this huge structure. Whether the earlier, western passage grave had been built before or after the rotunda grave was unclear, however.

Human bones were found in all three of the megalithic tombs at Prissé-la-Charrière. The remains of three individuals were recovered from the rotunda grave, and although the western passage grave had been badly destroyed by later quarrying at the long mound in more recent times, the archaeologists recovered the bones of eight individuals (four adults and four children) in and around its burial chamber and sherds from a ceramic "vase support." The eastern passage grave was well preserved and contained the remains of eight people, and two intact vase supports were also found in its burial chamber, with Roger Joussaume describing the moment he first entered this ancient place: "It was a dive into the past that gave me a great shock. . . . It was a really unforgettable moment."[2] Interestingly, scientists were able to extract mitochondrial DNA from three of the individuals found in the passage grave. Analysis of this DNA suggested that their ancestors had been immigrants whose origins lay in the Linear Pottery/Linearbandkeramik (abbreviated to LBK) culture of central Europe.[3]

LA CHAUSSÉE TIRANCOURT

Another famous French megalithic tomb outside Britany is La Chaussée Tirancourt gallery grave, which was discovered in 1967 by a farmer plowing his fields near the city of Amiens in northern France (*département* of Picardy). La Chaussée Tirancourt was subsequently excavated by French archaeologists Claude Masset and Jean Leclerc. Meticulous investigation of the gallery grave took almost ten years to complete and represents "one of the most spectacular and complete accounts of a French megalithic monument."[4]

La Chaussée Tirancourt was constructed about 3300 BCE and essentially comprised a megalithic subterranean chamber or gallery, measuring 11 meters long by 3 meters wide, which was used as a place of collective burial for about a thousand years. The walls of the chamber were constructed in a deep trench (about 1.7 meters deep, 3.5 meters wide, and 15 meters long) that was dug into the limestone bedrock. The excavations recovered a small assemblage of artifacts typical of the French Late Neolithic "Seine-Oise-Marne" culture, such as a greenstone pendant in the shape of a Neolithic axehead, a small pottery vessel, a perforated seashell, and two bone awls or points that were probably used for piercing animal hides.

Although La Chaussée Tirancourt was relatively modest in size, the remains of nearly four hundred individuals were found inside its burial chamber, representing different episodes of burial activity at the monument between the second half of the fourth millennium BCE and the end of the third. The earliest was represented by only a few bones, but not long after a thin layer of sediment had accumulated over them, sixty individuals were buried successively in three separate groups within the chamber. Intriguingly, different genetic abnormalities were identified in the bones of two of the groups, and as these were inherited, they "suggest that people from particular households were being buried in distinct parts of the tomb."[5]

After these burials, there was a hiatus in the use of La Chaussée Tirancourt as a place of collective burial as revealed by the thick deposit of loam (approximately 15 centimeters in depth) that had accumulated over the bones of the dead. This was followed by the final phase of burial at La Chaussée Tirancourt in the later third millennium BCE. This involved the internment of more than three hundred individuals who seem to have been originally placed in eight separate wooden compartments or cases, although these had long since decayed by the time of Masset and Leclerc's excavation of the gallery grave. However, somewhat remarkably, two or three distinct clusters of bones displaying different genetic abnormalities were also discovered in this upper burial layer, again suggesting the burial of kin-based groups or families within the chamber at La Chaussée Tirancourt.

At some point around 2100 BCE, in the Early Bronze Age, people closed off or "decommissioned" La Chaussée Tirancourt by filling it with loam; the final act in this closure was the partial destruction of the tomb by a fierce fire lit on its roof. This fire destroyed the roof and the top half of the chamber uprights, covering the monument with a thick layer of ash and debris. After this destructive episode, "subsequent inundation by alluvium hid La Chaussée Tirancourt, preserving its fascinating secrets for posterity."[6]

PETIT-CHASSEUR

Switzerland is not particularly blessed with an abundance of megalithic monuments, but it is home to one of the most important megalithic sites in Europe: the Petit-Chasseur necropolis, which lies in the town of Sion in the canton (like an American state) of Valais in southwestern Switzerland. Petit-Chasseur was discovered accidentally in 1961 and subsequently excavated over the next thirty years or so. Swiss archaeologists uncovered a complex site, comprising both dolmens, simple boxlike burial chambers or cist graves, and an alignment of nine standing stones measuring some 28 meters long. A few other alignments or stone rows are known in Switzerland, such as the one discovered near the shore of Lake Genève, which comprises twenty-four menhirs in a 15-meter line, or the twelve-stone row found on the northern side of Lake

Neuchâtel. Two of the stones in this alignment are statue menhirs featuring anthropomorphic decoration.

The earliest monuments at Petit-Chasseur (dolmens MXII and MVI) were built around 3000 BCE and resemble those found in the Franche-Comté region of central-eastern France, bordering Switzerland. These megalithic tombs consist of square or rectangular chambers set in long triangular cairns that are considerably narrow at their ends, which means that, in plan, they somewhat resemble giant wedges of cheese. Dolmen MXII was the first monument to be constructed at the necropolis, with dolmen MVI built a couple hundred years later. Along with human remains (representing around 150 people), various grave goods, such as flint arrowheads and daggers, engraved pendants, beads, spindle whorls, and perforated pig canines, were recovered from the two dolmens. Following the construction of dolmens MXII and MVI, between approximately 2450 and 2200 BCE, people of the Beaker culture constructed several cist graves at the site. The people buried in their chambers were accompanied by the distinctive pottery vessels that give this famous prehistoric culture its name, and numerous seashells were also recovered, which had adorned the bodies of the dead.

As has been noted, "The particular importance of Le Petit Chasseur derives from the decorated anthropomorphic stone stelae [found] at the site."[7] These stelae, or statue menhirs, were erected by both the Late Neolithic and the Beaker communities who built the dolmens and cist graves at Petit-Chasseur. In

Figure 3.3.   Le Petit-Chasseur dolmen MVI (© Muséees cantonaux du Valais, H. Preisig, CC BY-SA 4.0).

fact, one of the larger cist graves (MXI) was constructed entirely of fragments recycled from earlier Late Neolithic stelae that had been deliberately toppled and broken up. Many postholes were also uncovered around the edges of this cist grave, indicating that it had once stood within some sort of wooden structure, which may also have been roofed.

There are differences between the decoration on the Late Neolithic and Beaker statue menhirs, which archaeologists refer to as type A and B, respectively. The former stelae are quite plainly decorated, featuring simple depictions of belts and the distinctive, triangular copper daggers with semicircular bone pommels that are a characteristic feature of the Remedello culture[8] of northern Italy. The type B stelae erected by the later Beaker communities are much more richly decorated, with one example particularly well carved and

Figure 3.4.   Le Petit-Chausseur statue menhir (image courtesy of Ordrade123, CC BY-SA 3.0).

probably depicting a warrior, probably male, dressed in a garment featuring the triangle and lozenge patterns more typically found on Beaker pottery. A bow can be seen slung across his chest, and a necklace and belt are also depicted. The garment this figure is depicted as wearing may represent "quilted armor." As pointed out, this type of armor "is particularly effective against archery and there are numerous examples of it in the ethnographic record; perhaps its last appearance in action was at the battle of Omdurman in Sudan."[9] Alternatively, this geometric decoration may represent a woven garment made from a textile of some sort.

The symbolism of the Petit-Chasseur stelae can never be completely grasped, and "the question of whether these human portrayals represent high-ranking persons, divinities who protect these persons, or gods remains unanswered."[10] The depiction of weaponry on the menhirs also perhaps suggests that violence and conflict were not unknown among the communities who used the Petit-Chasseur necropolis and that elite warrior groups may have existed at this time. Whatever these decorated standing stones symbolize, there can be little doubt that they provide us with a fascinating reminder of the unknown prehistoric communities who raised them in this quiet and beautiful corner of southern Switzerland several thousand years ago.

MEGALITHS OF MAINLAND ITALY

Megalithic tombs are even thinner the ground in mainland Italy, although whether this is because of their later destruction in the face of agricultural and urban expansion or simply because "megalithic culture" did not fully take root there, as it did in other parts of Europe, is hard to say for sure. Whatever the case, Italian megalithic tombs are largely confined to the southeastern Apulia region (also known as Puglia), although an important group of dolmens and decorated menhirs resembling those found at Petit-Chasseur survive at Saint Martin de Corleans in the Italian part of the Aosta Valley (which is bordered by France and Switzerland).

The Bisceglie and Giovinazzo Gallery Graves

The dolmens found in the countryside around the port of Bari, the capital of Apulia, are the most impressive of the megalithic tombs found in mainland Italy. The best-known example is probably the Dolmen di Bisceglie (also known as the Chianca dolmen), which is also one of Italy's most famous megalithic monuments. The Bisceglie dolmen comprises a long megalithic gallery, approximately 10 meters long and 2 meters wide, that runs from east to west, with only one large capstone of its roof surviving today at the western end. Bisceglie was discovered and excavated by Italian archaeologists Franceso Samarelli, Angelo Mosso, and Michele Gervasio between 1909 and 1913. The evidence they uncovered at Bisceglie suggests that the dolmen had been constructed in the Early Bronze Age (ca. 2300 BCE) and continued to be used as place of burial and ritual for many hundreds of years, down until the Late Bronze Age (ca. 1200 BCE). The bones of at least thirteen individuals were recovered from Bisceglie along with a rich collection of artifacts that included items such as bone points, fragments from flint and obsidian blades, part of a limestone axe, a decorated copper or bronze disc, five amber beads, a small ivory disc, and several complete pottery vessels.

The largest and most striking of these Apulian megalithic tombs is the Giovinazzo cairn, another gallery grave built around the same time as the Dolmen di Bisceglie. Measuring nearly 30 meters long, this is quite a sophisticated structure; its megalithic gallery is covered by a low cairn composed of well-laid dry-stone masonry, running east-west, with a circular forecourt area at its western end, marking the entrance to the tomb. The Giovinazzo cairn was discovered by a local farmer, who unfortunately also cut it in half when he drove his bulldozer through the middle of the cairn, which at the time was hidden below the mound of earth that he was trying to level. Nevertheless, many human remains were recovered from within its long gallery or chamber, as were various grave goods such as Bronze Age pottery from Greece that had been made by artisans of the famous Mycenean civilization.

The Piccolo San Bernardo Cromlech

This fascinating stone circle, or cromlech, is impressively situated in the Aosta Valley, at the top of the Piccolo San Bernardo Pass, on the Italy-France border at an impressive height of nearly 2,200 meters above sea level (offering visitors stunning Alpine views). The circle, which has a very impressive diameter of about 72 meters, has been damaged by the modern mountain road that bisects it, but more than forty (sources quote either forty-three or forty-six) low-standing stones of an original fifty or so survive on either side of the road (in fact, one half of the circle lies in Italy, the other in France, and therefore, strictly speaking, it has "dual nationality"). Although archaeologists have been unable to obtain any firm evidence for the date of the Piccolo San Bernardo Cromlech, and it could possibly have been erected in the Iron Age by a Celtic tribe (Iron Age coins have been found within the circle), its appearance suggests a more probable construction date at some point in the third millennium BCE. Stone circles are something of a rarity in mainland Europe, as these mysterious megalithic monuments are primarily concentrated in Britain and Ireland, where many hundreds of examples still survive, with the majority of these erected between the Late Neolithic and Early Bronze Age (approximately 3000–1500 BCE).

The Pogio Rota Megaliths

Finally, there is the Pogio Rota "stone circle" in southern Tuscany, which was discovered on a hilltop overlooking the River Fiora in 2004 by researcher Giovanni Feo. Although the date of Pogio Rota has not been pinned down, its stones are thought to have been raised by people of the Rinaldone culture around the middle of the third millennium BCE. Pogio Rota covers an area of about 15 meters and comprises a roughly circular arrangement of five bulky standing stones, measuring approximately 3 meters high, around which are spread five smaller stones about half as high. The upper surface of one of these lower-lying stones appears to have been deliberately hollowed out to form a rough oval "bowl" that may well have been used to hold water used in rituals and ceremonies performed at the site. Italian researchers have suggested that Poggio Rota was originally an "astronomical temple" and that its builders aligned its stones on significant astronomical events (e.g., winter solstice sunset and the setting of the star Sirius). Whether or not this was the case, somewhat predictably, Poggio Rota has been dubbed the "Italian Stonehenge," and while this is "overegging the pudding" somewhat, this monument remains an enigmatic and unique reminder of Italy's prehistoric past.

• 4 •

Megalithic Iberia

There can be little doubt that one of the greatest achievements of Europe's megalith builders was the construction of the Menga dolmen in Spain. Situated some 22 miles north of the popular holiday resort of Málaga on the coast of Andalusia in southern Spain, Menga is a masterpiece of megalithic engineering that has been captivating people for many hundreds of years. Antiquarian accounts dating from the sixteenth to nineteenth centuries reveal that Menga has been variously interpreted as an ancient, pre-Roman refuge that protected people from pirates and wild animals, as a monument built by "supernatural beings in which men carried out sacrifices and demonic practices,"[1] and as an Iron Age druid shrine or temple. In the earlier twentieth century, archaeologists proposed that Menga was built in the Copper Age, but radiocarbon dating of charcoal found at Menga revealed that it was built as some point between 3800 and 3400 BCE in the later Neolithic.

Menga was built on top of a low hill and comprises a huge earthen tumulus (approximately 50 meters in diameter and 3.5 meters high), covering a megalithic chamber or gallery measuring about 27 meters long and 6 meters at its widest point (representing the largest megalithic chamber in Europe). Massive slabs of stone were used in its construction, and the three unique pillars that run down the center of the chamber were probably (but not definitely) inserted by Menga's builders as a supporting device for its capstones (they may perhaps have had a religious significance of some sort). It has been estimated that in total, the architectural components of Menga's chamber weigh about 840 tons, and the mind boggles as to how the massive stones used to build it were transported and moved into place, although the same could be said for many of Europe's megalithic monuments.

Adding to the unique character of Menga is the impressive circular shaft located just behind the third pillar at the back of the chamber, which was only

Figure 4.1.   Interior of the Menga dolmen (image courtesy of Pedro J. Pacheco, CC BY-SA 4.0).

discovered by archaeologists from the University of Granada in 2005. Measuring about 1.5 meters wide and around 13 meters deep, this intriguing feature may perhaps be a ritual shaft[2] dug by Menga's builders or could perhaps have even been there before the dolmen was built, providing the "sacred focus" of the monument. However, it is also quite possible that it was dug by the antiquarian Rafael Mitjana, who explored Menga in the nineteenth century, reputedly finding hundreds of skeletons in its chamber.

Standing just inside the entrance to Menga, the visitor to this exceptional megalithic structure will probably notice that its stones "frame" the small mountain of La Peña de Los Enamorados (Lovers Rock), some 4 miles to the north. This distinctive peak has been a familiar landmark for travelers throughout history (and no doubt prehistory too) and is famed for its striking silhouette or profile, which, when seen from the east or west, "evokes clearly the image of an upturned sleeping human head."[3] The mountain is also known as Montaña del Indio, as it is seen as resembling the head of a Native American Indian, and in local folklore it was said to be the head of a sleeping giantess. Many archaeologists are of the opinion that Menga's builders deliberately oriented their monument to this prominent landscape feature. In fact, using Geographical Information Software (GIS), archaeologists precisely plotted the axis of the Menga dolmen, which, when projected as a line, was found to pass directly through its steep northern cliffs.[4] This indicates that for the people who built Menga, La Peña de

Figure 4.2.   Pena de los Eñamorados (image courtesy of Grez, CC BY-SA 3.0).

Los Enamorados had special significance and was "an ideologically prominent place within the surrounding landscape."[5] In other words, La Peña de Los Enamorados was probably viewed as a sacred place by Menga's builders and a home to supernatural forces, with its anthropomorphic profile surely also not escaping their attention and perhaps lending the mountain its sacred importance.

THE VIERA AND EL ROMERAL DOLMENS

The Menga dolmen does not stand alone in the landscape, as two other fine megalithic tombs lie nearby; the closest, the Viera dolmen, is situated only about 70 meters from its more celebrated neighbor. Dated to ca. 3500–3000 BCE, Viera basically consists of a 19-meter-long megalithic gallery or corridor of twenty-five slab-like uprights and four capstones under a covering mound of a similar size to that of Menga. The gallery is divided into three sections by two slabs that have square openings, or "portals," cut into them near their bases, which a person can pass through, although only by stooping down. At the end of the gallery is a small, square chamber with a hole cut in its rear slab, pointing to the presence of later tomb robbers at Viera.

Some half a mile from Menga and Viera is the El Romeral dolmen. Unlike Menga and Viera, which are classed as gallery graves, El Romeral is a passage tomb of the "tholos" type, consisting of a long passage or corridor (about 26 meters), leading to a corbelled chamber at its end. Unusually, the dry-stone walls of

Figure 4.3. The megalithic gallery at the Viera dolmen (image courtesy of Olaf Tausch, CC BY-SA 3.0).

the passage, which is roofed by eleven huge slabs, lean slightly inward, creating a somewhat disorienting sense of being "funneled" toward the chamber, which was probably the desired intention of El Romeral's builders. The chamber is quite substantial, measuring 5 meters in diameter and 4 meters high, with smaller slabs and boulders used in the construction of its walls, which gradually curve inward the higher they go, to form the dome-like tholos chamber. A smaller, raised chamber lies just off the main one and has been assigned a gruesome purpose in local folklore, with the slab on its floor said to be a sacrificial altar on which prehistoric people were ritually murdered. El Romeral is the "youngest" of the tombs of the Antequera Necropolis, being constructed around five thousand years ago in the Early Copper Age.

Unfortunately, little in the way of archaeological finds was made by the various antiquarians and archaeologists who investigated the Menga, Viera, and El Romeral dolmens, and it is likely that we have later tomb robbers to thank for this scarcity. The only artifacts recovered from the three monuments were a few polished stone axes, long flint blades, and small tools (used for drilling and scraping), a copper punch or awl, a pottery bowl, and part of a possible stone quern used for processing grain.

Figure 4.4. El Romeral Tholos chamber (image courtesy of Ángel M. Felicíísmo, CC BY-SA 2.0).

MEGALITHIC TOMBS OF LOS MILLARES

In addition to boasting the three famous megalithic monuments of Menga, Viera, and El Romeral, the province of Andalusia is home to one of Europe's most famous prehistoric settlements: Los Millares, the type site of the well-known Millaran culture. Discovered in the late nineteenth century by two Belgian mining engineers, brothers Henri and Luis Siret, this large, fortified Copper Age site (covering some five hectares) dates to ca. 3000–2300 BCE and was built in a defensive position on the highest point of a promontory between the Andarax and Rambla de Huéchar rivers.[6] Three massive walls were built around its houses and workshops, some of which were used for copper working (the "wealth" of Los Millares was likely founded on the production and circulation of copper items). Just outside the outer wall, there is an extensive cemetery of around eighty surviving megalithic tombs, which are mainly small passage graves with domed chambers like that of El Romeral. The passages of many of the tombs are divided into two or three sections by upright slabs, which have large "porthole" openings cut into them.

Today, the Los Millares tombs are generally poorly preserved, but previous excavations unearthed the remains of around one hundred individuals in their

Figure 4.5.   Model of a Los Millares passage grave (image courtesy of Tuor123, CC BY-SA 3.0).

chambers. These people were buried with numerous and diverse grave goods such as copper axes, daggers, saws, chisels, small spearhead-like objects known as "palmella" points, flint arrowheads, stone and bone anthropomorphic "idols," and pottery vessels decorated with a distinctive motif that has been interpreted as representing either the sun or the eyes of a deity (this motif also appears on some of the so-called idols). A small number of tombs also yielded "prestige" grave goods such as boxes, combs, and idols made from ivory, ostrich eggshells, and amber. These artifacts point to the existence of an elite and powerful group at Los Millares tied in to long-distance exchange networks.

THE VALENCINA DE LA CONCEPCÍON TOMBS

The prehistoric "mega-site" of Valencina de la Concepcíon is located on the outskirts of Seville, the capital of Andalusia; covering some 450 hectares, it is the largest Copper Age settlement in Iberia, if not Europe. Several megalithic tombs are located within the boundaries of the settlement, such as the La Pastora and Montelirio tholos-type passage tombs. The former has a very impressive approximately 40-meter-long passage with dry-stone walls, leading to a stone-built corbelled chamber, while Montelirio has a passage of similar length, although it has two corbelled chambers, and these are roofed by sun-dried mud bricks.

Montelirio

Excavation of the Montelirio tomb also yielded "an extraordinary set of sumptuous grave goods"[7] that were probably buried with high-status members of Copper Age society. Among the grave goods were many thousands of beads, some of them made from amber, which had been used to decorate the long since decayed clothes or shrouds of the people buried in the tomb (some twenty-five individuals were found), as well as long flint arrowheads, fragments from four gold daggers, tiny crystal "micro-blades," and ten beautiful arrowheads made from rock crystal. A large fragment or "core" of rock crystal was also found, which had probably been used as the raw material to make the miniature crystal blades and arrowheads.

Structure 10042-10049

However, even more extraordinary were the grave goods that came to light during the excavation of the Valencina de la Concepcíon megalithic tomb that has the rather scientific moniker of "Structure 10042-10049." This monument is another example of a two-chambered passage tomb, with the burial deposit in its first chamber apparently disturbed by later activity. Just outside its entrance, archaeologists recovered the remains of four people, as well as grave goods that included flint arrowheads and blades, more than eight hundred sherds of pottery, a pottery figurine, and more than two thousand perforated beads covered in red powder (made from toxic cinnabar ore). In the second chamber, there was the skeleton of a young man (seventeen to twenty-five years old) who had been laid in the fetal position on his right side, with his head pointing toward the passage. The superb collection of grave goods found with him surely suggests that he was no "commoner" and was a person of some significance honored with a prestigious burial. Cinnabar powder had been scattered over the man's bones, and he was buried with a large ceramic plate, twenty-three flint blades, many small and fragmented ivory objects, a flint dagger blade with an amber pommel, and, rather remarkably, an elephant tusk. The tusk measures some 60 centimeters long, had been cut into three parts of a roughly similar size, and had been placed behind the young man's head, presumably during his funeral.

Above the young man, there was a secondary burial deposit, which appears to have been separated from the primary one by twenty-two horizontal slate slabs. The most notable object found in this deposit was an exquisite dagger made from rock crystal, which is ogival in shape and measures around 21 centimeters long, looking like something out of a fantasy film. Only a few centimeters from the dagger archaeologists found the ivory hilt and sheath of the dagger, which had been decorated with carved zigzag motifs. Another elephant tusk, or at least part of one, was recovered from the secondary deposit; it featured carved parallel lines and chequerboard motifs. Also discovered was a small ivory bowl, thirty-eight flint blades, and an ostrich eggshell.

MEGALITHIC PORTUGAL

The Alto Alentejo region of south-central Portugal, or the Évora district, as it is also known, after its ancient and picturesque capital city, has the densest concentration of megaliths in Iberia and was a core area of the megalithic phenomenon in Europe, perhaps also representing the place where it was "born." As Roger Joussaume has noted, "Many archaeologists see Alto Alentejo as a centre of megalithic creativity, and some would like to see in it the cradle of Atlantic megalith-building."[8] Whether or not Europe's first megaliths were built in this region, some examples date back to the very beginnings of the megalithic phenomenon, around seven thousand years ago. It could perhaps even be the case, as some archaeologists have proposed, that the earliest of these monuments date back as early as ca. 5500 BCE. Whatever the case, as in Brittany, the other core area of "megalithism" in Europe, the earliest megaliths of Alto Alentejo may have been the work of final Mesolithic hunter-gatherer communities who were reacting somehow to the new, incoming Neolithic lifestyle. One such monument is the Almendres cromlech, or megalithic enclosure, which lies about 10 miles west of Évora on the slopes of Monte dos Almendres (known locally as "the hill of the stone amphorae"). This is Portugal's largest megalithic monument, covering an area of some 70 by 40 meters, and has been nicely described by Simon Broughton:

> The Cromlech of the Almendres is only 15km west of Evora, down a maze of unmade lanes in a forest of cork trees. In spring, the open fields that surround it are a carpet of wild flowers and on midsummer's day, people come here to celebrate the solstice. . . . [T]here's no visitor centre and no amenities, just a lovely feeling of being in a sacred grove of stones. . . . There are about 90 huge, granite stones in what looks now like a sort of horseshoe, although originally it was probably a circle adjoining an ellipse. They are rounded and smooth, unlike the hewn stones of Stonehenge. Standing among them, you feel like you are in a corpulent crowd of granite friends, jostling to see something. The shapes are natural, weathered and softened by the elements, although several have decorations, which are difficult to make out without guidance.[9]

The "shepherd's crook" motif also features on the decorated standing stones of the Almendres enclosure. As we have already seen, this motif also appears on decorated Breton menhirs and strongly suggests connections between Early Neolithic communities in Brittany and Portugal. Somewhat surprisingly, it was not until 1966 that the Almendres cromlech emerged from obscurity, when a local geologist and amateur archaeologist, Henrique Leonor Pina, stumbled across its fallen and neglected stones while conducting a geological survey in the area. These were later re-erected by archaeologist Mario Varela Gomez, who endeavored to locate them as faithfully as possible in their original positions.

Although the Almendres cromlech is the standout example, other megalithic enclosures can be found in the Évora district (only twelve remain in total), such as the well-known and impressive Vale Maria do Meio monument, with its thirty-four standing stones, or the smallest of the Portuguese cromlechs, Vale d'el Rei, with its twelve stones arranged in a "perfect horseshoe shape."[10] It is thought

Figure 4.6. The Almendres cromlech (image courtesy of Ángel M. Felicíismo, CC BY-SA 2.0).

likely that the Early Neolithic communities who built the Portuguese cromlechs deliberately aligned them on various astronomical events such as the rising full moon around the time of the equinoxes.

PORTUGUESE MEGALITHIC TOMBS

Thousands of megalithic tombs, or *antas*, as they are generally known, can be found in Portugal, with two major concentrations in Évora/Alto Alentejo and the northern part of the country (i.e., the provinces of Beira, Douro, Minho, and Trás-os-Montes). Many of these monuments are passage graves, with the first examples being built as early as ca. 4500 BCE (if not a couple hundred years before this time), and typically comprise low passages with tall chambers, the walls of which are formed from megalithic uprights that often lean inward toward the interior. One of the earliest passage tombs to be built in Portugal was *anta* 1 at Poço da Gateira (Évora), which was excavated in 1948 by the famous German archaeologists Georg and Vera Leisner, a husband-and-wife team whose extensive work on the megalithic tombs of Iberia is unparalleled and remains a valuable source of information for researchers. Like many other early passage graves in Portugal, *anta* 1 at Poço da Gateira, which may have been built as early as ca. 4800 BCE, is a modest affair, with a small burial chamber and short passage covered by a circular mound measuring some 12 meters in diameter. Inside the chamber, acidic soil had put paid to any human remains, but the Leisners discovered eleven undecorated pottery vessels that had been arranged in a single line on the floor of the chamber, as well as several polished stone axes.

Georg and Vera Leisner also undertook excavations at the well-known Comenda da Igreja passage tomb (Évora), which today, thanks to erosion around the top of the burial chamber, has a unique "double-decker" appearance, looking

Figure 4.7. Comenda da Igreja passage grave (image courtesy of Dr Phillip C. Lucas, Stetson University, Florida).

like two separate tombs, one stacked on top of the other. This superb monument is probably the second-largest passage tomb in Portugal and has a total length of 16 meters, with the eight massive slabs used for its burial chamber standing 4.5 meters high. The capstone of the chamber, which broke in two at some point in the past, is equally impressive, measuring about 4.5 meters long by 4.5 meters wide. The 10-meter-long passage leading into chamber is only about 1 meter high, meaning that people would have had to crawl into the chamber when making burials. Included among the numerous artifacts uncovered by the Leisners were more than one hundred polished stone axes, a stone pendant in the shape of a rabbit, more than sixty decorated slate plaques (one of which was unusually large and measured 14 centimeters in height), pottery bowls, a copper awl, large flint daggers, and hundreds of perforated beads made from various materials such as amber, amethyst, and variscite.

The Great Dolmen of Zambujeiro

The largest passage tomb in the whole of the Iberian Peninsula is the Great Dolmen of Zambujeiro, although sadly this mighty megalithic monument is today in somewhat poor condition, thanks in part to neglect by the Portuguese authorities. Located in a peaceful olive grove some 3 miles from the Almendres cromlech, Zambujeiro was built about a thousand years later than its near neighbor and comprises a long, low passage (12 meters long and 2 meters high), leading to a polygonal burial chamber about 5 meters in width. The seven enormous slabs used for its walls rise to a height of 8 meters, making the megalithic burial chamber of Zambujeiro the tallest example known in Europe. The remains of the tumulus or mound of earth and rubble that once covered the passage and chamber can still be seen at the site, with this tumulus originally measuring about 50 meters in diameter. The massive capstone of the burial chamber now lies broken in pieces on the western slope of the mound, and a huge and narrow slab of stone with a concave surface lies on the ground near the entrance to the tomb. The original purpose of this prostrate slab is unclear, as is the meaning of the numerous "cupmarks" that have been carved into its surface. These small, concave circular carvings can be found on many of Europe's megalithic monuments and also on open-air rock outcrops. Their true meaning is lost in the dim shadows of prehistory, but they perhaps symbolize the sun, moon, or stars (or possibly all three).

Zambujeiro was discovered by Henrique Leonor Pina, who uncovered the remains of several people in its burial chamber, along with numerous artifacts such as polished stone axes, long flint blades, pottery vessels, and engraved stone plaques and "croziers" resembling the crook motif found on some Portuguese and Breton menhirs. More than a thousand stone plaques (which are normally made from schist or slate) have been found in Portugal, with the majority found in the passage tombs of Alto Alentejo. These intriguing objects are decorated with geometric shapes, and some also feature motifs resembling wide, staring eyes, giving them a somewhat owl-like appearance. It has been remarked that the plaques with the probable eye motifs "may be linked symbolically with the moon implying a lunar cult among the people responsible for erecting the monuments."[11] With this in mind, it has been noted, "An examination of . . . published ground plans of passage tombs in the administrative district of Évora in central Portugal reveals an exceptional conformity in the orientation of their passages. It is here suggested that observations of the rising of the first full moon, or sightings of the first lunar crescent, which followed the vernal [Spring] equinox, were instrumental in orienting the passages."[12]

Unfortunately, Pina's excavation of Zambujeiro in 1965 and 1966 was rather careless, and his removal of a large part of the tumulus from around its passage and chamber destabilized the monument. There is also a suspicion that Pina removed the capstone of Zambujeiro's chamber by blasting it with dynamite, although he always denied this. Whatever the truth, the "temporary" and unsightly metal roof that was erected over Zambujeiro in 1984 has not helped in its preservation, as it is still in place, and the rain that runs off it is further weakening the dolmen's stability. In fact, the Great Dolmen is now in real danger of collapse unless some serious restoration work is soon carried out at this remarkable but overlooked monument.

Figure 4.8.   The burial chamber of the Great Dolmen of Zambujeiro in 1971, shortly after its excavation (image courtesy of John Atherton, CC BY-SA 2.0).

"Star Dolmens" of the Mondego Valley

Like those in other parts of Europe, some of Portugal's megaliths may have been aligned on certain stars or constellations in the night sky rather than on the sun or moon or on parts of the landscape that were held sacred. An example of this could be provided by a group of passage graves that cluster in the Mondego Valley (also known as the "Mondego Platform") of north-central Portugal, with the Dolmen da Orca being the largest and best known of these monuments. An archaeological analysis of the Dolmen da Orca and several other of the Mondego Valley tombs has shown that their passages face the mountain range on the horizon known as Serra da Estrela (Mountain Range of the Star). More specifically, this analysis revealed that "within this mountain range there is a particular region that was specifically targeted by the dolmen builders."[13] This region of the horizon does not correspond to the highest peak of the Serra da Estrela, as perhaps might be expected, with all the tomb passages aligned to the left of this peak, with no significant lunar or solar events taking place in this part of the sky. The Mondego Valley tombs were constructed ca. 4300–3700 BCE, and, intriguingly, one of the brightest stars in the night sky, Aldebaran, "would have risen exactly within the band of the horizon that is visible from within all [these] corridor dolmens [passage graves]."[14] It is also interesting to note that in one of the chambers of the tombs, there is a faded motif painted in red ocher that looks like a five-rayed star, and Aldebaran has a reddish color when it appears in the sky.

It could perhaps even be the case that the folktale associated with the "Mountain Range of the Star" has ancient roots and provides us with an echo of Neolithic life in the Mondego Valley. This tale tells that the Serra da Estrela was named by a shepherd from this area who traveled to the top of a nearby mountain range with his dog after becoming fascinated by the very bright star that he had seen illuminating its peaks. Intriguingly, archaeological evidence suggests that the Neolithic communities that constructed the Mondego Valley passage graves were pastoralists who lived near these monuments in the fall and winter but moved their herds of sheep and goat to the high passes of the Serra da Estrela in the kinder spring and summer months.

Even though the architectural evidence of the Mondego Valley passage tombs literally points in this direction, we can never say for sure whether they were deliberately aligned by their builders on the rising of the giant red star, Aldebaran. However, it is worth considering that in many ancient and more recent nonstate societies around the world, the stars were an integral part of religious beliefs and practices. For example, shamans of the famous Inca civilization of western South America regularly made sacrifices to the distinctive Pleiades star cluster, which was believed to be a sacred place, or *huaca*, inhabited by powerful spirits; the Incas also believed that the stars protected animals on earth. The

Figure 5.1. Model showing the remains of the Ġgantija temple complex, National Museum of Malta, Valetta (image courtesy of Ethan Doyle White, CC BY-SA 4.0).

aligned not only with the rising sun at the equinoxes but also with sunrise at both the summer and the winter solstices. Whether or not this was the case at Mnajdra, this temple complex certainly stands in a beautiful and peaceful location, "with no modern development in sight, only the flowery slopes, the sea and the rocky islet of Filfla in the distance."[2]

It is hard to say for sure why the Maltese archipelago became home to such distinctive and elaborate structures in the middle of the fourth millennium BCE.[3] Their abrupt *Mary Celeste*–like abandonment about a thousand years later also remains something of an archaeological mystery. Some scholars, however, have proposed that the temples were built by rival clans or tribes who were competing with each other for good agricultural land and water, which was becoming increasingly scarce as a result of severe soil erosion ultimately caused by the first Neolithic settlers, who cleared the land of its natural vegetation; eventually the environmental situation became so dire that the later temple builders were forced to leave Malta and Gozo to seek out new, fertile lands. An alternative and darker scenario is that warlike invaders from outside the Maltese archipelago aggressively drove the temple-building communities from Malta and Gozo. Whether or not this was the case, archaeological evidence found at the temple complexes and other sites on the islands attests to the arrival of newcomers in around 2500 BCE. Although the identity of these people remains a mystery, unlike the temple builders, they cremated their dead and had a different material culture, which included novel items such as axes and daggers of copper or bronze, as well as strikingly decorated pottery and figurines.

Archaeologists think these newcomers also constructed the megalithic burial chambers found on Malta and Gozo, which resemble the Neolithic dolmens found further west along the Atlantic facade. Although they only survive in small numbers, there were once probably many more of these Maltese dolmens, which tend to be modest in size and somewhat crude in appearance, although some examples have quite substantial capstones covering their chambers (e.g., the Wied Filep dolmen on Malta, which has a capstone measuring almost 4 meters long).

When it comes to the driving forces that lay behind the construction of the Maltese temple complexes, we are somewhat in the dark. However, it seems unlikely that these magnificent megalithic monuments were built by a society without leaders, and ruling groups or families were probably responsible for their construction, also using them as means of maintaining and reinforcing their elevated position in society. Much the same can probably be said for many other megalithic monuments in Europe.

Ġgantija

The famous site of Ġgantija (Giant's Tower), located on Gozo's Xagħra plateau, is one of the most impressive of the Maltese temple complexes, with some of the megalithic slabs used in the construction of its massive wall measuring more than 5 meters long and weighing about 50 tons. The wall encloses two separate temple buildings: the southern one is the larger and earlier of the two, built around 3600 BCE in the early temple-building period, and the northern one was constructed some five hundred years later. Within the five apses of the southern temple building are decorated rectangular "altar" blocks featuring spiral-like motifs, although these are now badly weathered. A slab-like menhir, which has a relief carving of a snake on one of its edges, once stood within the southern temple, but this now resides in the Victorian Museum on Malta. What snakes meant to the Maltese temple builders can never be known for sure, but it seems highly likely that this carving has some sort of religious symbolism.

Regrettably, a great deal of archaeological evidence must have been lost during the "excavation" of Ġgantija in 1827 by John Otto Bayer, the lieutenant governor of Malta. Bayer haphazardly cleared out the debris that filled its interior and kept no records of any finds, with a similar approach taken at the other Maltese temples explored by his fellow antiquarians. Nevertheless, some important artifacts have survived from the site, such as the famous sculpted human heads discovered in one of the apses of the southern temple building by General de la Marmora in 1832. Although the faces on these limestone sculptures are badly weathered, traces of the eyes and noses of the two individuals they represent can still be discerned, as can their rather modern-looking bobbed haircuts. The symbolism of these sculpted heads, however, remains a mystery.

Tarxien

Tarxien is the most complex and celebrated of the Maltese megalithic temple complexes, with the various excavations carried out here yielding "some of the most important art works . . . created during Mediterranean prehistory."[4] Although Tarxien is now surrounded by modern buildings in the small town of Tarxien in southeastern Malta, it still opens a wonderful window onto the temple-building culture of Late Neolithic Malta and rightly attracts many thousands of visitors every year.

Dating from ca. 3600–2500 BCE, Tarxien lay undiscovered for more than four thousand years, only coming to light again in 1913, after a local farmer had mentioned to the "father" of Maltese archaeology, Sir Themistocles "Temi" Zammit, that he had often snagged his plow on huge stone blocks lying just below the surface of his fields. Zammit subsequently visited Tarxien but had to wait for two years to begin its excavation, as at the time of its discovery he was working at the amazing "hypogeum" of Ħal Saflieni (more of which below) nearby. His excavation campaign at Tarxien ran from 1915 to 1919 (although work at the site was interrupted for a while between 1916 and 1917 because of World War I), with Zammit uncovering four adjacent temple units: Tarxien Far East (Tarxien FE), Tarxien South, Tarxien East, and Tarxien Central. Tarxien FE, the smallest and earliest building, dates to ca. 3600 BCE, with the other three built during a major phase of construction that took place between ca. 3000 and 2500 BCE.

Inside the Tarxien Temple Complex.   As has been rightly noted, Tarxien South contains "one of the most important repositories of art works known from world prehistory."[5] The most remarkable of these works is the famous "fat lady" statue that Zammit discovered in the outer right-hand chamber, just inside the huge trilithon entrance (which is a modern reconstruction). Originally, the statue would have stood nearly 3 meters high. Sadly, however, it was broken in two by local farmers, with the remaining lower half showing a figure wearing a pleated skirt; perhaps (but not definitely) female, her "monstrous calves and tiny feet hardly match modern standards of beauty."[6] Faint traces of red and black pigment can still be seen on the statue, reminding us that the temple complexes were originally much more colorful places than they are today (wall fragments painted with red ocher have also been found at some temple sites such as Ġgantija). A replica of the Tarxien "fat lady" statue today stands in the apse, with the original removed for safekeeping to Malta's National Museum of Archaeology. The true meaning of the "fat lady" lies lost with the Neolithic temple builders of Malta, but scholars have often interpreted this figure as a representation of a "mother goddess" who was central to their religion.

Smaller versions of the Tarxien "fat lady," in the form of figurines or statuettes, have been found at Tarxien and several other Maltese temple complexes.

Figure 5.2. The famous "fat lady" statue from Tarxien (image courtesy of Briangotts, CC BY-SA 3.0).

For example, at Ħagar Quim five examples were found hidden below the steps within the temple's interior, perhaps representing a votive offering made to the deities worshipped here. Another discovery made at the site was the Venus of Ħagar Quim. This small but intriguing pottery figurine (nearly 13 centimeters high) is missing its head and feet but depicts a standing and naked female figure with shortened arms folded under drooping, overexaggerated breasts, somewhat resembling the famous Venus figurines made by the peoples of Upper Paleolithic (Old Stone Age) Europe between 35,000 and 10,000 BCE. It is a highly unusual, naturalistic piece, and nothing else like it has been found at the Maltese temples apart perhaps from a much cruder example (7 centimeters high) recovered from Tarxien. Somebody had jabbed small bone splinters into the clay of this grotesque and misshapen figure before it was fired in a kiln. It is suspected that it represents an early version of a voodoo doll, with the person who made this somewhat sinister object trying to inflict pain or harm on a rival or enemy through sympathetic magic.

Also found in the outer eastern apse of Tarxien South was a finely decorated rectangular altar with spiral motifs carved in relief on its front surface and a small, boxlike structure with a central opening on its top. Temi Zammit first came across this altar in 1915, and after clearing the rubble surrounding it, he

Figure 5.3.   Decorated block from the outer eastern apse at Tarxien South (image courtesy of Berthold Werner, CC BY-SA 3.0).

subsequently discovered that it was hollow. Inside he discovered an intriguing collection of objects that included sheep and ox bones, several seashells and flint blades, a long, bone "spatula," and a large flint knife measuring nearly 12 centimeters long. Archaeologists think that this curious cache of artifacts relates to animal sacrifices that were carried out within Tarxien South.

There are also two beautifully carved blocks showing animal figures in the western chamber of Tarxien South; one features twenty-two horned sheep or goats, and the other, fragmentary one depicts four sheep/goats, a pig, and a probable ram. Two upright stone slabs about 1.5 meters in height also flank the short, paved passageway that leads into the interior of the apse, on which are the famous ship "graffiti," which were only discovered in 1956. Around thirty-six crudely inscribed carvings depicting prehistoric ships or boats like those seen in ancient Egyptian and Greek art can be seen on the slabs. Although the exact date of these ship carvings is unclear, it has been suggested that they were executed shortly before the abandonment of the temples in around 2500 BCE, representing "the votives of those who escaped from storm and shipwreck, and who, reaching shelter in the prehistoric backwater of Grand Harbor, paid their vows to some deity unknown to us, in the temples of Tarxien."[7]

Tarxien Central

Tarxien Central is unique among the Maltese temple complexes in that it contains six apses or chambers, rather than the usual three to five, and it also displays fine, sophisticated stonework in its architecture. Interestingly, some of this stonework shows clear signs of a fierce fire that swept through the building at some point in the past. This fire may possibly have been deliberately started by the newcomers who arrived in the Maltese archipelago in the middle of the third millennium BCE. As in Tarxien South, several decorated stones are incorporated into the layout of Tarxien Central, such as the low-lying rectangular block decorated with two spiral motifs that look like staring eyes, which lies in the middle of the entrance leading to the rear chambers (like many of the decorated stone blocks of the Maltese temples, this is a replica of the original). This stone perhaps symbolizes a powerful deity and was put in place to ward off unwanted intruders.

In a secluded chamber close to a paved passage that links the Tarxien Central and Tarxien South temple units, there are badly weathered relief carvings depicting two bulls and a sow with piglets. As with the carvings of the sheep/goats, pig, and probable ram at Tarxien South, these carvings likely reflect the importance of domesticated livestock in the Neolithic economy of the temple builders.

MALTESE UNDERGROUND TEMPLES: THE XAGĦRA/ BROCHTORFF CIRCLE AND ĦAL SAFLIENI HYPOGEUM

The well-known and unique site known alternately as the Xagħra or Brochtorff Circle lies on the summit of the Xagħra plateau, only some 300 meters away from the Ġgantija temple complex. The Xagħra Circle was first recorded by King Louis XVI's official engraver, Jean Houel, in his *Voyages pittoresque des ilses de Sicile, de Malta, de Lipari* (1787) and explored in 1826 by John Otto Bayer. Unfortunately, like that at Ġgantija the following year, Bayer's exploration of the Xagħra Circle may have been "enthusiastic," but it was far from "scientific," and he basically destroyed any surface features at the site, also leaving no record of his work or finds.

However, the talented artist after whom the site is sometimes named, Charles Brochtorff (a German infantry officer who settled in Malta in the early nineteenth century), was fortunately on hand to make several detailed watercolors and engravings during Bayer's "archaeological excavation." One of these shows a megalithic enclosure or circle (approximately 45 meters wide) of large, roughly shaped stones standing side by side, with a gap in the enclosure to the east flanked by two even larger, pillar-like standing stones, which may originally have been capped by a lintel to form a monumental trilithon entrance. This entrance faced directly east toward Ġgantija, indicating a link between the Xagħra Circle and the nearby temple complex, with the group who used Ġgantija as their place of worship probably using the Xagħra Circle as their place of burial. Another of Brochtorff's paintings shows the large cavernous hole that Bayer dug in the center of the site, inside which can be seen megalithic uprights and a few trilithon altars. In the same scene, a man with a human skull in one hand can be seen climbing out of a cave that lies to the left behind these megalithic structures.

Aside from a few nineteenth-century accounts of the Xagħra Circle by people such as William Henry Smyth (a Royal Navy officer who was also something of an antiquarian), it remained all but unknown until 1964, when its three surviving megaliths were identified as the remains of a megalithic enclosure by a well-respected local historian, Joseph Attard Tabone. It was not until 1987, however, that a joint team of archaeologists from the Universities of Malta, Cambridge, and Bristol returned to begin re-excavating Xagħra Circle. Although the megalithic settings uncovered during Bayer's excavations had long since been destroyed, what they subsequently discovered here during seven seasons of arduous archaeological excavation probably exceeded all their expectations.

The Anglo-Maltese team uncovered a series of caves and interconnecting chambers, at the entrance to which they found the remains of a megalithic pavement flanked by two trilithon altars, or "shrines."[8] A pit adjacent to these contained many hundreds of human bones (mostly belonging to males) that had been taken from already decomposed bodies. These altars "may have been used for preliminary sacrifices and obeisances before the priest and the assembled mourning community ventured down into the foul, reeking caves of the dead."[9]

Below ground, megalithic pillars were erected on the edges of the smaller caves and chambers, while in the center of the main cave, two trilithon altars, a curved megalithic screen, and a square slab with a central carved hole were set up around a huge stone bowl that had been placed in a pit. Two large pits adjacent to this central "shrine" and a cavity in the cave contained thousands of human bones that had been carefully sorted and stacked into piles according to type, with, for example, skulls placed in one area of the pit and femurs (thigh bones) in another. Scientific analysis of some of the bones from the pits revealed that the people to whom they belonged had been healthy and little troubled by illness or disease; fifteen "fat lady" figurines were also found mixed in with the bones.

One of the most exciting objects recovered from the caves was the finely carved stone sculpture found near the stone bowl in the central shrine area, which depicts two "fat ladies" sitting side by side on a wickerwork bed or couch decorated with curvilinear designs, which had been daubed with red ocher before it was buried. Both "ladies" wear pleated skirts that still have traces of black paint on them, and while one of the figures is missing its head, the other is complete and has a ponytail. A tiny clothed person (perhaps a baby) can also be seen sitting in the lap of the complete figure, while the headless figure holds a cup in his or her lap. A fragmentary "fat lady" figurine that had originally measured at least 2 feet high was also found on the edge of one of the burial pits near the shrine and may have been placed here to protect the dead.

Another notable discovery was the so-called shaman's cache comprising nine carved-stone "idols," which was also found near the stone bowl in the

Figure 5.4.   The "Shaman's Cache" found at the Xagħra Circle (image courtesy of Hamelin de Guettelet, CC BY-SA 3.0).

central shrine. Six of these small sculptures or figurines take the form of simple but rather haunting human figures with flat triangular bodies and carved human heads. They measure some 16 centimeters in height and are just the right size and weight to fit into a human hand. Although one example seems to be unfinished and is crude in appearance, the others are finely carved with distinct faces and bobbed haircuts; the two finest figures wear pleated skirts, belts, and headdresses of some sort. The three smaller figurines are rather curious and consist of a boar's head on a vertical stump, a well-carved human head with a bobbed haircut sitting atop a vertical curved stand with a sloping base, and a human head with two projecting stumps.

THE ĦAL SAFLIENI HYPOGEUM

The Xagħra Circle is a remarkable reminder of how Europe's megalith builders sometimes built their ritual and religious sites underground, but it pales in comparison to the spectacular Ħal Saflieni Hypogeum. This world-famous and unique masterpiece of subterranean megalithic engineering was discovered in 1902 on the outskirts of Casal Paola in southeastern Malta, where much-needed new houses were being built for a growing population. The first excavations at Ħal Saflieni were conducted in 1904–1906 by a man of the church who was also a leading authority on Malta's antiquities, Father Emmanuel Magri. Unfortunately, Father Magri died unexpectedly while away on missionary work in Tunisia, and Sir Themistocles Zammit took over the archaeological exploration of the site, concluding his excavations at Ħal Saflieni in 1911.

Basically, Ħal Saflieni is a huge underground ritual and funerary complex consisting of three distinct levels (with the lowest some 10 meters below ground level) of interconnecting rock-cut chambers, built and used between ca. 3300 and 2500 BCE. The earliest activity at Ħal Saflieni dates to around six thousand years ago, when a now destroyed megalithic building of some sort was probably built on the surface. This vast and atmospheric underground space must have had a considerable impact on any Neolithic "initiates" who were granted access to its labyrinthine arrangement of chambers and galleries: "Any visitor to the Hypogeum soon appreciates the remarkable resonance qualities of the subterranean complex; the echo of a voice or handclap can rumble on through the chambers and galleries in a most eerie fashion. There can be no doubt that the people who created and used the Hypogeum would have been equally aware of the acoustics of the place—it would have been impossible for it to have been otherwise."[10]

The oldest, upper level of the Ħal Saflieni Hypogeum was carved out of a limestone hill that overlooks Malta's Grand Harbor and is represented by several roughly finished rock-cut chambers and a monumental trilithon setting of two uprights and a lintel. The middle level is the most architecturally complex and sophisticated of the hypogeum's three levels, with its most notable components being the main chamber and the famous Holy of Holies chamber, which has become an iconic symbol of Malta. Both are beautifully carved in relief and mimic the architecture of the temples above ground, comprising curved trilithon settings and corbelled roofs, revealing the supreme skills of the people who laboriously created these atmospheric spaces out of solid rock. The main chamber is built on two levels (with the Holy of Holies reached through a superbly carved doorway in the upper one), and when viewed from the exterior "lobby" area, this underground space is visually striking: "The effect is similar to that often experienced in a modern day fish-eye camera lens only in the case of the Hypogeum, the illusion was achieved by a thoughtful arrangement of relief carvings."[11]

To the right of the main chamber is the Painted Room, with cruder, roughly cut walls. However, its domed ceiling was more smoothly finished so that it could be decorated in red ocher with the spirals and closely set swirls that cover it, looking somewhat like vine tendrils. Ħal Saflieni's lower level is reached by a series of steps that are accessed from an entrance in the Holy of Holies chamber. The main chamber of the lower level is the so-called Oracle Room, which also

Figure 5.5.   Photo of the entrance to the "Holy of Holies" chamber at Ħal Saflieni, taken by Richard Ellis in 1910 (CC public domain).

features red-ocher decoration on its roof, similar to that seen in the Painted Room, although here solid circular blobs or discs are set among the spirals and swirls and look like fruit of some sort. There is a roughly oval niche measuring about 0.5 meters deep carved into one of the Oracle Room's walls, which produces an eerie, deep echoing sound when someone speaks into it. It could be that the niche was deliberately designed so that it would magnify the utterances of Neolithic priests or priestesses, although most scholars are of the opinion that it was a receptacle for a sacred object of some sort.

The excavations undertaken at the Ħal Saflieni Hypogeum by Father Magri and Temi Zammit uncovered thousands of human bones (from approximately seven thousand individuals) and a huge collection of artifacts in its chambers and passages, revealing how this amazing place had been used as an underground cemetery for around a thousand years. The Tarxien temple complex only lies about half a mile away from Ħal Saflieni, suggesting that the hypogeum was the burial ground of the communities who built and used Tarxien as their "place of worship." Among the small finds from Ħal Saflieni were objects such as finely crafted bowls and pots; huge numbers of buttons, beads, and pendants made from seashells; stone "mallets" (one of which, rather remarkably, still had its wooden handle attached); stone axe pendants; small animal figurines; and two small limestone heads sporting bobbed haircuts. Also found were a small number of "fat lady" figurines, with the finest and most remarkable of these the now

Figure 5.6.   The "Sleeping Lady" of Ħal Saflieni (image courtesy of Jan van der Crabben, CC BY-SA 3.0).

famous "Sleeping Lady" of Ħal Saflieni. This ample female figure (approximately 12 centimeters in length) is depicted lying on her right side on a bed or couch, with her right hand tucked under her cheek, which rests on a small pillow; she is naked to the waist and wears a fringed skirt that reaches down to her calves. As has been pointed out, "We can enjoy the superb artistry of the 'Sleeping Lady' of Ħal Saflieni, even if we are completely baffled in trying to divine her meaning."[12]

MEGALITHIC SARDINIA, MENORCA, AND CORSICA

No megalithic monuments matching the magnificence of the Maltese temples can be found on any other of the Mediterranean islands, but some spectacular megaliths nevertheless survive on Sardinia, Menorca, and Corsica. Many of the holidaymakers who flock to these beautiful sun-kissed islands every year are unaware of these fascinating monuments, which bear witness to the various prehistoric peoples who once lived here.

Sardinian Megaliths

The prehistoric communities of the Italian island of Sardinia left behind many megalithic reminders of their lives. One of the earliest, the Neolithic necropolis

Figure 5.7.   Sa Coveccada dolmen (image courtesy of Giovanni Sue, CC BY-SA 3.0).

of Li Muri, sits in the rocky hills above the town of Arzachena, near the island's northeastern coast in the province of Sassari. Although not particularly well preserved, this fascinating site began life in ca. 3500 BCE and continued to be in use for some eight hundred years. It comprises four interconnected stone circles with slender upright slabs, with each circle surrounded by a low platform of stones. Within the center of each circle is a burial cist, and during the 1939 excavation of Li Muri, each of these yielded fragmentary human bones and a fine collection of artifacts, including flint knives, pottery, stone axes and mace heads, obsidian arrowheads, beads, and a bowl made from steatite (soapstone). The bones and the objects had also been covered with red ocher when they were originally placed in the cists, and a fifth cist without a stone circle can also be seen at the necropolis, along with a later *allée couverte*, or gallery grave, located on its perimeter.

Numerous megalithic tombs also survive in Sardinia, with the largest and most impressive, the Sa Coveccada dolmen, also in Sassari province. This monument is thought to date to ca. 3000 BCE and consists of a rectangular burial chamber or gallery that measures nearly 3 meters in height and 5 meters long, with massive slabs of volcanic rock used for its walls and capstone. The front slab of the tomb features a low, carved doorway, or "soul hole," and just to the left is a curious carved niche in the base of the huge slab used for the wall of the chamber. It is possible that this marks a place where offerings were left for the dead by the living.

The Tomba dei Giganti

The most distinctive Sardinian megalithic tombs are the Bronze Age *tomba dei giganti* ("giants' tombs"), with many examples built by people of the sophisticated Nuragic culture (ca. 1800–500 BCE). These monuments are often located near the famous stone towers, or *nuraghi*, of Sardinia, which the Nuragic people built as fortified residences or refuges. The earliest giants' tombs date to before the building of the *nuraghi* (which can be found in the hundreds across Sardinia), however, and were constructed by people of the Bonnanaro culture, which archaeologists see as marking the embryonic stage of the Nuragic civilization.

A typical *tomba dei giganti* comprises a low rectangular burial chamber with a curved end, made of either megalithic uprights or dry-stone walling and fronted by a taller, semicircular megalithic facade of standing stones or large stone blocks. The large forecourt areas in front of the tombs were also clearly used as places where people gathered to perform rituals and ceremonies, as revealed by the thousands of pottery sherds unearthed in the forecourts of the *tomba dei giganti* that have been excavated by archaeologists. One of the finest and best-known examples is Coddu Vecchiu, near the Li Muri stone circles. As with several other giants' tombs, the people who constructed Coddu Vecchiu in the earlier second millennium BCE reused an earlier gallery grave as its burial chamber, which they enclosed within a low cairn made from courses of dry-stone walling. The monumental facade of menhirs at the front of the monument measures about 12 meters wide and has a central entrance stone, or stele, that stands about 4 meters high. This stele consists of two massive slabs of stone, one on top of the other, with the upper stone having a rounded top. A small, curved doorway or porthole in the center of the lower stone provides access to the burial chamber (although this would have entailed crawling).

Sardinia is also home to numerous rock-cut tombs known as *domus de janus* ("houses of the fairies"). Constructed between the Neolithic and Copper Age (ca. 3500–2500 BCE), many of these tombs are decorated with carvings and paintings, representing the densest concentration of "megalithic art" in all of Europe. Typically cut into slopes or cliffs overlooking river valleys and located next to each other in clusters or necropolises, the *domus de janus* vary considerably in design, but the classic type comprises an entrance passage and antechamber leading to a large central chamber, off which can be found several smaller ones (some examples feature as many as twelve subsidiary chambers). Sometimes the main chambers imitate domestic dwellings, with features such as roof beams, doorways, and columns or pillars carved in relief into the rock. The walls of the

Figure 5.8. Coddu Vecchiu giants' grave (image courtesy of Heinz-Josef Lücking, CC BY-SA 3.0 DE).

domus de janus were often decorated with geometric motifs such as zigzags and spirals, along with "bucrania" motifs representing horned cattle or bull's heads. A popular idea holds that these motifs symbolize a male deity who was the counterpart of a female mother goddess.

Corsican Megaliths

The island of Corsica has some superb megalithic monuments, such as the well-known Fontanaccia dolmen and the many striking "statue menhirs," standing stones carved to represent anthropomorphic warrior figures with weapons. The most famous Corsican statue menhirs are undoubtedly those found at the renowned site of Filitosa in the southwestern part of the island. The site is located on a rocky spur overlooking the beautiful Taravo Valley and was excavated in the mid-twentieth century by the French archaeologist Roger Grosjean, a colorful character who led a very interesting life. Before he became an archaeologist, Grosjean was a member of the Free French Air Force during World War II and worked as a double agent for the British Security Service (MI5), codenamed "Fido." Tragically, Grosjean died of a heart attack at just fifty-five years old, by which time he was an established authority on Corsican prehistory and at the height of his career. Today, he is widely regarded as one of the most significant figures in the founding of modern Corsican archaeology.

At Filitosa, Grosjean uncovered a complex archaeological sequence dating from the Mesolithic to the Iron Age. Various architectural features can be seen at the site, such as the remains of stone huts and two circular stone towers, or *torri*, but it is the statue menhirs that provide the biggest draw for Filitosa's numerous visitors today. Carved in relief on the surfaces of many of these standing stones are swords, daggers, and simple but rather haunting human faces, with some statue menhirs standing around 4 meters high and weighing as much as 21 tons. Grosjean came up with the interesting (but disputed) theory that they had been seen set up by the Bronze Age inhabitants of Filitosa to "magically"

protect them from the invading "Torrean" people who built the *torri* that can
be found scattered in their hundreds across Corsica. Grosjean further suggested
that the statues had failed to serve their purpose and were cast down after Filitosa had been attacked and taken over by Torrean invaders; many of them had
been broken and were subsequently recycled as building material for the stone
towers erected at the site.

Figure 5.9.   Statue Menhir V, Filitosa (image courtesy of Clemensfranz, CC BY-SA 3.0).

Grosjean also uncovered two alignments of menhirs near the above Fontanaccia dolmen while working on the Cauria plateau in 1964. Included among the forty-five stones in these two stone rows were several statue menhirs. Two of the carved standing stones (Cauria II and IV) are particularly impressive and depict warriors wearing short swords on their chests that are slung in scabbards hanging from their shoulders, with what look like loincloths also seen around the waists of the figures. Both statues also feature holes on their tops on the left and right sides, and it seems likely, as Grosjean suggested, that these holes originally held real or model horns. He also noted the striking resemblance between the warriors depicted on these statues and those carved in relief into the wall of the famous Egyptian temple of Medinet Habu, which shows a sea battle fought between Egyptian forces and one of the mysterious "Sea Peoples"—the "Sherden" or "Shardana." The Sea Peoples are thought have been a confederation of Late Bronze peoples from various parts of the Mediterranean, and Grosjean (not implausibly) concluded that the Sherden or Shardana warriors depicted at Medinet Habu were in fact Torrean warriors from Sardinia.

Menorcan Megaliths

Some scholars would probably disagree that the Balearic Island of Menorca has "the most evocative megalithic monuments on Spanish soil,"[13] but the *naveta* and *taula* monuments found there undoubtedly provide us with outstanding and unique examples of late megalithic architecture. The evidence from the small numbers of *navetas* and *taulas* that have been excavated suggests that these monuments were mainly built between 1400 and 800 BCE by Late Bronze Age communities of the Talayotic period (ca. 1700–125 BCE).

A typical *naveta* is shaped somewhat like the hull of an upturned boat, with the front of the monument flattened and the rear rounded or pointed. Horizontal courses of huge stone blocks were used to construct the *navetas*, with their builders also going to the trouble of carefully dressing the blocks so that they had smooth surfaces. The *navetas* functioned as collective burial places, with their chambers accessed through narrow doorways. Immediately behind the doorways are small antechambers leading to a main lower room or chamber, above which there can be a smaller chamber that may have been used to dry out the corpses of the recently deceased. The largest and best preserved is the Naveta d'Es Tudons ("boat of the woodpigeons"), which measures nearly 15 meters long and about 6 meters wide and today reaches a height of about 4 meters, although originally it would have stood closer to 6 meters high. The ceiling of the lower chamber is made of massive slabs, with the ceiling of the upper one containing what appear to be ventilation holes. Es Tudons was excavated in 1959 and 1960, and the skeletal remains of more than one hundred people were found in this superb monument, with simple grave goods such as bronze bracelets, bone buttons, and a decorated bone disc interred with the dead.

Figure 5.10.   The Naveta d'Es Tudons (image courtesy of Daniele Paccaloni, CC BY-SA 3.0).

The Menorcan *taulas* ("tables") are magnificent and rather "eccentric" structures that are somewhat like Stonehenge in appearance. Their main architectural component, the *taula*, is a very broad, massive stone slab or pillar, on top of which sits a huge table-like capstone. Together these form impressive megaliths that look like a giant capital letter *T*. Each *taula* stands within a precinct or enclosure consisting of several large standing stones encircled by a horseshoe-shaped dry-stone wall, with entrances marked by two upright pillars supporting a lintel stone. One face of the broad uprights of the *taulas* is usually carefully worked so that it is very smooth and oriented to look toward the entrances of the enclosure wall.

The majority of the *taulas* are found in the southern half of the island and are always located on level ground, with their entrances facing toward the sea and the southern horizon, perhaps indicating an interest in the night sky on the part of the communities who built these Menorcan megaliths. In the Talayotic period, when the *taulas* were being built and used, "the southern sky . . . witnessed a nightly procession of stars: the Southern Cross . . . would rise and begin to trace a shallow arc across the sky, soon to be followed by the bright star β Centauri and then by α Centauri, the second brightest star in the Menorcan sky."[14] Therefore, it may be the case that "these southern *taulas* were constructed so that the Southern Cross and these two bright stars . . . could be seen from the taula through the precinct entrance."[15] If so, it seems likely that these stars played an important role in the religious cosmology of the *taula* builders.

The best-known and most impressive of the Menorcan *taulas* are the Trepuco and Talatí de Dalt monuments. The former is located on the outskirts of the island's capital, Mahón, with its T-shaped megalith approximately 4 meters in height and capped by a slab measuring around 4 meters long by 2 meters wide. Nearby are the remains of the settlement inhabited by the people who built the Trepuco *taula* enclosure, where four stone *talayot* towers (similar to the *nuraghi* and *torri* of Sardinia and Corsica) can be seen along with the remains of houses made from dry-stone walling and a defensive wall that protected the village.

Talatí de Dalt is a more complex site that includes the remains of five *talayot* towers, underground chambers, semicircular enclosures of standing stones, and a large solitary standing stone that has a hole carved in its upper end. The Talatí *taula* is not as tall as that of Trepuco, but its more massive slabs give it a "thunderous presence,"[16] and it is also one of the few *taulas* that feature an extra upright pillar. At Talatí, however, this leans against the capstone of the T-shaped megalith at an odd diagonal angle, with a smaller stone also inserted between the top of the pillar and the underside of the capstone.

Excavations carried out at various *taulas* have uncovered an abundance of animal bones, pointing to ritual sacrifice or communal feasting at these megalithic sites. It is likely that the *taulas* functioned as religious shrines or

Figure 5.11.   The Talati de Dalt *taula* (image courtesy of Rene Boulay, CC BY-SA 3.0).

sanctuaries, but, as with the other megalithic monuments of Europe, we can never know for sure what religious beliefs lay behind their construction. It has, however, been suggested that the *taulas* were religious centers connected with healing, and, interestingly, an ancient Egyptian bronze figurine representing Imhotep, the god of medicine, was found within the enclosure of the Torre d'en Galmés *taula*. The idea that the *taulas* were places of healing is a nice one, but it is a theory that can never be proved. Nor will we ever find out how a bronze figurine from ancient Egypt ended up in a Menorcan *taula*.

· 6 ·

The Stone Circles of Britain and Ireland

$\mathscr{A}$round five thousand years ago many Neolithic communities throughout Britain and Ireland began raising stone circles in the landscape, marking the emergence of a widespread megalithic tradition that replaced tomb building and which lasted for some two thousand years from the Late Neolithic to the Middle Bronze Age, ca. 3200–1200 BCE. Well over a thousand stone circles have survived in varying states of preservation in Britain and Ireland, and countless more have been lost as a result of later farming and building activities. Archaeologist and broadcaster Neil Oliver has nicely captured the great appeal of these enigmatic prehistoric monuments: "Archaeologists are usually scientists and therefore uncomfortable talking or writing about how places make them feel. But there is no denying that stone circles have an atmosphere all of their own. Perhaps we bring that feeling ourselves, in the expectation that such sites must have once mattered and had power; but it is surely impossible to walk around those, touching stones set in place 5,000 years ago, without sensing something strange?"[1]

Why the first stone circles appeared at the end of the fourth millennium is something of a mystery. However, one interesting possibility in this respect is that they began to be built because severe climate change caused by a volcanic eruption in Greenland was threatening the existence of later Neolithic farming communities in Britain and Ireland: "For as long as men could remember, and their fathers, and their fathers before them, the weather had been bad, with long periods of rain, dark clouds, cold and winds blowing across desolate fields. Crops would not ripen. Cattle sickened. It was as though the skies were angry. . . . Helpless in a seemingly never-ending calamity, they turned away from the ancestors they believed had once protected them and, instead, looked to the threatening skies. Stone circles were born of desperation."[2]

Whether or not desperation was the driving force behind the emergence of the first stone circles in Britain and Ireland, the evidence for worsening weather at the time when the first stone circles began to be built is certainly there: "Annual growth-rings in ancient Irish oaks show a sudden contraction around 3190 BC caused by colder, wetter weather."[3]

STONE CIRCLES OF THE FAR NORTH

The two most northerly stone circles in Britain are the Orkney Islands' Ring of Brodgar and Stones of Stenness, which were raised by Late Neolithic communities some five thousand years ago. This windswept archipelago lies some 10 miles off the coast of mainland Scotland and is rightly famed for its wild beauty and its rich wildlife. It is probably best known, however, for its exceptional and abundant collection of prehistoric monuments, many of them megalithic in nature, with the Ring of Brodgar and the Stones of Stenness counted among the most spectacular.

The Ring of Brodgar and the Stones of Stenness are situated on Mainland Orkney, the largest and most important island of the Orkney archipelago, and stand about a mile apart on two narrow and opposing promontories that divide Loch Stenness and Loch Harray.[4] The Ring of Brodgar is the more impressive of the two circles, having a diameter of more than 100 meters and surrounded

Figure 6.1. Standing stones in the Ring of Brodgar, with Loch Harray in the background (image courtesy of Steve Keiretsu, CC BY-SA 3.0).

by a massive rock-cut ditch measuring about 140 meters in diameter and up to 3 meters deep. Today, some of the sixty or so standing stones that form the circle are mere stumps or lie toppled on the ground. However, twenty-two thin and angular menhirs made of Orkney flagstone (a type of sandstone that splits easily) remain standing.

Most of the standing stones that formed the Stones of Stenness circle are now lost (only four remain standing), and its surrounding rock-cut ditch is no longer visible; it is possible that a low bank originally surrounded both ditch and circle, although the evidence for this is inconclusive. However, although there are only a few stones remaining from the original circle, they have an imposing presence and a rather modern feel, looking more like "an art instillation than an archaeological site,"[5] with the three tallest ones reaching about 5 meters high.

Excavations carried out at the site in 1972 and 1973 by archaeologist Graham Ritchie and his team confirmed that at least eleven stones originally stood in a circle measuring about 32 meters in diameter, with a socket hole for a twelfth apparently never used. This hole is in the southeastern arc of the circle, and it could be that a gap was intentionally left here to mark the midwinter sun rising over the nearby hills. Only a few hundred meters to the northeast of the Stones of Stenness are the circular and contemporary stone dwellings of the well-known Neolithic village of Barnhouse, showing that stone circles were not always isolated in the landscape and were sometimes built alongside the homes of the living.

Figure 6.2.   The Stones of Stenness (image courtesy of Steve Keiretsu, CC BY-SA 3.0).

In the central area within the Stones of Stenness, there is a monumental, square stone hearth (about 2.5 by 2.5 meters) built from four stone slabs; it is like the one that can be seen in one of the Barnhouse dwellings (Structure 8, known as the "big house") and those found in the houses at the world-famous prehistoric site of Skara Brae.[6] In fact, Graham Ritchie's excavations at the Stones of Stenness uncovered strong evidence to suggest that the Stenness hearth was once part of a destroyed building that had resembled Structure 8 at Barnhouse. Just to the north of the hearth are two small upright stones that stand close together at the end of a longer flat slab lying on the ground. This was once thought to represent the remains of a small, Neolithic dolmen-like structure, but it is in fact "modern" and was erected in the nineteenth century. The 1970s excavations also uncovered Neolithic Grooved Ware pottery as well as large quantities of animal bones (cattle, sheep, and dog/wolf) and, curiously, two cremated bones from a human hand. Some 120 meters northwest of the circle is the famous Watchstone, a lofty standing stone that is approximately 5 meters high.

Archaeological research has also identified that the Ring of Brodgar and the Stones of Stenness were built using stones extracted from different "quarries" on Mainland Orkney. It thus may be the case that the quarried menhirs were "brought to the circles by different groups occupying those different areas, implying competition between villages and communities."[7] It is also possible that both circles were "a microcosm of landscape,"[8] with their standing stones and ditches, which may have been deliberately dug to hold water, mimicking the surrounding lochs, hills, and mountains.

CALLANISH

Located on the west coast of the Isle of Lewis in the Outer Hebrides, Callanish (or Calanais) is a unique and fascinating monument, and it has been said that "no other megalithic site exceeds the lyrical beauty of Callanish's setting above Loch Roag."[9] Callanish measures approximately 13 by 11 meters in diameter. Standing roughly at its center is a large menhir about 4.5 meters in height, behind which are the remains of a tiny chambered tomb with a short passage, although it is probable that this tomb is a later addition to the circle. Running northeastward for some 80 meters from the circle is a damaged double row, or "avenue," of standing stones, with the remains of another avenue (about 28 meters long) of five stones extending from the southern arc of the circle; extending west and east, there are also two shorter single rows, both consisting of four stones. Thus, in plan, Callanish somewhat resembles a giant Celtic cross, and various astronomical alignments have been proposed for its avenues over the years.

Figure 6.3.   Callanish stone circle (image courtesy of Thilo Rose, CC public domain).

The stones of Callanish are made from a type of stone known as gneiss and come in many shapes and sizes, having a fantastical quality that comes from the swirling and striped banding and the black hornblende (a type of mineral) eye-like inclusions that are a feature of this type of stone. These distinctive features cannot have escaped the attention of the people who raised Callanish's standing stones, which may have been perceived as somehow "magical."

SCOTTISH RECUMBENT STONE CIRCLES

These superb megalithic monuments, which date from ca. 2700–2200 BCE, are clustered in northeastern Scotland in the foothills of the Grampian Mountains, Aberdeenshire. They take their name from the huge, horizontal stones, or "recumbents," laid between the two tallest "portal" stones in the southwestern or southeastern arc of these striking stone rings. The recumbents are often made of different types of stone than the others in the circles, and in some cases these "foreign" stones came from considerable distances away. For example, at the Old Keig circle, the recumbent stone, estimated to weigh between 30 and 40 tons, was transported to the site from a valley that lies 6 miles away.

Archaeologists have often viewed these striking and unusual stone circles as sites connected to the movement of the moon, with the "major standstill,"[10]

Figure 6.4.   Easter Aquhorthies recumbent stone circle (image courtesy of Stu Smith, CC BY-SA 2.0).

or midsummer full moon, "framed" between the recumbents and their flanking stones as it moved through the sky. Interestingly, scatterings of white quartz pebbles have been found around the recumbents at several sites, and carved cupmarks can also be seen on the surfaces of some of these megalithic blocks. As has been noted, "If the symbolism is correct then the cupmarks are lunar motifs and the quartz pieces of white rock that epitomized the distant land of death would have been entirely appropriate placed close to the recumbent stone in family rings at whose hearts human offerings lay."[11]

Whether or not there is a lunar link at the Scottish recumbent circles, confirmation that they were used as burial places is shown by discoveries such as that made at Loanhead of Daviot, where the cremated remains of some thirty individuals (both adults and children) were found. Some of these remains were placed in simple graves, others in upturned pottery vessels, while in the center of this cremation cemetery lay the partially cremated remains of a man, who appears to have been clutching a stone pendant when he was placed on his funeral pyre. It could be that this man was a leader of some sort within his community and was thus given the honor of being laid to rest in the central space of Loanhead of Daviot. Cremation burials have also been found at several other Scottish recumbent stone circles.

CUMBRIAN CIRCLES

The county of Cumbria in northwestern England is the home of the Lake District National Park, an area of outstanding natural beauty that has long been a source of inspiration for artists and poets alike. Every year it attracts thousands of visitors who come to soak up its glorious countryside. Some of the earliest and largest stone circles erected in Britain and Ireland can also be found in Cumbria, with several examples located within the national park itself. One of the best-known and largest of the Cumbrian stone circles is Long Meg and

Her Daughters, which was the subject of a poem ("The Monument Commonly Called Long Meg and Her Daughters," 1833) written by the Lake District's favorite son, the nineteenth-century Romantic poet William Wordsworth.

Long Meg and Her Daughters is located on a low hill that rises above the Eden Valley near the town of Penrith on the eastern edge of the Lake District. The curious name of this stone circle comes from local folklore, with its huge standing stones said to be a local coven of witches petrified by a saint incensed by their pagan practices. This massive monument has a diameter of about 100 meters and consists of fifty-nine standing stones (not all of which remain upright). The heaviest stone in the circle weighs about 28 tons, and it has been estimated that at least 120 people would be needed to drag and lift it into position.

Long Meg and Her Daughters has a "portaled" entrance comprising two pairs of menhirs, like a rough stone porch, and at the highest point of the site, there is an outlying slender standing stone (Long Meg), which at about 4 meters high is taller than any of the other stones (her "daughters") in the circle proper. Unlike the granite stones that make up the circle, Long Meg is made of red sandstone that was probably dragged from the banks of the River Eden some 2 miles to the west. It is also possible that this tall stone, which stands at the top of the slope on which the circle is situated, is positioned in line with the midwinter sunset in the southwest (the entrance of the circle also faces southwest). Bearing this in mind, it is interesting to note that one of Long Meg's smooth faces features carved concentric circles and a spiral motif, which are often seen as sun symbols by archaeologists. Similar symbols are seen in the art of many "primitive" peoples, such as the famous Anasazi, or "Ancestral Puebloans," of the American Southwest.[12]

Many of the Cumbrian stone circles are sited in glorious landscapes,[13] but in terms of scenic beauty, one stone circle in Cumbria stands out above all others: Castlerigg. Described as "perhaps the most atmospheric and dramatically sited of all British stone circles,"[14] Castlerigg is situated on the level top of a low hill close to the market town of Keswick in the heart of the Lake District. The huge number of people who visit Castlerigg annually are rewarded with a wonderful 360-degree panorama of Lakeland mountains and fells that form a natural amphitheater around the site.

Like Long Meg and Her Daughters, Castlerigg is one of the earliest stone circles in Britain, having been built around 3000 BCE. Measuring about 30 meters in diameter, Castlerigg is a lot smaller than Long Meg and Her Daughters, today consisting of thirty-eight standing stones varying in height from about 1–2.5 meters. There is also a curious rectangular arrangement of ten standing stones within the eastern half of the circle, the function of which is unclear. A carved spiral motif, like the one found on the Long Meg menhir, can also be seen on one of the standing stones in the eastern arc of the circle. Three Neolithic stone axes quarried from the Neolithic stone axe "factory"[15] located high on the rocky fells,

Figure 6.5.   Castlerigg stone circle (image courtesy of Mike Peel, CC By-SA 4.0).

or "pikes," of the Great Langdale valley were found inside the circle in the nineteenth century. Stone axes from Great Langdale traveled far and wide in Britain during the Neolithic and were deposited at various ritual and ceremonial monuments, particularly those found in the Thames Valley, the Midlands, and eastern England. Archaeologists have plotted the probable mountain tracks along which the unfinished stone axe "roughouts" from the Langdale axe factory traveled to the grinding and polishing sites where they were turned into finished stone axes. Several of these sites lie close to the Cumbrian stone circles, suggesting that the latter were places where Neolithic people gathered (some of whom may have traveled from hundreds of miles away) to barter and trade for these finished axes.

Neolithic and Bronze Age communities may also have gathered at stone circles to perform dances that were of a ritual nature and connected to religious beliefs. It is interesting to note that many of the names of British and Irish stone circles have a firm connection to dancing, and in local folklore the circles are often said to be people who had been turned to stone as a punishment for dancing or playing games on the Sabbath. For example, there are the Merry Maidens and Trippet stones in Cornwall, the Piper's Stones in County Wicklow, southern Ireland, and the Nine Ladies stone circle in northern England's Peak District. Whether or not the names of stone circles such as these "contain memories of ancient practices,"[16] the interiors of the larger examples would certainly have been ideal locations for Neolithic and Bronze Age ritual dances.

The practice of ritual dancing has been documented in many nonstate cultures around the world; for example, there is the famous Ghost Dance of the American Great Plains tribes, which was "introduced when the white colonists eliminated the buffalo herds upon which they depended practically and symbolically."[17] When performing this tragic and ultimately futile dance, people circled sunwise, dancing and chanting for "an immediate regeneration of the earth, with the disappearance of the White Man, and the resurrection of both the buffalo and all the Indian dead."[18]

STONE CIRCLES OF THE SOUTH: STANTON DREW AND THE ROLLRIGHT STONES

Although many of the stone circles of Britain are concentrated in groups that cluster in the western and northern parts of the country (i.e., Cornwall, Devon, Wales, northern England, and Scotland), there are outlying examples in southern England. In fact, the most famous stone circles of Britain and Ireland are Stonehenge and Avebury in the southern English county of Wiltshire, and we will return to these megalithic behemoths in the next chapter. After Stonehenge and Avebury, the best-known stone circles in southern England are the Great Circle of the Stanton Drew megalithic complex and the Rollright Stones.

Stanton Drew

There are three stone circles at Stanton Drew, the largest of which is the Great Circle, measuring 113 meters in diameter and today consisting of twenty-seven standing stones, although originally there may have been more. Massive limestone blocks dragged from a source 3 miles away were used in the construction of the Great Circle, and a megalithic avenue comprising two rows of standing stones was built against its northeastern arc, although the stones of the avenue now lie prostrate. One of the two smaller "circles" (strictly speaking, both are ovals) stands about 40 meters to the northeast of the Great Circle and measures some 32 by 30 meters in diameter, with eight stones used in its construction. It also has the remains of a megalithic avenue on its northeastern side, which perhaps originally linked up with the one running from the Great Circle to form a processional way down to the River Chew. Some 140 meters to the southwest of the Great Circle is the second smaller circle (about 43 by 40 meters), although all its twelve remaining stones have long since tumbled to the ground, where they now lie somewhat forlornly and in danger of being lost beneath the grass of a quiet water meadow.

Figure 6.6.   Stanton Drew great circle (image courtesy of Rodw, CC BY-SA 3.0).

Another feature of the Stanton Drew complex is the megalithic monument known as the Cove, which has the added attraction of being situated in the beer garden of the Druid's Arms public house. The Stanton Drew Cove consists of three huge stones that once formed an unroofed, three-sided, boxlike structure, with the rear stone of this monument having long since fallen to the ground. A few other cove monuments are known in Britain, and it has been suggested that they may have been "symbolic representations of megalithic tomb entrances."[19] However, a geophysical survey undertaken at the Stanton Drew Cove in the summer of 2009 by the Bath and Camerton Archaeological Society identified evidence below the ground to suggest that it may in fact be the remains of a ruined Neolithic tomb. It is also worth noting that an earlier geophysical survey undertaken at Stanton Drew by English Heritage in 1997 revealed that nine concentric rings of huge wooden posts had once stood within the Great Circle.

The Rollright Stones

The Rollright Stones are situated on the edge of the Cotswold Hills, on the border between the counties of Oxfordshire and Warwickshire, and this famous stone circle was originally erected next to a prehistoric trackway. Unfortunately, this has now disappeared beneath the tarmac of the modern highway that somewhat mars the peaceful atmosphere of this secluded and pretty site. The circle may derive its name from the Anglo-Saxon term *Hrolla-landriht*, meaning "the land belonging to Hrolla" (the Rollright Stones are also known as the King's Men), and today it consists of seventy-three stones forming a perfect circle, measuring 33 meters in diameter. However, this is probably not the original number of stones used in the construction of the Rollright Stones, as many of the smaller stones that can be seen in the circle today are probably fragments that have weathered from larger ones, subsequently being placed in handy gaps in its circumference in the nineteenth century.

Some five thousand years of weathering have left their mark on the limestone boulders that were used in the circle, and they have been pitted and corroded by the elements so that they have a rotted appearance, giving them something of an eerie quality. The antiquarian William Stukeley memorably described the Rollright Stones as "the greatest Antiquity we have yet seen . . . corroded like wormeaten wood by the harsh jaws of time."[20]

In the early twentieth century, photographer Henry W. Taunt provided an atmospheric description of the Rollright Stones, where, along with his companions, he spent the night waiting for midsummer sunrise (readers will be left to make up their own minds about the fairies that were also apparently in attendance during this midsummer vigil!):

> Taking the circle as whole, what a quaint assemblage of stones it is; in the dead of the night it is very weird indeed, when the grey stones can only just be made out in the dimness, and the trees are black against the twinkling stars, and a fairy-light here and there, like a glow-worm amid the long grass, and the twitter of some small bird whose rest is disturbed yet is too sleepy to seek refuge in flight; then imagination goes back to the olden times when the place was thronged with worshippers, who perhaps like ourselves watched through the waning night waiting for the glorious sun to rise in the east and shed his beneficent rays upon the open temple and those gathered within.[21]

Taunt's idea that prehistoric people came to the Rollright Stones to worship the rising sun was probably not far from the truth. The circle may also have been associated with the Neolithic stone axe "industry" of the Lake District. With its closely set stones and portaled entrance, the design of the Rollright Stones is like that of its Cumbrian counterparts, particularly the fine Swinside circle on the southwestern edge of the Lake District near the market town of Broughton in Furness. Therefore, it could be that Neolithic settlers from Cumbria erected the Rollright Stones, with the circle being used as a "staging post" for stone axes quarried from the Great Langdale axe factory.[22]

Some 75 meters northeast of the Rollright Stones, at the top of a steep slope, is the King Stone, an outlying standing stone of substantial size (about 2.5 meters high) that is twisted and bent so that it resembles some strange, hunchbacked creature.[23] The original purpose of the King Stone is unclear, but it may have been set up as an astronomical marker or, alternatively, to guide prehistoric travelers to the nearby stone circle. Another possibility is that it was raised to mark the location of an Early Bronze cemetery, as cremation burials dating to this time were discovered around the stone during excavations carried out here in 1979. About 360 meters east of the Rollright Stones are the remains of a ruined megalithic tomb known as the Whispering Knights, which was probably erected about a thousand years before the stone circle ca. 4000 BCE.

Arthur Evans, the English archaeologist who discovered the remarkable Bronze Age Minoan civilization of Crete as a result of his excavations at the now famous palace of Knossos, said of the Rollright Stones (i.e., the King Stone, the King's Men, and the Whispering Knights), "The folk-lore of which the Rollright stones have become the center is of the highest interest, and it would be difficult to find any English site in which it is more living than at the present day."[24] This folklore tells of an unnamed king and his knights who were turned to stone by a witch over whose land they had marched, uninvited, with the circle representing his knights; the King Stone, the king himself; and the Whispering Knights, a small group of traitors who had been plotting against him. The witch was said to have turned herself into a nearby elder tree that bled when cut, and witches reputedly carried out naked ceremonies at the stone circle in Tudor times. Local people told Evans that it had once been a custom to come to the King Stone on Midsummer's Eve and stand in a circle around it while the elder tree was cut and that fairies had also been seen dancing around the stone at night.

We also have an account of some rather sinister goings-on at the King Stone, which reads like a scene from a Hammer Horror film or a Dennis Wheatley novel. On the night of a full moon on May 12, 1949, about half a dozen people were observed dancing around this curiously shaped menhir: "There was more a mumbling than any talking or singing. . . . When they were still the leader appeared to make signs and gestures as he stood by the King Stone. He had some kind of disguise. I could have sworn it was a goat's facemask . . . but I did not mention this before as I thought someone would think I was suffering from some kind of madness, or hallucinations."[25]

Figure 6.7. The Rollright Stones/King's Men stone circle (image courtesy of the Locster, CC BY-SA 3.0).

IRISH AND WELSH STONE CIRCLES

> On the summit of this hill . . . stands a Druidical temple somewhat
> resembling that at Stonehenge in size and structure. . . . The place is
> called Baltony, a name not uncommon in some districts of Ireland.
> It is supposed to be a corruption of Baal tinné, the "fire of Baal,"—
> intimating a spot where that deity was particularly worshipped in
> Ireland. Among the rigid Presbyterians of the North, such remains
> of antiquity are lightly regarded because they are deemed remnants
> of superstition and idolatry.
>
> —S. C. Hall and A. M., *Ireland: Its Scenery, Character, &c.*, 260

Ireland and Wales have no great stone circles like the Ring of Brodgar or Long
Meg and Her Daughters, but some fine examples of these mysterious monuments are nevertheless scattered throughout their beautiful, legend-filled landscapes. The Beltany Tops stone circle in County Donegal, Northern Ireland, can
be counted as one of the best of the Irish and Welsh stone circles. This monument stands on a rounded hill (Tops Hill) and commands fine views of Donegal's countryside, perhaps being constructed as early as the middle of the fourth

**Figure 6.8.   Sunset at Beltany Tops stone circle (image courtesy of Mark McGaughey,
CC BY-SA 4.0).**

millennium BCE. Today, sixty-four of a possible eighty closely set standing stones survive in a circle measuring about 45 meters in diameter. These surround a ru-ined cairn (possibly the remains of a Neolithic tomb) that was rifled by treasure seekers in the 1930s, leaving it a confused mass of grass-grown humps, bumps, and hollows. Forty-three cupmarks are carved into the surface of a triangular-topped stone located in the northeastern arc of the circle that lies opposite the tallest stone in the circle (about 3 meters high) to the southwest. Intriguingly, an imaginary line drawn through these two stones points to Tullyrap Hill some 5 miles distant, above which the sun rises on and around May Day, the time of the ancient spring festival of Beltaine (hence the name of the circle), when fires were lit throughout the countryside to ward off evil spirits. Two Neolithic stone axes were found near the circle, as was a curious carved stone head with rather fierce features that probably dates to the Early Iron Age (ca. 500 BCE), pointing to ritual activity at Beltany Tops long after its builders were dead and gone.

Another notable northern Irish circle is Ballynoe, County Down, "a reward-ing site to visit in its sloping field with the dramatic peaks of the Mourne moun-tains to the south-west."[26] The Ballynoe circle (about 34 meters in diameter), which may have originally contained as many as seventy closely set standing stones, surrounds a low mound with a boulder curb that may be an earlier monu-ment. The southwestern entrance of the circle is formed by two pairs of standing stones, and there are two pairs of outlying stones to the northeast and southwest. Excavations carried out at the site in 1937 and 1938 uncovered a cist grave be-low the eastern end of the mound, which contained the bones of about sixteen individuals, most of them children. It was evident that the skulls and long bones of the dead had been neatly and carefully stacked by the people responsible for their burial. Ballynoe is also similar in size and design to the early stone circles of the Lake District such as Swinside. This suggests that Neolithic communi-ties from the two areas were in contact with each other or even that a Neolithic group from Cumbria settled in Northern Ireland (or vice versa).

IRISH RECUMBENT CIRCLES

It was not just prehistoric communities in northeast Scotland that built re-cumbent stone circles, as they are also found in southwestern Ireland (again suggesting links between Neolithic communities in Britain and Ireland). These monuments, known as the Cork/Kerry circles after their location in the counties of Cork and Kerry (although the majority are found in Kerry), are somewhat smaller than their Scottish "cousins." At least ninety examples survive, many of them well preserved, and there are two distinct types: the "multiple stone circles," which contain up to nineteen stones, and the "five-stone circles," which always—

and somewhat curiously—consist of just five stones. The recumbents are often located in the western or southwestern arc of the circles, although in contrast to their Scottish counterparts, they are not set between the tallest "portal" stones, which lie opposite in the northeastern arc.

The best known of the Cork/Kerry circles is probably Dromberg in County Cork, a very well-preserved monument situated on a natural terrace that overlooks a shallow valley clothed in a pretty patchwork of Irish fields, beyond which can be seen the Atlantic Ocean. The monument comprises fifteen stones (originally there were seventeen) that form an almost perfect circle measuring about 9 meters in diameter. The portal stones in the northeast of the circle are quite substantial, measuring about 2 meters high, with the low recumbent stone opposite being about 2 meters long. The site was excavated in 1957, and below the interior of the circle, which its builders had carefully leveled and covered with pebbles and gravel, a Bronze Age pottery urn containing some burnt human bone was found. It seems probable that the circle's recumbent is aligned on the midwinter sunset, with one of the founding fathers of "astroarchaeology," Boyle Somerville, who visited Dromberg in the early twentieth century, the first person to propose this.[27] In fact, at Dromberg, the midwinter sun sets in a cleft in a hillside, which can be seen directly behind the recumbent on the horizon. Interestingly, two cupmarks can also still faintly be seen on the upper surface of the recumbent stone at Dromberg, perhaps carved into the stone as solar motifs.

Figure 6.9.   Dromberg recumbent stone circle (image courtesy of Ingo Mehling, CC BY-SA 3.0).

WELSH STONE CIRCLES

Stone circles are not found in great numbers in Wales, but there are nevertheless some notable examples, such as Gors Fawr ("great marsh"), with this monument lying below the Carn Meini ridge in Pembrokeshire, the likely source of some of the stones used in Stonehenge, or Ysbyty Cynfyn ("Cynfyn's hospice") in mid-Wales. Here, a stone circle was probably Christianized by being incorporated into the wall of a pretty country church, with the magnificent 3.5-meter-high standing stone that can be seen in the wall today one of the finest in Wales. There is also the unusual Four Stones stone circle in the Walton Basin, Powys, with the four huge stones of this small but impressive monument thought to represent an isolated example of a "Four-Poster" ring, more commonly found in Aberdeenshire in northeastern Scotland. The most notable of the Welsh stone circles, however, are the Bryn Gwyn Stones, Bryn Cader Faner, and the Druids' Circle.

The Bryn Gwyn Stones

The lofty standing stone found in the wall of Ysbyty Cynfyn is not the tallest in Wales, as this honor goes to one of a pair, known as the Bryn Gwyn ("white hill") stones, that today act as monumental gateposts in a farmer's field on the Isle of Anglesey, North Wales. The larger stone is immense, measuring 4 meters high and 3 meters wide, although, at about 3 meters high and 3 meters wide, its megalithic neighbor is almost as impressive. These two stones represent the remains of a relatively unknown stone circle first recorded in 1723 by a Welsh antiquarian and native of Angelsey, the Reverend Henry Rowlands. The reverend described a ruined stone circle featuring three standing stones and the stump of a broken fourth, estimating that originally there were eight to nine stones in a circle measuring about 12 meters in diameter.

Nearly two hundred years later, in 2008 and 2010, the Gwynedd Archaeological Trust (GAT) carried out two excavations at the circle, with this work largely confirming that Reverend Rowland had been correct. Pits that had once held another six standing stones were uncovered, and, along with the two surviving stones, it was evident that they would have stood in a circle measuring about 16 meters in diameter. If the lost standing stones of the circle (which were removed or broken up in the nineteenth century) were of a similar size to the two that suffered the somewhat ignominious fate of being used as gateposts, then, when complete, this must have been a very imposing monument.

The GAT excavations also uncovered within the center of the circle a pit still containing the bottom half of a broken standing stone estimated to have been at least 2 meters in height, which would originally have faced northeast/

Figure 6.10.   The Bryn Gwyn stones (image courtesy of Richard Keatinge, CC-BY SA 3.0).

southwest, toward the midwinter sunrise and sunset. Also recovered from within the circle were the cremated remains of at least four individuals: two infants, one a newborn; a child aged five to eight years; and a young adult aged about eighteen to twenty years. These burials, however, were associated with a circular setting of pits or postholes that predated the circle by about a thousand years, which seems to have been erected in the Early Bronze Age ca. 2000 BCE.

Bryn Cader Faner

Although, strictly speaking, Bryn Cader Faner ("the outlook post on the hill") is not a true stone circle, this famous monument is undoubtedly one of the wonders of prehistoric Britain. Located in the lonely uplands above Harlech on the northwest coast of Wales and commanding breathtaking views of the hills and mountains of northwestern Snowdonia, this unique monument looks like the grim crown of some Welsh giant or a thicket of huge, bristling spears. Today, Bryn Cader Faner consists of a circle of fifteen tall and thin standing stones measuring around 2 meters in height (there may have been as many as thirty originally), which lean markedly outward from the edge of a Bronze Age burial cairn. The remains of a damaged cist grave can be seen at the center of the cairn,

Figure 6.11.   Bryn Cader Faner cairn circle (image, author).

although this is now empty, having been pillaged in the nineteenth century by treasure hunters and soldiers on an exercise during World War II, who mindlessly damaged Bryn Cader Faner by removing stones from its eastern side.

Although the sequence of construction at Bryn Cader Faner is not certain, it is perhaps more likely that the stone circle originally stood alone on the dominant spur of land on which it is located, with the burial cairn added later, the weight of its stones subsequently pushing those of the circle outward. As Bryn Cader Faner is approached along the trackway (which is prehistoric in origin) and seen from a distance, it forms a striking silhouette against the sky, which was probably the desired intent of its builders.

The Druids' Circle

The Druids' Circle, or Y Meini Hirion ("the long stones"), is located above the North Welsh coastal town of Penmaenmawr on Cefn Coch, a windy upland expanse that is rich in prehistoric monuments and also the location of an important Neolithic axe "factory," with the stone axes made here found in many parts of Britain. This monument is probably the most famous of the Welsh stone circles and stands alongside an ancient trackway that provided prehistoric travelers with a route across Cefn Coch (now the popular North Wales

Path hiking trail). There are about thirty stones surviving in the Druids' Circle, although there may well have been more, and these are set into a low and broad stony bank with a diameter of around 25 meters, providing an example of a Welsh "embanked" stone circle.

The Druids' Circle was excavated by W. E. Griffiths in 1958,[28] and although the date of its erection is unclear, Griffiths discovered that two pairs of portal stones had probably once stood in its southwestern entrance (which may have been astronomically oriented), recalling those seen in the early stone circles of the Lake District. This perhaps suggests that the Druids' Circle was contemporary with these monuments, being built around 3000 BCE. Whatever its date, Griffiths made some fascinating finds during his excavation of the Druids' Circle. The first to be mentioned, the "primary burial," was found in a stone cist near the center of the circle, inside of which was a finely made, decorated Bronze Age pot of the food vessel type, containing the cremated remains of a child who had probably been aged ten to twelve years at death. Two more food vessels were found in pits inside the circle, one containing the cremated remains of another child (about twelve years old) and the blade of a small bronze knife, its handle long since crumbled to dust. Another cremation burial was found in a shallow pit lined with whetstones (one of which showed traces of knife sharpening), although the bones were in a very poor condition, and nothing could be said about the age or sex of this individual.

Figure 6.12. The Druids' Circle (image, author).

Griffiths suggested that the cremation burials found at the Druids' Circle could have been sacrificial in nature, and interestingly, in local folklore, one of the stones in the circle, which features a curious ledge-like indentation, was said to have to been used as an altar on which infants were sacrificed. Of course, this is probably nothing more than a gruesome tale made up thousands of years after the Druids' Circle was built, but could it perhaps contain an element of truth? As Aubrey Burl has remarked, "It may be wondered whether the cremations at the Druids' Circle are . . . evidence of sacrifice . . . relics of a darkening past that the visitor to the stone circle must remember, telling him he may be standing . . . in a place where people, fearful in a precarious world, offered fire and death in return for protection."[29]

· 7 ·

Stonehenge and Avebury

Set among the rolling chalk downs of rural Wiltshire in southern England are two of the most spectacular prehistoric monuments in Europe, if not the world: Stonehenge and Avebury. Stonehenge, of course, is world famous, and the unique and sophisticated architecture of this towering stone circle is an iconic reminder of prehistoric life. Avebury is less well known around the globe, but it is more impressive than Stonehenge, at least in terms of size, and contains not one but three huge stone circles.[1] In fact, Avebury is so vast that half a village lies within its interior, and a busy modern road linking the towns of Swindon and Devizes also bisects the monument. For the famous eighteenth-century antiquarian William Stukeley, Avebury was "the most extraordinary work in the world."[2] Stukeley was guilty of over-exaggeration,[3] but the same cannot be said for his earlier counterpart, the notable seventeenth-century antiquarian John Aubrey, who wrote that Avebury "does as much exceed in greatness the so renowned Stonehenge as a Cathedral doeth a parish church."[4]

Whatever the different merits of Stonehenge and Avebury, which, strictly speaking, are classified by archaeologists as "circle henges,"[5] it is interesting that, in terms of their origins and subsequent architectural development over many centuries, they are roughly contemporary, dating to ca. 3000–2000 BCE. In fact, it may well be the case that social competition lay behind the construction and elaboration of Stonehenge and Avebury, with prehistoric tribes or polities seeking to outdo each other by building the "pre-eminent ceremonial centers within their respective regions."[6]

Figure 7.1.   Aerial view of the Avebury monument (image courtesy of Detmar Owen, CC BY-SA 4.0).

AVEBURY

> Nowhere was like Avebury . . . nowhere was there a ditch so deep inside a bank so vast around a stone circle so enormous. There was nowhere like Avebury, a Texas of prehistory.
>
> —Aubrey Burl, *Prehistoric Avebury*, 2

The first thing that visitors see as they approach Avebury is its colossal bank, which would have been even more impressive when complete. Measuring about a quarter mile in diameter and made from chalk rubble, with larger chalk blocks used as rough retaining walls in some places, the bank is about 20–30 meters wide at its base and stands some 5 meters high. Originally, however, it would have been about 7 meters in height and not covered with grass, as is it today. In its pristine condition, the bank must have been a dazzling sight, particularly when the sun was shining brightly on the chalk, and it must have been visible from some distance away.

The chalk used for the construction of the bank was quarried from the immense ditch that closely follows its inner circuit, which today measures about 20 meters across at the top and some 4 meters deep. However, the weathering and silting up of the ditch that have taken place over the many long centuries since it was completed have altered its original dimensions. Harold Saint George Gray's excavation of the ditch in the early 1920s, which he recorded in a series of famous photographs, revealed that it originally reached 7–10 meters in depth and

Figure 7.2.   A section of the bank and ditch at Avebury (image courtesy of Stevekeiretsu, CC BY-SA 4.0).

was around 9 meters wide at the top. Four entrances pierce the bank at Avebury, with causeways of earth across the ditch providing access to the interior of the monument from the north, south, east, and west.

It almost staggers belief that some 200,000 tons of chalk were dug from Avebury's ditch by prehistoric people who only had rudimentary tools at their disposal. This mammoth task was mainly achieved using picks made from red deer antlers, as Gray discovered during his excavation. He recovered forty-four antler picks from the base of the ditch, and it was evident that these had not just been casually tossed there by tired prehistoric workers after a hard day's digging; rather, they had been carefully placed in specific groups. In one case, two dog jaws had been placed alongside a group of antler picks, suggesting a votive offering, perhaps to subterranean spirits who needed to be placated because the digging of the ditch had "wounded" the earth. A curious deposit of antler picks was also found buried deep within Avebury's bank during Sir Henry Meux's earlier excavations at Avebury in 1804, and these had been deliberately placed within a boxlike arrangement of large chalk blocks that resembled a stone cist grave.

The Avebury Stone Circles

The outer stone circle at Avebury, which follows the inner edge of the ditch around the interior of the monument, is the largest stone circle in Europe and measures some 165 meters in diameter. Lying within its circumference, in the southern and northern halves of the monument, are a further two stone circles, which, although smaller than the outer circle, both measure around 103 meters in diameter and thus are no mean monuments themselves. Unworked blocks of sarsen (a very hard, local sandstone) that vary considerably in size (with the tallest measuring about 4 meters high), shape, and texture were used in the construction of the Avebury stone circles, and these would have somehow been dragged from the nearby Marlborough Downs, which were littered with sarsen stones in prehistoric times. Significant concentrations of sarsen can still be found on the downs today, with the most notable at the Fyfield Down nature reserve, where there are some twenty-five thousand stones. These stones are known as the "Grey Wethers," with *wether* being the Old English word for sheep. Incidentally, there are two fine stone circles known as the Grey Wethers on Dartmoor in the county of Devon, southwest England, both of which measure around 33 meters in diameter and stand less than 5 meters apart.

Originally, there were about one hundred standing stones in the outer circle, but today only thirty survive; the two smaller circles both had about thirty stones originally, although many of these no longer exist. Small, triangular concrete pillars in the outer and southern circles mark the locations of sockets of missing

Figure 7.3.   Standing stones in the Outer Circle, Avebury (image courtesy of Adrian Farwell, CC BY-SA 3.0).

standing stones that were discovered by Alexander Kieller[7] during his notable excavations at Avebury between 1934 and 1939. Kieller was obviously a rather "racy" character, as archaeology was just "one of a number of obsessions that included skiing, fast cars, sexual experimentation and witchcraft."[8]

The northern circle is now a shadow of its former self, with only four stones remaining in its circumference, but at its center are two standing stones that represent the remains of a three-sided megalithic cove like the one seen at Stanton Drew and a few other sites in Britain. They are huge sarsen stones, with the tallest measuring almost 5 meters high and about 2.5 meters wide; the other stands about 1.5 meters lower but is nearly 5 meters wide and weighs around 100 tons. This cove may have been one of the earliest components of the Avebury monument.

Although it has long since gone, there was also once a massive standing stone within the center of the southern circle, which had long since fallen when William Stukeley came across it in the eighteenth century. The "Obelisk," as Stukeley called the fallen stone, measured some 6.5 meters high and 2.5 meters wide and would have stood more than 5 meters high when erect. Some 12 meters west of the Obelisk, a mysterious line of small standing stones (about 1 meter in height) measuring approximately 30 meters in length and roughly aligned from north to south, was uncovered by Alexander Kieller in 1939. It has been suggested that this stone row could have perhaps been aligned on the midwinter and midsummer moonsets. However, a recent geophysical survey carried out by the Universities of Leicester and Southampton made the exciting discovery that this row formed part of a very unusual square setting of standing stones that originally enclosed the Obelisk.

Also recorded by Stukeley was the "Ring-Stone," which once lay between the perimeter of the southern inner circle and the southern entrance, although only its stump remains today. Stukeley described it as a relatively small stone pierced by a natural hole and came up with a rather gruesome (and imaginative) interpretation of this holed megalith, suggesting that it had been used to tether prehistoric people brought to Avebury to be sacrificed.

The Avebury Avenues

In addition to the three stone circles at Avebury, there are also the remains of the West Kennet and Beckhampton megalithic avenues. The former is the much better preserved of the two and runs from Avebury's southern entrance for about 1.5 miles toward the River Kennet and then curves upward onto Overton Hill, where it links up with the "Sanctuary." Given this name by Stukeley, the Sanctuary seems to have been built around the middle of the third millennium BCE. Modern excavations here recovered the remains of a monument comprising a larger outer circle and a smaller inner one, with multiple timber circles set within and around the latter. It is not clear whether the timber circles preceded the stone ones or it is a composite monument, but it is perhaps more likely that they were contemporary.

William Stukeley was the first person to record the existence of the Beckhampton Avenue, but many British archaeologists have, until quite recently, been skeptical of Stukeley's claim, pointing to the lack of stones along the route he proposed for it. However, a geophysical survey undertaken in 1999 confirmed—some 150 years later—that Stukeley was right, although there is some doubt as to where the Beckhampton Avenue ends after it leaves the western entrance of Avebury. Most archaeologists probably agree that the avenue terminates at two opposing standing stones known as "Adam and Eve" or the "Longstones." Standing 4 meters high and weighing about 60 tons, Adam represents the sole survivor of a four-sided cove, while Eve is smaller and likely to have once formed part of the avenue. William Stukeley, however, recorded that the Beckhampton Avenue continued for about another half mile from the cove and ended at a place called "Fox Covert," next to a group of Early Bronze Age burial mounds.

Silbury Hill would also have been clearly visible to prehistoric peoples as they walked from Avebury to the Sanctuary (and vice versa) between the stones of the Beckhampton Avenue. This amazing and highly enigmatic monument, which is only 2 miles from Avebury, was built in stages between ca. 2400 and 2000 BCE; it is the largest man-made prehistoric mound in Europe, measuring nearly 40 meters high and about 160 meters across at its base, with various layers of turf, soil, and chalk used in its construction. Silbury Hill is also one of the greatest enigmas of prehistoric Europe, and we will probably never know its true purpose. However, this is not for want of trying, as there have been various antiquarian and archaeological investigations of this massive mound over the last three hundred years or so, with various shafts driven into its center. These have not found any spectacular prehistoric burials, as might be expected, although a rather ambiguous late eighteenth-century account mentions that Colonel Edward Drax and the Duke of Northumberland sank a shaft into the mound and found a small piece of oak and a man at its base. Presumably, the "man" was a skeleton, and the piece of oak may perhaps have been the remnants of a wooden coffin. Future large-scale excavation of Silbury Hill and its surrounding ditch, however, may perhaps unlock its prehistoric secrets. One of the most interesting suggestions to be made about Silbury Hill is that it could have been inspired by the early pyramids or ziggurats of ancient Egypt and Mesopotamia: "Fashionable consensus presently requires prehistoric people to have been largely rooted in local domesticity, but there is nothing to have prevented individuals from moving about. . . . Had someone from southern Britain seen one of these wonders? Or had word gone down wind of their existence, filtered and embroidered in numerous retellings?"[9]

Also located a short distance (about 1.5 miles) from Avebury is one of the most famous and largest (about 104 meters long) of Britain's finest megalithic

Figure 7.4.   The enigmatic Silbury Hill (image courtesy of Greg O' Beirne, CC BY-SA 4.0).

tombs, West Kennet Long Barrow, an outstanding example of a Cotswold-Severn tomb that was built ca. 3700 BCE. West Kennet was excavated in the mid-nineteenth century by John Thurnam and in the twentieth century by Stuart Piggott and Richard Atkinson. We will return to West Kennet in the next chapter to examine the fascinating discoveries that they made within its chambers.

Buried and Broken Stones: Avebury's Missing Megaliths

Modern visitors to Avebury cannot fail to be impressed by its standing stones, but they are only seeing a fraction of the numerous sarsen stones that were somewhat remarkably hauled to the monument by its prehistoric builders. This is because many of Avebury's stones were buried in pits or destroyed in earlier times, robbing the monument of some of its prehistoric majesty, although Alexander Kieller did re-erect many of the buried stones that he found during his excavations at the site.

During the medieval period (perhaps as early as the twelfth century), stone burial began at Avebury, as revealed by Kieller's discovery in the outer circle of the famous (and unfortunate) "barber-surgeon":

> During the excavation of the buried stone 16, a complete skeleton was found within the narrow space between the stone and the unfinished part of the side of the burial-pit. It is evident that the remains were those of an individual who

had been accidentally killed while engaged in completing the pit for the burial of the stone, which had apparently slipped or fallen owing to a support giving way, fracturing the victim's pelvis, and breaking his neck. The right foot was wedged beneath the fallen stone and it had consequently been impossible at the time to remove the corpse. It had therefore been covered over and the pit filled in. . . . [N]ear the man's left hip [was a] discoloured patch of soil, doubt-less representing the remains of a leather pouch, upon which were three coins: two silver pennies of Edward I, minted at Canterbury in 1307, and sterling of the City of Toul [France]. Other finds beside the skeleton included a pair of pointed scissors, which from their form were definitely those rather of a barber than a tailor, and a small iron object, with the vestigial remains of a wooden handle, which had apparently been a lancet or probe.[10]

Some doubt, however, has been cast on Kieller's original interpretation of "death by megalith" for the barber-surgeon. A recent reanalysis of the skeleton suggested that he may not have been crushed to death by the stone and was already dead when placed in its burial pit. It is possible, then, that murder raises its ugly head in the strange case of the barber-surgeon.

Whatever the cause of the barber-surgeon's death, the burial of the Avebury stones is often seen as a reaction by the church against stones that were deemed the focus of pagan (and thus undesirable) practices carried out by superstitious medieval villagers. However, some stones may also have been buried by villagers who simply needed to free up more land for the cultivation of crops and pasture, evidence of which archaeologists have found within the interior of Avebury.

Many "megalithic crimes" have been perpetrated over the years, with numerous monuments damaged or destroyed, but one of the most pernicious took place at Avebury between 1650 and 1730. During this period, many of its standing stones were destroyed as the village began to expand into the in-terior of the monument, with some of the stones not only getting in the way of this expansion but also providing a convenient source of building material for houses and farm buildings. Some stones were also removed or destroyed during the nineteenth century; one was blown up with gunpowder, with some of its fragments sent sailing over a nearby barn by the force of the explosion. William Stukeley has left us with a melodramatic yet vivid description of the destruction of one of Avebury's ancient and irreplaceable standing stones: "The massacre of a stone here with levers and hammers, sledges and fire is as terrible a sight as a Spanish Atto de fe [execution by burning]. The vast cave they dig around it, the hollow under the stone like a glass-house furnace or a baker's oven, the huge chasms made through the body of the stone, the straw, the faggots, the smoak, the prongs, and the squallor of the fellows looks like a knot of devils grilling the soul of a sinner."[11]

The expansion of the village also resulted in irreparable damage to some parts of Avebury's bank and ditch. For example, in the later seventeenth century, the owner of Avebury Manor, Ralph Stawell, leveled an area of the bank and filled in the ditch near the western entrance so that a barn could be built and trees planted, while in 1762 the bank near the southern entrance was quarried for material to be used in the village road.

Nonetheless, despite all the damage and destruction done to Avebury in the past, it has survived into modern times and remains a truly magnificent monument that exudes a great sense of prehistoric power and mystery. However, somewhat unfairly, Avebury has always lived in the long and famous shadow cast by its near neighbor, Stonehenge, which lies some 20 miles to the south on Salisbury Plain.[12]

STONEHENGE

Archaeologists have long been aware that the monument that arguably represents the greatest achievement of megalithic Europe is a complex structure comprising several phases of construction or remodeling, and it has been noted that "each of [Stonehenge's] different parts may well have had different purposes and meanings. An analogy is sometimes drawn with Europe's great medieval cathedrals, each of which contains a huge array of symbolically meaningful architectural components that are called into play for performances such as christenings, weddings, funerals, harvest festivals, saints' days, observances of the birth, death and resurrection of the central deity, and many other events that both celebrate life and commemorate death."[13]

Stonehenge: The Early Years

Stonehenge began its long and complicated life around 3000 BCE, when a Late Neolithic community decided to construct an atypical henge monument that consisted of a low inner bank and an external ditch. This earthwork enclosure has an overall diameter of around 110 meters and features a main entrance in the northeast, with a smaller entrance in its southern part; cattle and red deer bones that were already several hundred years old were placed at the base of the ditch shortly after it was dug. A prehistoric deposit of a more disturbing nature was found in the ditch in 1978, when archaeologists accidentally found a crudely cut grave dating to ca. 2300 BCE that contained the skeleton of a healthy young man who was about twenty-five or thirty years old when he died. It subsequently became clear that he had not died peacefully, as the tips of flint arrowheads were found lodged in his bones. Lying alongside him in the grave were three broken arrowheads with snapped off tips that had been fired from close range, with the one that killed him probably passing through his heart. Why this young man's life was brutally cut short, however, will remain an unsolvable prehistoric "cold case," but the archer's stone wrist guard or bracer, found near his left arm, marked him out as a member of the Beaker culture.

Hugging the inner circuit of the bank around the inside of the earthwork enclosure are the fifty-six "Aubrey holes," named after antiquarian John Aubrey, who discovered them in 1666 (the year of the notorious Great Fire of London), when England was basking in an extremely hot, Mediterranean-like summer, with a few of the holes showing up as darker marks in the sunbaked turf. There has been a long-standing archaeological debate as to whether the Aubrey holes once contained timber posts (perhaps of a roofed building) or standing stones. Whatever the truth, what is not in doubt is that cremation burials were deposited inside many of the Aubrey holes around 2800 BCE, before the erection of Stonehenge's megalithic settings. These cremations represented the burnt bodies of more than two hundred people, who were buried with artifacts such as long bone pins, antlers, and curious ball-like carved lumps of chalk.

The Sarsen Settings

Roughly three to four hundred years after the construction of the bank and ditch, ca. 2600–2450 BCE, Stonehenge was transformed from a prehistoric monument that was nothing out of the ordinary into one that was unique and spectacular, as in the mid-third millennium BCE its two major components were built: the Sarsen Trilithon Horseshoe and the Sarsen Circle. The former came first and comprises five pairs of huge sarsen uprights capped by equally impressive lintels—hence the term "trilithon" ("three stones"). As the name suggests, the trilithons are arranged in a horseshoe shape, and they are graded in height, with the tallest, the "Great Trilithon" (about 7.5 meters high) to the southwest, probably marking the midwinter sunset (in fact, at midwinter the sun can be seen setting between its two uprights). The Trilithon Horseshoe is open to the northeast, facing the main entrance of the earthwork enclosure and the direction of the midsummer sunrise. The famous Heel Stone (a crude sarsen pillar that lies just outside the main northeastern entrance of the bank) at Stonehenge also probably marks the rising sun at midsummer. It may well have originally been one of a pair between which the midsummer sun rose on the horizon, as an empty hole that once held an adjacent standing stone was found here during an excavation in 1979. The Heel Stone stands at the end of the Stonehenge Avenue, its two parallel banks forming a long approach that was linked to the nearby River Avon, with the first part of the avenue oriented northeast toward the midsummer sunrise. In the early eighteenth century, William Stukeley, the first antiquarian to recognize the Stonehenge Avenue, noted that stone holes were still visible in the remains of its low banks, suggesting that—like its counterparts at Avebury—it was once lined with parallel rows of standing stones.

The Great Trilithon only has one remaining upright today, as at some point in the more recent past, the other collapsed on top of the so-called Altar Stone, which lies half buried under this huge stone in the center of the Trilithon Horseshoe. It is not clear whether this 5-meter block ever stood upright, but royal architect Inigo Jones came across the Altar Stone in 1620 and, as was often the way with antiquarian ruminations on megaliths, speculated that it was a place where people had been sacrificed.

Measuring some 30 meters in diameter, the Sarsen Circle is almost double the size of the Trilithon Horseshoe, which it surrounds. Originally, it probably consisted of thirty sarsen uprights measuring some 4 meters high that were linked at the top by thirty lintels. The main entrance or focal point of the circle appears to be in the northeast, as the gap between the two uprights situated there is about a meter wider than the gaps between the others.

As there were none of a suitable size in the immediate vicinity of Stonehenge, the great sarsen boulders used in the Trilithon Horseshoe and Sarsen Circle had to be hauled from the Marlborough Downs, which lay some 17 miles to the north. The route used for this hugely impressive feat can never be known for sure, but it would not have been a direct one owing to the wide marshes and dense, tangled forests that lay between the Marlborough Downs and Stonehenge in prehistory. Furthermore, there would also have been dangerous hills and slopes to contend with on the rolling chalk downs.

Once the sarsens arrived at the site of Stonehenge, they were fashioned into the rectangular uprights and lintels that are so familiar and famous today. This must have been arduous and boring work for the Stonehenge workers, as they only had rounded sarsen mauls of varying sizes (some as large as a pumpkin, others as small as a tennis ball) to batter, grind, and smooth the unworked sarsens. Numerous sarsen mauls have been found during excavations undertaken at Stonehenge; for example, in 1901 Professor William Gowland discovered around one hundred examples, which had been used as packing material around the one remaining upright of the Great Trilithon. When work was in progress at Stonehenge, which would surely have taken years rather than months, it would have been little more than a prehistoric building site: "In the turmoil of those years Stonehenge must have been a bustling, dirty, rowdy place, with the crashes of the hammerstones, the rhythmical scrape and screech of the grinding mauls, the chatter, the bellowing of orders over the noise as the stones were levered upright, cries of warning, the distant shouting of a team dragging yet another sarsen across the last mile of the plain."[14]

Rather ingeniously, the builders of Stonehenge secured the lintels and the uprights of the Trilithon Horseshoe and Sarsen Circle together using simple mortise and tenon joints. During the working of the sarsens, they left two bulbous, peg-like stone tenons in place at the top of each upright, while on the undersides

Figure 7.5.   Stonehenge (image courtesy of Guenter Wieschendal, CC public domain).

of their corresponding lintels, two deep mortise holes were pounded and ground out to receive the tenons. Measures were also put in place to secure the lintels together in the Sarsen Circle with beak-like, inverted-V-shaped projections and corresponding V-shaped grooves left at their ends so that they could be socketed together into the curving and rather graceful ring that is seen today. These techniques are more commonly seen in carpentry, and they suggest that the builders of Stonehenge were skilled carpenters. In fact, "it has long been realized . . . that Stonehenge was a stone skeuomorph of temples and shrines built elsewhere in wood."[15] Well-known examples of these timber circles include Woodhenge near Stonehenge and, further afield, Sarn-y-bryn-caled in Powys, Mid Wales.

A few of the uprights of the Sarsen Circle also feature mysterious prehistoric carvings that, somewhat surprisingly, were not discovered until 1953. Although these are now very faint, the carvings depict more than fifty Early Bronze Age (ca. 1800 BCE) axes and one dagger, probably of a native British type. As has been noted, "The weaponry displayed could have been deliberate defacement; stamping a new warrior authority over an earlier ritualised, more passive one."[16] Two carvings (in bas-relief) of Early Bronze Age axeheads can also be seen at the base of the central standing stone in the well-known Boscawen-un stone circle in Cornwall. A large, abstract rectangular motif accompanied by a semicircle and a crook motif can also be seen on one of the Stonehenge uprights; curiously, these abstract carvings find parallels in the megalithic art of Brittany.

THE STONEHENGE BLUESTONES

Although Stonehenge's great sarsens are very familiar to a worldwide audience, its smaller "bluestone" settings are not so well known. Bluestone is a catch-all term for a variety of different rock types that are not local to Salisbury Plain and include spotted diorite, nonspotted diorite, rhyolite, and tuffs. Stonehenge experts now think that the first of these settings was the Double Bluestone Circle erected around the Trilithon Horseshoe ca. 2550 BCE, probably before the building of the Sarsen Circle. As many as ninety standing stones may once have stood in this double circle, although some or all were removed and rearranged in the later Outer Bluestone Circle and Bluestone Oval, which were both raised ca. 2200–2000 BCE. The former was erected between the Sarsen Trilithons and the Sarsen Circle, but many of its stones have been stolen or smashed in more recent times; today only thirty remain, but at least double that number probably stood in the circle when it was complete. The Bluestone Oval stands inside the Sarsen Trilithons and originally consisted of an arrangement of twenty-four or twenty-five standing stones that were graded in height toward the southwest. At some point, five or six of its standing stones were removed from the northeastern segment of the Bluestone Oval, creating a horseshoe-shaped setting of stones, although the date of this event is not known for sure.

Preceding the Bluestone Oval within the interior of the Sarsen Trilithons, perhaps by a couple hundred years, was the Central Bluestone Circle. The plan of this monument is ill defined, however, and the only traces of it that remain are five standing-stone sockets, maybe from a circle originally containing about twenty-five standing stones.

The Bluestone Controversy

As early as the 1720s, William Stukeley realized that the distinctive bluestones of Stonehenge were "foreign" to Salisbury Plain and must have come from elsewhere. Subsequent antiquarians of the nineteenth century continued to puzzle over the origin of the bluestones, but it was not until the early twentieth century that this elusive "elsewhere" was identified as the Preseli Hills of north Pembrokeshire, southwest Wales, by Henry Herbert Thomas, a petrographer with His Majesty's Geological Survey. More specifically, Thomas pinpointed Carn Menyn as the major source of the Stonehenge bluestones, "realizing that the spotted dolerite from this outcrop with its characteristic white spots of feldspar,

Figure 7.6.   Bluestone outcrops on Carn Menyn (image, author).

was identical in appearance"[17] to that used for the bluestone settings at Stonehenge. As has been noted, the Preseli Hills "are the only part of the British Isles where this type of distinctive spotted dolerite can be found. It is the most common of Stonehenge's bluestones."[18]

Thomas's discovery was a landmark moment in the study of Stonehenge, and in 1923 he published his findings in a now famous paper,[19] arguing that it was highly unlikely that the bluestones were glacial erratics carried to Salisbury Plain by ice and that they must therefore have been transported there by prehistoric people. Thomas's theory has since become widely accepted by archaeologists and geologists, although more recent archaeological and geological research suggests that Carn Menyn was just one of several places in the Preseli Hills, such as the Carn Goedog outcrop opposite Carn Menyn, that were quarried for the Stonehenge bluestones. However, some archaeologists and geologists today find it just too hard to accept that prehistoric people transported some eighty bluestones weighing at least 1–2 tons each by land and sea from the Preseli Hills to Salisbury Plain, which represents a journey of about 150 miles. Instead, like some of their earlier counterparts, they have argued that ice rather than prehistoric people transported the bluestones from Pembrokeshire to Stonehenge, with a glacier that moved from South Wales to southern Britain carrying them to Salisbury Plain thousands of years before the famous monument was built.

The incredulity of those who favor the glacial over the human-transport theory is understandable, as it does seem hard to believe that such an amazing feat could ever have been pulled off by prehistoric people who had no modern machinery to aid them. Indeed, it would still be a very difficult task today to transport eighty or so bluestones from the Preseli Hills to Salisbury Plain. However, the fact remains that archaeological evidence has been found at both the Carn Menyn and the Carn Goedog outcrops of the quarrying of bluestone "monoliths" (standing stones); furthermore, no glacially derived material from the Preseli Hills has been found in the rivers on Salisbury Plain.[20]

Between 2014 and 2016, Mike Parker Pearson and his colleagues carried out excavations at Carn Goedog, targeting an area where the outcrop contained striking in situ natural pillars of rock that resembled the bluestones at Stonehenge. They subsequently discovered a recess from which four bluestone pillars appeared to have been quarried as well as a pair of large stone slabs set lengthways about 1 meter apart, which were interpreted as a "classic trestle arrangement on which monoliths can be perched before being transferred to a wooden sledge."[21] An artificial stone platform of flat slabs was also uncovered at the base of Carn Goedog on its southern side, onto which bluestone pillars may have been laid after they had been quarried from the outcrop, ready to begin their remarkable journey to Stonehenge.

Two wedge marks, which probably represent the unsuccessful removal of standing stones from the rock outcrop, were identified at Carn Goedog by the archaeologists, and large numbers of crude stone tools were also unearthed during the excavations. The most common of these were wedge-shaped implements that displayed clear signs of use on their wider ends, or "blades." These tools have been "interpreted as wedges that were used for opening up the joints between each naturally formed pillar so that it could be levered away from the outcrop."[22]

Parker Pearson and his team also investigated another possible bluestone quarry at Craig Rhos-y-felin, some 2.5 miles from Carn Goedog, uncovering further possible evidence of the quarrying of bluestones. Although the existence of this putative bluestone quarry has been seriously questioned by some geologists,[23] scientific analysis of some of the stone-working debris found at Stonehenge provides a close match with the rock type (rhyolite) at Craig Rhos-y-felin.

The jury remains out on the Craig Rhos-y-felin "bluestone quarry," but Carn Goedog is now probably favored as the major source of the Stonehenge bluestones. However, the archaeological evidence found at Carn Menyn by Geoffrey Wainwright and Timothy Darvill during their archaeological fieldwork on this atmospheric hilltop perhaps suggests that this was also an important bluestone source: "Investigations in 2004 revealed a stone wall defining the area of ancient stone extraction at the top of Carn Menyn, and broken monoliths of exactly the same size and proportions as those at Stonehenge are found scattered below the craggy summit—blocks of stone won from the quarry but abandoned because they broke before they could be carried far down the mountainside."[24]

Wainwright and Darvill identified other stone extraction sites and bluestone pillars that had been left abandoned on the slopes of Carn Menyn, as well as hammerstones like the ones used to shape the Stonehenge sarsen stones, during subsequent seasons of fieldwork. On a hillside to the west of Carn Menyn, there is also an oval setting of bluestones known as Bedd Arthur (Arthur's grave) and from this intriguing monument, which stands alongside a prehistoric trackway, Carn Menyn is clearly visible. Bedd Arthur is so similar in size, shape, and orientation to the more famous bluestone oval at Stonehenge that "it is difficult to believe that they are not the work of the same people."[25] Is this just a coincidence? If so, it is a very curious one, given the link between Stonehenge and the Preseli Hills.

Exactly when the bluestones arrived at Stonehenge is unclear, although radiocarbon dates obtained during the excavations at Carn Goedog and Craig Rhos-y-felin suggest that this might have happened around 3000 BCE. It is therefore possible that there was once an earlier bluestone circle (or, alternatively, a megalithic tomb comprising bluestones in its architecture) somewhere in the Preseli Hills, which was dismantled and transported to Stonehenge, with its stones subsequently erected within the Aubrey holes.

Figure 7.7.   Bedd Arthur bluestone oval, with Carn Menyn seen in the distance (image, author).

The Meaning of Stonehenge: Some Suggestions

Many theories have been put forward regarding the purpose of Stonehenge, and the antiquarians of the seventeenth to the nineteenth centuries often interpreted the monument as a temple built by Iron Age Celtic druids, although it was also viewed as a Roman temple or a court built for Viking royalty during this time. Jumping forward to the 1960s, the astronomer Gerald Hawkins came up with the rather esoteric theory that Stonehenge was something akin to a Stone Age computer built to predict solar and lunar eclipses, and his book, *Stonehenge Decoded*, became something of a sensation on its publication in 1965. There have also been some theories about Stonehenge that, at best, can be described as odd, with that of W. S. Blacket undoubtedly one of the oddest of all. In his *Research into the Lost Histories of America* (1884), Blacket proposed that Native American Indians from the Appalachian Mountains crossed the Atlantic to build Stonehenge and other British megalithic monuments!

In more recent times, however, Mike Parker Pearson, Geoff Wainwright, and Tim Darvill have come up with what are perhaps the most thought-provoking and plausible theories to date regarding the time-honored question of what Stonehenge was for. Writing in the respected archaeological journal *Antiquity*, Parker Pearson and his Madagascan colleague Ramilisonina drew on ethnographic evidence from Madagascar, where menhirs known as *Vatolahy* ("man stones") are intimately linked to the ancestors. The basic premise of the article is that Stonehenge was built for the ancestors, "a stone version for the dead of the timber circles used for ceremonials by the living."[26] Parker Pearson later expanded on the theory of Stonehenge as a place belonging to the ancestors and suggested that the Sarsen Trilithon Horseshoe was "the meeting place of the ancestors of the people of Britain" in which the trilithons symbolized "five tribal lineages charting their descent from five original households or founding ancestors."[27] Perhaps the trilithons also "represented ancestral deities watching over activities taking place in the central arena"[28] of Stonehenge. A similar scenario has been suggested at Avebury, which, rather than being built *for* the ancestors, was built *of* them, with some of the sarsen stones representing specific ancestral deities who were gathered together within its massive bank and ditch.[29]

Geoff Wainwright and Tim Darvill theorized, however, that Stonehenge was not the domain of the dead or the ancestors, but rather a place for the living—albeit people who were not in the best of health. They proposed that prehistoric people believed that the bluestones possessed healing powers and were thus drawn to Stonehenge in its heyday, in much the same way medieval pilgrims visited places such as the shrine of Saint James in Santiago de Compostela Cathedral, hoping to cure their ills: "Bluestones from Carn Menyn and other nearby outcrops in west Wales were brought to Stonehenge and set up within a temple whose structure had already been built from sarsen stones. From that time on-wards, pilgrims and travellers were drawn to Stonehenge because of the special properties that had empowered Stonehenge to provide pastoral and medical care of both body and soul: tending the wounded, treating the sick, calming troubled minds, promoting fecundity, assisting and celebrating births and protecting people against malevolent forces in a dangerous and uncertain world."[30]

This theory has not found that much favor with Stonehenge experts, but local folklore holds that the many springs around Carn Menyn (and other out-crops in the Preseli Hills) have healing powers. Interestingly, Wainwright and Darvill found that not only are some springs on Carn Menyn located close to where bluestones were quarried, but some also have low stone walls surrounding them, creating pools (some of which were subsequently turned into Christian holy wells). A few of the stones used in these walls also feature prehistoric "art" in the form of carved cupmarks.

It could be that the bluestones were attributed healing powers because the people who probably transported them to Stonehenge, in "one of the greatest achievements of human prehistory,"[31] believed that they came from the sacred home of the gods or the ancestors, with these stones thus brought to Stonehenge to "supercharge" the great stone circle with their supernatural power. It is not

Figure 7.8.   Bluestone pillar and Carn Menyn (the bluestone was brought down from Carn Menyn by an RAF Chinook helicopter) (image courtesy of Helge Klaus Rieder, CC BY-SA 1.0).

hard to see how prehistoric people—with no knowledge of geological processes—viewed the unusual and dramatic peaks of the Preseli Hills in this way. Carn Menyn is the largest and most visually impressive of these peaks, and seen from a distance "as you approach from the south, it resembles an ancient ruined city of broken walls and towers."[32] Furthermore, "when you reach its summit, [Carn Menyn] has the atmosphere of a liminal place between earth and sky, [which] is enhanced by the evocative, primordial shapes of the rocky outcrops that form the 'walls and towers' of this city in the clouds."[33] As has also been noted, the spotted dolerite outcrops in the Preseli Hills, which were probably used for many of the bluestones, "reveal patterns of white spots looking like stars and constellations as if the night sky is mirrored and fixed for ever in the face of the earth."[34]

Finally, there is Geoffrey of Monmouth's account in his *Historia regum Brittaniae* ("history of Britain," published ca. 1136) to perhaps take into account when considering the origin of the Stonehenge bluestones. In this classic and entertaining work of pseudo-history, Geoffrey records that giant stones with healing powers were transported from the "Giant's Dance" monument in Ireland to Salisbury Plain by the legendary magician Merlin for the Dark Age British ruler Aurelius Ambrosius. Its dismantled stones were subsequently re-erected at "mount Ambrius" (Amesbury, near Stonehenge) as a cenotaph to the native Celtic nobility who had been treacherously murdered there by warriors of the Saxon leader Hengist, with this infamous event known as the "Treachery of the Long Knives." Of course, this is a fantastical account from many hundreds of years ago, but could it perhaps contain a grain of truth, preserving an echo of a real and remarkable prehistoric event that involved the transport of stones with special powers from a land far to the west of Stonehenge?

English Megalithic Tombs

$\mathscr{L}$ocated in the southern English counties of Wiltshire and Oxfordshire, respectively, are two of the finest megalithic tombs in Britain, if not Europe: the West Kennet and Wayland's Smithy long barrows. Both West Kennet and Wayland's Smithy have yielded fascinating evidence about the burial rites of the shadowy Early Neolithic communities who raised their great stones in the landscape. As will be seen, strong hints that southern England's first farmers lived in a time troubled by violence and warfare have also been recovered from the burial chambers of these two famous megalithic tombs.

These two monuments represent superb examples of the Cotswold-Severn group, a distinctive type of megalithic tomb built ca. 3800–3400 BCE and mainly concentrated in the lovely Cotswold Hills of Gloucestershire, though they are also found in other southern English counties and also in parts of South and North Wales. The characteristic features of the Cotswold-Severn tombs are long, wedge-shaped or trapezoidal, carefully constructed long mounds with projecting "horns" enclosing deep forecourts at their wider ends (finely laid courses of dry-stone walling were also used in the lower halves of the mounds). The burial chambers are set in either the wider ends or the sides of the mounds, and a few examples also have small additional chambers in their narrower ends. Some Cotswold-Severn tombs also have what at first sight look like blocked-up entrances to burial chambers at the rear of their forecourts. However, excavation has shown that these are "false" entrances beyond which there is no chamber and only the material used to construct the mound. A fine example can be seen at the northern end of Belas Knap long barrow in Gloucestershire, another impressive and well-known Cotswold-Severn tomb.[1] The purpose of these false entrances is unknown, but they perhaps functioned as "spirit doorways" through which the dead could pass, perhaps to receive offerings left for them by the living.

Figure 8.1. The "false" entrance at Belas Knap (image courtesy of Ethan Doyle White, CC BY-SA 4.0).

WEST KENNET LONG BARROW

> The great old mound, with its time stained stones, among which bushes of the blackthorn maintain a stunted growth, commanding as it does a view of the great part of the sacred city of Avebury, has still a charm in its wild solitude, disturbed only by the tinkling of the sheep bell, or perhaps the cry of the hounds.
>
> —Excerpt from a paper read by John Thurnam to the Society of Antiquaries of London on March 15, 1860[2]

The West Kennet Long Barrow was built on a ridge of chalk downland and commands fine views of gently rolling Wiltshire countryside, with the famous Silbury Hill and the unexcavated, and even larger, East Kennet long barrow visible from the site. Constructed about 3700 BCE, West Kennet is one of the largest Neolithic long barrows in Europe, its trapezoidal mound (which survives to a maximum height of approximately 4 meters) measuring about 103 meters long and 25 meters across at its wider eastern end, where a central passage or gallery (approximately 7 meters long) leads from the entrance into the interior of the barrow. This "transepted" passage terminates at a western chamber and has two pairs of opposing chambers opening off its southern and eastern sides, and "while the chambers are for crouching in, the passage is big enough to enable a man to walk upright and the whole interior, dimly illuminated by a small pane of modern toughened glass in the roof, is reminiscent of a chapel. [West Kennet] somehow demands, and usually receives, respectful quiet."[3]

The wider end of West Kennet features a monumental facade of huge sarsen slabs set in a row, with the two largest and most impressive ones symbolically blocking the entrance to the tomb. The remains of dry-stone walling made from oolite (a type of limestone) can also be seen between the stones of the facade, and, interestingly, most of the stone used came from a source about 19 miles to the southwest of West Kennet. The massive "blocking" stones of the facade were seemingly erected when the forecourt of the barrow was filled in with rubble, during the "closing" of the tomb around 2500 BCE. This was perhaps carried out by people of the Beaker culture who may have seen this by-then-ancient monument as a threat to their new religious traditions because it was still "redolent with powerful associations."[4]

West Kennet has long been a source of fascination for scholars, and the earliest sketches and descriptions of the long barrow were made in the seventeenth and eighteenth centuries by the famous English antiquarians John

Figure 8.2. The megalithic facade at West Kennet (image courtesy of Dickbauch, CC BY-SA 3.0).

Aubrey and William Stukeley. Aubrey's sketches also revealed that the perimeter of its great mound was once surrounded by standing stones. Some of
these stones were still standing when William Stukeley visited West Kennet
in the eighteenth century, but the missing ones were probably removed by the
infamous "Farmer Green," with Stukeley recording that this local farmer had
taken stones from another long barrow nearby for use in his sheepfolds. People
have been digging at West Kennet since at least the seventeenth century. However, as was often the way in earlier times, they were opportunists looking for
treasure or building materials rather than knowledge about its builders, and the
pitted appearance of the top of West Kennet's mound points to the activities
of these earlier barrow diggers. The most notorious of these was a Dr. Toope,
from the nearby town of Marlborough, who in the late seventeenth century
dug into the West Kennet mound looking for human bones to be ground down
and used as an ingredient in his potions and medicines.

It was not until 1859, when the well-known antiquarian John Thurnam
partially excavated its chambers, that the first scholarly exploration of West
Kennet took place. Thurnam was employed as medical superintendent at "The
Retreat," a progressive mental hospital in Yorkshire founded by the Quakers,
but his leisure time was devoted to archaeology and anthropological pursuits.
In fact (and perhaps questionably), patients from the hospital were used as
laborers by Thurnam during his excavation at West Kennet in the fall of 1859,
helping him to shed light on the lives and religious practices of Wiltshire's
Stone Age farmers.

Although Thurnam only partially explored West Kennet, failing to notice
its side chambers (he was not helped in this respect by the local landowner, who
placed restrictions on Thurnam's digging), he nevertheless dug into the western
chamber and part of the adjoining passage. There he found the skeletons (not all
which were whole) of four adult males and the large part of a child's skull lying
on the chamber floor. According to Thurnam, two of the men had died violently, as he recorded that their skulls displayed lethal fractures, although a more
recent analysis suggests that these fractures were more likely post-depositional
breakages that occurred after burial. Antiquarians of the nineteenth century, and
particularly John Thurnam, all too often viewed any fractures on Neolithic skulls
as evidence of violence. However, as we will see below, later excavations at West
Kennet in the mid-twentieth century did uncover evidence to suggest that at
least one of the individuals buried in the long barrow had met a violent death.
Thurnam also found animal bones (e.g., boar, ox, sheep, or goat), heaps of pottery
sherds, a fine flint dagger or knife, numerous sharp flint flakes that had probably
been used as knives (perhaps at a Neolithic funeral feast), and human remains in
the western chamber, with a bone pin (possibly from a funeral shroud), a single
shale bead, and more pottery sherds recovered from the passage.

Nearly one hundred years after John Thurnam's excavations, Professors Stuart Piggott and Richard Atkinson carried out further excavations at West Kennet in 1955 and 1956, digging through the deposits of chalk rubble and soil that prehistoric communities had deliberately dumped into the tomb over many hundreds of years, eventually filling its passage and chambers to the roof. Once this infilling had been removed, further human remains were found in the side chambers, representing nearly forty men, women, and children who had probably been buried over a period of about fifty years, after which the "shutting down" of West Kennet began as people began filling its chambers and passage with debris. Perhaps the most interesting burial came from the northeastern side chamber, where the crouched skeleton of "an elderly man occupied the western corner."[5] Lying very suggestively in the region of his throat was a leaf-shaped flint arrowhead, which "was no gift from a grieving relative but more than likely his ticket to a place in hallowed ground—a fallen hero, killed defending hearth and home."[6] Leaf-shaped arrowheads are a characteristic feature of the earlier Neolithic in Britain and Ireland, and these have traditionally been interpreted as grave goods when found in megalithic tombs. However, many archaeologists now agree that a fair percentage of these arrowheads probably entered Neolithic burial chambers not as grave goods but rather in the bodies of the people they had killed.

Later scientific analysis of the bones of the men, women, and children recovered from West Kennet revealed that their lives cannot have been easy in a world without modern medicine and hospitals. This analysis revealed that arthritis was widespread among the older adults, and there were also dental abscesses and fractures; there were even signs of spina bifida observed on the bones of several adults from West Kennet. It should also be pointed out that, as archaeologists have found at many other megalithic tombs in Europe, not all the skeletons were complete at West Kennet, with many skulls and larger leg and arm bones missing from the chambers. This probably reveals that "[Neolithic] people had removed the skulls and long bones for their rituals, speaking to them and invoking their ghosts to assist the living."[7]

Numerous artifacts were recovered during the 1955–1956 excavations at West Kennet, most of which were mixed in with the secondary filling in the chambers and passages. This assemblage contained, among other things, a broken chalk mace head that had been turned into a pendant, an abundance of pottery sherds from Late Neolithic vessels and Copper Age beakers, flint scrapers and knives, bone pins, many stone, bone, and shell beads, a leaf-shaped arrowhead, boar tusks, and infant and animal bones. A crushed and complete Early Neolithic pottery bowl was also recovered from the northeast chamber, while an almost complete, finely decorated, high-quality Beaker vessel was found high up in the fill of the northwestern chamber, where it had been carefully placed upside down.

WAYLAND'S SMITHY

Wayland's Smithy Long Barrow lies some 16 miles to the northeast of West Kennet on the famous Ridgeway, an ancient route that has been used since at least the Neolithic. This route follows a chalk ridge that runs through some 90 miles of the finest countryside that southern England has to offer, with many remnants of ancient life lying along its route.[8] Wayland's Smithy itself is located in the county of Oxfordshire, in a peaceful and bucolic corner of the English landscape, with the best time to visit the monument being the summer, when the tall and graceful beech trees surrounding the site dapple its ancient, time-worn stones with shifting shadows.

Although, at about 55 meters long, Wayland's Smithy is smaller than the West Kennet Long Barrow, its Neolithic architecture is just as impressive, if not more so, as its Wiltshire counterpart's. At the front of its trapezoidal mound of earth and chalk, there is a megalithic facade comprising two pairs of massive sarsen slabs interspersed with dry-stone walling that stand on either side of its entrance (there were originally three flanking stones on either side of the entrance), with many of the smaller sarsens that formed a curb around the edges of the barrow also still visible. A short and narrow transepted passage measuring about 7 meters long leads from the facade to a pair of burial chambers, which lie opposite each other at its end.

Figure 8.3.   Entrance at Wayland's Smithy (image courtesy of August Schwerdfeger, CC BY-SA 4.0).

The first mention we have of Wayland's Smithy comes from an Anglo-Saxon charter of King Eadred dated to 955 CE, with the Saxons naming it after Weland the Smith, the legendary supernatural metalworker of Norse and Germanic mythology. This mythological figure can be seen on the famous Franks Casket, a beautifully carved whalebone box dating to the eighth century that now resides in the British Museum. The Anglo-Saxons also likely viewed Wayland's Smithy as a supernatural portal to the spirit world, a boundary between the worlds of the living and the dead. In addition, there are various antiquarian accounts of Wayland's Smithy dating from the seventeenth to the nineteenth centuries, with John Aubrey the first to document the long barrow around 1670. Wayland's Smithy was partially excavated in 1919 and 1920 by C. R. Peers and R. A. Smith, who discovered the remains of around eight people in the western chamber and evidence to suggest that there may have been two phases of construction at Wayland's Smithy.

It was not until 1962 and 1963 that Wayland's Smithy became the subject of a more thorough and scientific archaeological investigation, with the excavators of West Kennet, Stuart Piggott and Richard Atkinson, directing the excavations and also undertaking restoration work at the monument. It was discovered that Wayland's Smithy was indeed a two-phase monument, with the trapezoidal long mound and megalithic burial chamber (Wayland's Smithy II) built over an earlier wooden mortuary structure (Wayland's Smithy I, ca. 3580 BCE), which lay below a smaller oval barrow made from chalk rubble. The larger and more impressive Wayland's Smithy II was built about 130 years after Wayland's Smithy I, ca. 3450 BCE, although no further human remains were found in its chambers during the 1962–1963 excavations.

This was not the case with Wayland's Smithy I, as on the flat sarsen slabs that had been used to pave the floor of the wooden mortuary structure (which may have resembled a ridge tent), the excavators unearthed the remains of fourteen individuals: eleven males, two females, and a child. At either end of the paved mortuary area, to the north and south, D-shaped postholes (about 1 meter deep) were uncovered, and each of these had originally held timbers from the base of a tree trunk that had been split in two. Just in front of the southern end of the barrow, a rectangular arrangement of four postholes was also found. It is possible that these represented the remains of a timber excarnation scaffold or platform on which dead bodies were laid prior to burial, a practice recorded among several nonstate peoples around the world. The Sioux and Lakota tribes of North America, for example, sometimes performed "sky" or "air" burials, with corpses placed on wooden scaffolds or even in the limbs of trees. Traditionally constructed by the female members of tribes, these scaffolds were normally reserved for warriors who had fallen in battle. The dead were tightly wrapped in blankets and laid to rest with their weapons and valuables, sometimes remaining on the scaffolds for as long as two years before their decomposed bodies were retrieved for burial. As has been noted of this Native American funerary practice, "The motive was not solely to encourage the dead person's spirit to depart into the sky: Sioux and Lakota people feared the dead as well as the diseases they can spread, so it was an also an attempt to minimize contact with the body."[9]

A NEOLITHIC WAR GRAVE?

Richard Atkinson noted that the only grave goods found with the burials in Wayland's Smithy I were "three well-made leaf-shaped arrowheads of flint, the points of which had been broken off and discarded before burial."[10] However, it seems that Atkinson had misinterpreted these "grave goods," as a snapped tip from one of these arrowheads was later found embedded in the pelvis of one of the individuals buried in the wooden mortuary structure, probably representing the cause of death. Although no other arrow tips were found stuck in the bones from the primary barrow, the other arrowheads found here were likely also instruments of death rather than grave goods. Interestingly, the bones of two men bore marks relating to scavenging by dogs or wolves, indicating that these individuals had lain out on the surface for some time before their bones were interred in the mortuary structure. It could therefore be that the two men were recovered from the "battlefield" sometime after they died and that all of the individuals buried in Wayland's Smithy I were casualties of war. They may even have all died together in a single battle or massacre, as a recent radiocarbon dating program has indicated that the monument was only used for short space of time: "probably for only 1–15 years—less than a single generation!"[11]

THE MEDWAY MEGALITHS

Some of the earliest tombs to be built by Britain's Neolithic communities are those of the Medway group, which lie in two clusters to the west and east of the River Medway as it cuts through the beautiful countryside of the North Downs in the county of Kent in southeastern England. The nine long barrows that form this compact and important group, representing the only Neolithic mortuary monuments in Kent and constructed some six thousand years ago, are not well preserved due to later vandalism by medieval Christian zealots and opportunistic eighteenth- and nineteenth-century stone masons. It could be that the Medway megaliths were constructed by immigrants from northern France or, perhaps more likely, by native people who had connections with this area of the continent. The monuments consist of unusually tall H-shaped chambers measuring about 3 meters long by 2 meters wide, which are set in the eastern end of substantial long barrows fronted by megalithic facades. It has been said of these important reminders of Early Neolithic life, "It emerges that the Medway megaliths at their outset comprised a unique group of stone-built long barrows which were a concentration of the largest, and thus the most grandiose, of their kind in southern England."[12]

The Kit's Coty Monuments

The best known of the Medway group or megalithic tombs is the oddly named Kit's Coty House (nobody is quite sure where the name originates), with the three huge uprights and capstone seen at the site today originally forming the burial chamber of a barrow measuring some 70 meters long. The barrow was originally composed of chalk rubble, although this has now been virtually plowed away. About half a mile to the south is Little Kit's Coty House long barrow, although it is in a ruinous condition, being little more than a jumbled collection of huge sarsen slabs. Fantastic views of the rolling countryside of the North Downs and the Medway Valley are to be had from both monuments, with Neolithic people doubtless observing a landscape that was much more thickly wooded than that of today.

Figure 8.4.   Kit's Coty House (image courtesy of Simon Burchell, CC BY-SA 4.0).

Coldrum

The only Medway long barrow to yield any substantial human remains is Coldrum, located on the western side of the River Medway, about 4.5 miles from the Kit's Coty monuments. This is the best preserved of the Medway tombs and comprises a much-denuded, slightly trapezoidal rectangular barrow measuring around 20 meters long and 12–15 meters wide, with the four great sarsen slabs at its wider eastern end representing the remains of its burial chamber. Many large, prostrate sarsens can also be seen lying around the perimeter of the barrow. Contrary to a theory that was popular among nineteenth-century antiquarians, these represent not a toppled stone circle surrounding a dolmen but rather the remains of an enclosing curb and facade of upright stones. It is probable that these stones were felled by Christians in the fourteenth century, with the facade stones toppled by the digging away of the front of the terrace on which Coldrum is located. These can now be seen at the bottom of the steep slope that was the result of this digging, with the chamber stones set precariously above them in its top edge.

In 1910, F. J. Bennet excavated the burial chamber at Coldrum, uncovering human skulls and bones at two different levels, which he estimated represented around twenty-two individuals, although a recent analysis suggests that they belonged to seventeen men, women, and children. This analysis also revealed cut marks made by a sharp flint tool on two "proximal femur" fragments (the top of the upper thigh bone that forms the hip joint), which indicated that legs had been removed from two corpses.

The meaning of this strange evidence remains a mystery, but it is perhaps conceivable that the missing legs were taken as war "trophies" or that the bodies were mutilated by an enemy tribe. The taking of body parts as trophies from and the mutilation of enemies (not always dead ones) are practices well attested to in both the ethnographic and the historical records.[13] However, this seems unlikely in the case of the Coldrum thigh bone fragments, as the cut marks on them "are discretely and precisely located; they do not suggest frenzied hacking or mutilation,"[14] and they also indicate that the legs were probably cut from bodies that were already half rotted away. Intriguingly, though, two fine parallel cut marks were also found on a probable female skull from Coldrum, and these were located "just above and behind the external auditory meatus (the earhole)."[15] As there are no other cutmarks seen on the skull, it has been concluded that the cutmarks probably relate to the removal of the ear and that "it is difficult to see this in any other context than the taking of a trophy from a dispatched victim."[16] Whether or not the ear had been taken as a war trophy, clear evidence of a violent death was also present on the skull in the form of at least one (and probably two) lethal fractures on the frontal and parietal (side) bones.

PASSAGE GRAVES OF THE CHANNEL ISLANDS:
LA HOGUE BIE AND LE DÈHUS

Given that the British Channel Islands of Jersey and Guernsey lie close to the coasts of Normandy and Brittany, western France, it is hardly surprising that the islands were settled by Neolithic communities from there. This is shown by the similarities seen between the Neolithic material culture (e.g., polished stone axes, stone bracelets, pottery) and megalithic tombs found in Normandy, Brittany, and the Channel Islands. Included among these tombs

Figure 8.5.   Entrance at La Hogue Bie (image courtesy of Man vyi, CC public domain).

are several passage graves, with the most notable examples, La Hogue Bie and Le Dèhus, located on Jersey and Guernsey, respectively. Both monuments were constructed between ca. 4100 and 3900 BCE.

La Hogue Bie is an exceptional megalithic tomb and the largest and most spectacular example of the Amorican passage graves, which have their densest concentration in the *département* of Morbihan in southern Brittany. The massive earth and stone mound of the monument measures nearly 60 meters in diameter, some 12 meters high, and about 20 meters across at its summit, which is rather incongruously crowned by a medieval chapel. From the entrance, which comprises two uprights capped by a massive lintel, a 9-meter-long passage leads to the cross-shaped, or "cruciform," burial chamber, which comprises a main central chamber (about 9 meters long by 3 meters wide) with three smaller chambers or recesses opening on its sides and end. Some twenty-four cupmarks have been carved into the surface of one of the megalithic slabs forming the northern lateral chamber, with this slab perhaps reused or "appropriated" from an earlier megalithic monument.

Excavations undertaken at La Hogue Bie in 1924 by the Société Jersiaise recovered the scattered remains of around ten people in the chambers, as well as limpet and oyster shells, two intact pottery "vase supports," and sherds from some twenty others. The evidence of burning seen on the bowls of the intact vase supports indicates they were probably used as lamps by Neolithic people to illuminate the rituals and ceremonies that were carried out within the dark interior of La Hogue Bie.

Le Dèhus

Comprising a mound measuring about 18 meters in diameter and 3.5 meters high and an inner passage and central chamber that have a combined length of about 9 meters, Le Dèhus cannot compete with La Hogue Bie in terms of scale. However, carved into one of the capstones of its burial chamber is a unique and remarkable piece of megalithic art, which perhaps lends Le Dèhus a greater importance than its larger counterpart on the island Jersey.

Known as Le Gardien du Tombeau ("the guardian of the tomb"), this carving, discovered on the underside of the second capstone of the burial chamber by Lieutenant Colonel De Guérin in 1918, is "sometimes regarded as a pagan deity and the protector of the tomb."[17] The carving depicts a schematic male human figure with arms, hands, and a striking bearded face; he is equipped with a bow and what appear to be two arrows, below which is what looks like some type of belt or girdle. Under the right lighting conditions, this figure emerges like a Neolithic ghost from the capstone of the burial chamber, where it lay hidden for some six thousand years before its discovery. It is unlikely, however, that the carving was made after the capstone was put in place, as it is partially obscured by a

Figure 8.6.   Interior of Le Dèhus (image courtesy of Richard Scott-Robinson, CC BY-SA 3.0).

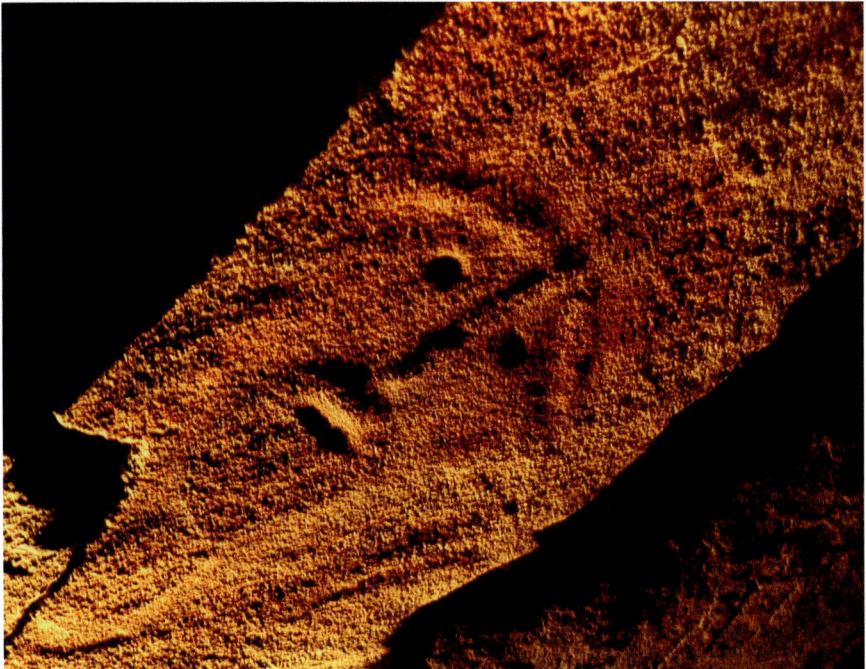

Figure 8.7.   A face from the past: "Le Gardien de Tombeau" (image courtesy of Richard Scott-Robinson, CC BY-SA 3.0).

slender standing stone in the center of the chamber, which was not put in place as a supporting device for the capstone above it. Furthermore, the image would have to have been carved from underneath on a horizontal surface some 2 meters from the ground. Therefore, the capstone probably began life as a decorated menhir that was subsequently incorporated into the architecture of the Le Dèhus passage grave and may have depicted a renowned or mythical Neolithic warrior figure.

The Guernsey antiquarian Frederik Corbin Lukis undertook excavations at Le Dèhus in the mid-nineteenth century. In its chambers he found human bones and artifacts such as a polished greenstone axe made from serpentine, Neolithic pottery, a copper dagger and three Beaker vessels (together revealing Copper Age ritual activity at Le Dèhus), animal bones (e.g., cattle, pig, sheep/goat, and horse), and a profusion of limpet shells. In one of the small side chambers opening off the passage, Lukis recorded that he found a rather remarkable burial featuring two adult male skeletons in an upright kneeling position, posed back-to-back and "looking" away from each other. Although his account cannot be totally relied upon, the abundance of limpet shells that were used to fill the chamber may have held the skeletons in position after the bodies of the two men had decomposed.

The Câtel and Saint Martin Statue Menhirs

The capstone of Le Dèhus is not the only prehistoric standing stone in Guernsey featuring a representation of a human figure, as there are also the Câtel and Saint Martin statue menhirs. While these decorated standing stones are difficult to date precisely, it is thought likely that they were raised at some point in the later Neolithic between ca. 3000 and 2500 BCE, although the Câtel menhir is more obviously Neolithic in character than the Saint Martin stone.

The Câtel menhir was discovered in 1878, buried beneath the chancel floor of the Sainte-Marie-du-Câtel church, but today it stands in an elevated position in the pleasant graveyard of the church. It measures nearly 2 meters high and 0.7 meters wide, and its surface has been carved to depict a stylized human figure with slight shoulders, a large, featureless head, and two small, rounded breasts carved in relief (one of which was probably chiseled off in the medieval period by the Christian iconoclasts who may also have buried the "pagan" stone underneath the floor of the church). Similar pairs of breasts carved in relief can be seen on some of the Late Neolithic megalithic tombs of both Brittany and the Paris Basin, and on the rear of the stone, a belt has been carved in raised relief.

The Saint Martin menhir, or La Gran'mère du Chimquière ("the grandmother of the church"), as this famous monument is more affectionately known, stands just outside the main entrance to Saint Martin's church. Measuring about 1.65 meters high and 0.5 meters wide, the menhir depicts the upper torso of a probable female figure, who has clearly defined facial features and a tightly

Figure 8.8.   The Câtel statue menhir (image courtesy of Man vyi, CC public domain).

fitting headdress with four central buttons, which drapes over her shoulders. As on the Câtel menhir, there is a small pair of breasts carved in relief on the front of the Saint Martin's menhir, with a pair of now eroded arms also recorded below these in 1925. It is these features that archaeologists think date to the Neolithic, with the face and the headdress representing a remodeling of the menhir, perhaps in the Iron Age or early Roman period around two thousand years ago, or maybe even later in the medieval period.

· 9 ·

Welsh Megalithic Tombs

Wales may be a small country on the western edge of Europe, but thousands of prehistoric sites and monuments survive in its glorious landscapes. Included among these abundant remnants of Welsh prehistory are many megalithic tombs, the most celebrated of which is probably Pentre Ifan in Pembrokeshire, an area of Britain with one of the densest concentrations of these compelling prehistoric monuments (the others being Anglesey, North Wales, and the Cotswolds in southern England). Pentre Ifan is a deserved icon of Welsh prehistory and Welsh heritage and a must-see for any megalithic enthusiast (figure 1.2). As has been noted, "The romantic setting and striking appearance of Pentre Ifan have long attracted the attention of visitors."[1]

PENTRE IFAN

Constructed during the earlier Neolithic in the first half of the fourth millennium BCE, Pentre Ifan represents a particularly fine example of a type of megalithic tomb known as a "portal dolmen," found on either side of the Irish Sea in both Ireland and Britain, with the majority located in Northern Ireland, western Wales, and southwestern England. Portal dolmens are simple but well-built structures that have a characteristic H-shaped setting of two megalithic uprights with a wider slab between them at the front (the portal), behind which are one or two further uprights forming a boxlike chamber. Huge capstones rest on the uprights of the portal stones and the succeeding chamber, and these are often at a rather precarious angle, sloping downward toward the back of the chamber, looking as though they could slide off and thud to the ground at any minute.

Figure 9.1. The author and "Oscar" at Carreg Coetan Arthur portal dolmen, Pembrokeshire (image courtesy of Pam Norman).

Many (but not all) portal dolmens are surrounded by low spreads of smaller stones, although there is no firm evidence to support the traditional idea that these represent the remains of robbed-out cairns that originally completely covered the uprights and capstones of the dolmens. In fact, many archaeologists now believe that these spreads of stone are low, surrounding stone platforms rather than the remnants of stone mounds, as may perhaps be seen at the well-known megalithic tomb of Dyffryn Ardudwy on the northwestern coast of Wales. This two-phase monument was excavated by Professor Terence Powell of the University of Liverpool in the early 1960s, with the remains of several Early Neolithic pottery bowls and a fragmentary stone bracer of the Beaker culture recovered. Professor Powell was of the opinion that most of the covering cairn of its two burial chambers had ended up being recycled into the dry-stone walls of nearby fields by local farmers.

In recent years, several archaeologists have also questioned the long-held view that portal dolmens were Early Neolithic tombs and instead have wondered whether their builders were more concerned with raising their great capstones into the air rather than constructing a burial chamber. If so, it could be that the primary function of portal dolmens was to celebrate a sacred or mythical stone and not the dead, as has often been assumed, with the human bones and arti-

Figure 9.2. The Dyffryn Ardudwy burial chambers and cairn (image, author).

facts found in their chambers representing secondary "offerings" placed beneath their capstones. Alternatively, it is possible that the capstones of portal dolmens were symbolic representations of sacred parts of the landscape, as is suspected at Pentre Ifan. Sharp-eyed visitors to the monument will notice the resemblance that its huge capstone bears to the profile of Carn Ingli mountain, which can be seen on the horizon through the tall and slender uprights of Pentre Ifan. Is this just a curious coincidence, or was this huge slab raised up by Pentre Ifan's builders because they wanted to pay homage to a part of the landscape that was venerated for some reason?

Other portal dolmens in Wales feature capstones that appear to mimic the local topography, and a strong candidate in this regard is Bach Wen on the northern coast of the beautiful Llŷn Peninsula in North Wales. The capstone of this well-known monument appears to echo the distinctive sloped profile of the pyramid-like peak of Gyrn Goch that rises dramatically behind Bach Wen. This Early Neolithic monument is well known for the numerous carved cupmarks (over one hundred) that can be found on the upper surface of its capstone. We might wonder whether the people responsible for creating these curious carvings would want to hide them below a covering mound, perhaps lending weight to the idea that portal dolmens were never completely covered by cairns.

Whatever the true purpose of portal dolmens, there can be little doubt that Pentre Ifan is a spectacular monument, with its massive, dart-like capstone

Figure 9.3.   Pentre Ifan, with Carn Ingli seen on the horizon (image, author).

Figure 9.4.   Bach Wen portal dolmen, with Gyrn Goch rising dramatically behind the monument (image, author).

appearing to "float" above its supporting uprights when seen from a distance, an optical illusion noted at other examples of these striking monuments. A famous lithograph of 1865 depicts two mounted horsemen sheltering beneath this massive capstone, illustrating the unusual height of Pentre Ifan, which adds to its visual impact.

The Early Neolithic community (or communities?) who constructed Pentre Ifan also chose a fine spot in which to locate their monument, which stands above the Nevern Valley, commanding fine views toward the northwest, with the small fields and woods of this lovely corner of southwestern Wales and the sea at Newport Bay providing a fine backdrop to the site. Four small but prominent rock outcrops can be seen to the west, with the larger and distinctive peak of Carn Ingli clearly visible beyond these, about 2.5 miles away on the horizon. This well-known local landmark sports one of the largest Iron Age hillforts of Wales on its slopes and takes its name, "Mount of Angels," from the legend that in the early sixth century, Saint Brynach communed with angels on its summit.

The famous Welsh archaeologist W. F. Grimes excavated Pentre Ifan during two seasons of fieldwork in 1936 and 1937 and in 1958 and 1959, subsequently uncovering its rather complex history. He found that it was a multiphase monument with three main phases of construction and that the earliest feature of the site was an approximately 3-meter-high standing stone erected next to a pit in which a fire had been lit. This stone was subsequently pushed over and sealed below the cairn or platform (about 16 meters long by 8 meters wide) that was added in the next phase when the portal dolmen was built. Its great capstone was probably a partly buried stone, or "grounder," removed from near the toppled standing stone and pit. The large pit Grimes uncovered in the ground below the capstone probably marks the spot where it was liberated from the earth. In the final phase of building, the cairn was enlarged to about 40 meters in length, with the monument now resembling a typical long barrow of the Neolithic of northwestern Europe, although whether the cairn completely covered the portal dolmen remains an archaeological bone of contention (despite being now overgrown with grass, the remains of this trapezoidal cairn can still be clearly seen). It was during this stage that two additional standing stones were erected on either side of the portal uprights, creating an impressive forecourt area, which was later blocked with stone rubble, effectively marking the end of Pentre Ifan as a "working" monument.

Grimes found no human remains at Pentre Ifan, and other finds were meager, with a flint arrowhead, some flint flakes, and a few sherds of Early Neolithic pottery the only objects recovered during his work, although tomb robbers may have rifled its chamber in later times. Although no burials were found at Pentre Ifan, the acidic Welsh soil could have put paid to any that had existed. It has been suggested that the megalithic slab, or "doorway," between the two portal stones at the front of Pentre Ifan "is set in such a way that human bone and associated offerings can be placed through the gaps between [it] and the uprights."[2]

COTSWOLD-SEVERN TOMBS IN WALES

Although Cotswold-Severn tombs are primarily found in southern England, there is a significant concentration of these distinctive megalithic tombs in the Black Mountains region of southeastern Wales. However, there are isolated examples in other parts of Wales, such as the Parc le Breos Cwm tomb,[3] which today lies on the grounds of an impressive country house on the beautiful Gower Peninsula, South Wales. Parc le Breos Cwm was excavated in 1869 by the wealthy Welsh industrialist Henry Hussey Vivian, Sir John Lubbock (an influential figure in the development of British archaeology),[4] and members of the Cambrian Archaeological Association, led by Lord Edwin Wyndham-Quin.

Parc le Breos Cwm was accidentally discovered by workmen who stumbled across human bones in what they thought was just an old and unremarkable large stony mound that would provide convenient material for road building. Its subsequent excavation by the group of nineteenth-century worthies uncovered the remains of a trapezoidal barrow measuring some 30 meters long by 17 meters wide, with a deep bell-shaped forecourt leading to a narrow central passage or gallery (about 5.5 meters in length) formed by ten megalithic uprights interspersed with courses of dry-stone walling. Opening off this passage are two pairs of small rectangular side chambers, although no capstones survive on either the top of the passage or the chamber stones. It is possible that the passage and chambers were originally covered with corbelled courses of flat stones, but these were removed during the rather "unscientific" excavation of 1869. Whatever the case, the bones of Neolithic men, women, and children were found in both the passage and the side chambers by the Victorian diggers: "Each set of bones were found in a small confused mass, just as would be if a body in a sitting position had collapsed, as it were, vertically within its own area."[5] Whether the dead had actually been "laid" to rest sitting up is debatable but not impossible. The nineteenth report on the bones estimated that around twenty-four individuals had been buried at Parc le Breos Cwm, but a more recent analysis suggests that this is an underestimate and that the number is probably closer to forty, with men, women, and children represented in the burials.

Professor Richard Atkinson, who carried out famous excavations at Stonehenge, reinvestigated (and restored) Parc le Breos Cwm in 1961 and 1962, discovering what were probably two ritual deposits made by Neolithic people in the forecourt area of the tomb. The western one contained flint "debitage" (waste material from the production of stone tools), a large leaf-shaped arrowhead, a pottery sherd, and eight pieces of quartz rock crystal, while the eastern one featured five pieces of quartz, thirty-four pottery sherds, and a small flint knife.

TY-ISAF

In 1938, after his initial excavations at Pentre Ifan, W. F. Grimes turned his attention to one of the Black Mountains Cotswold-Severn tombs. The tomb in question was Ty-Isaf, and in "rather less than three weeks' digging by four men,"[6] the remains of a trapezoidal or wedge-shaped cairn (about 33 meters in length), featuring a false entrance, two side chambers, and a smaller, circular "rotunda," or cairn, were revealed. The rectangular side chambers in the western and eastern sides of the cairn were arranged almost back-to-back and were accessed by short passages. The western chamber yielded the remains of at least seventeen Neolithic people, which "were found mostly in groups consisting frequently of the cranium, lower jaw and one or two long bones carefully placed against the side stones and sometimes [deliberately] pushed into angles and crevices."[7] Also recovered from the chamber were two leaf-shaped flint arrowheads, a complete stone axe, a bone pin, and a few sherds from an Early Neolithic pottery bowl. One end of a stone axe was also found in the tomb's forecourt area.

The remains of only one individual were positively identified in the eastern chamber, but large fragments from at least six bowls were uncovered, and these were associated with an area of charcoal, revealing that someone had entered its dark confines and lit a fire here some six thousand years ago. Just outside the entrance to the chamber, in the passage, were the badly broken long bones of two individuals, with a pierced sandstone pendant, found close by, perhaps once worn by one of these people in life. Ten roughly shaped sandstone discs of various size were also recovered from various parts of the tomb, although the purpose of these curious objects is unknown.

In architectural terms, the most sophisticated feature of the Ty-Isaf long cairn was the "rotunda" that Grimes uncovered in the southern half of the structure, which measured around 12 meters in diameter and featured two well-made circuits of dry-stone walling. Within its walls was an approximately 7-meter-long passage oriented southeast/northwest, with two opposing rectangular side chambers opening off its end. Poorly preserved human bones and sherds of Early Neolithic pottery were recovered from the chambers of the rotunda, with the long bones of at least two individuals also recovered from its passage. Just behind the outer wall of the rotunda near the southern end of the cairn was another smaller chamber, which yielded the base of an Early Bronze Age pot, which had probably contained a cremation, and part of the bone handle of a dagger, revealing ritual activity at Ty-Isaf some two thousand years after it was built.

PENYWYRLOD

Other notable Welsh Cotswold-Severn tombs can be mentioned, such as Penywyrlod, which is located about 5 miles northwest of Ty-Isaf. Penywyrlod was something of a "late starter" in archaeological terms as it was only discovered by accident in 1972. Excavations began in the same year and uncovered the remains of a massive trapezoidal cairn measuring 52 meters long and some 22 meters across at its broader southeastern end, making it the largest of the Black Mountains Cotswold-Severn long cairns. Although damaged by the quarrying for stone that led to its discovery, human skulls and bones were recovered from its chambers and forecourt area, along with a few grave goods, such as a flint knife and a stone disc like those found at Ty-Isaf. It also seems that all was not well in the Black Mountains area during the Early Neolithic when the Cotswold-Severn tombs were built there, as the tip of a flint arrowhead was later found embedded in a rib fragment from a young adult of uncertain sex. The arrow appears to have been fired from a distance and perhaps hit the individual in the side as he or she was trying to turn or run away from the incoming stone projectile; there is no evidence of healing on the bone, indicating that death followed soon after the arrow had hit home.

Perhaps the most intriguing find from Penywyrlod, however, was the broken section of a possible Neolithic bone flute, which had been made from the hollowed-out, broken thigh bone of a large sheep. This small artifact measured about 7 centimeters in length and was perforated with three small holes, giving it the appearance of a broken penny whistle. Although Early Bronze Age in date (ca. 2200 BCE), a similar "flute" was recovered by the antiquarian William Cunnington in 1808, after he dug into one of the burial mounds in the important Normanton Down Early Bronze Age barrow cemetery near Stonehenge. Made from a broken swan's leg bone that had been carefully smoothed and hollowed out and measuring some 20 centimeters in length, it featured at least two perforations or finger holes. It was found with the cremation burial of an individual who had also been sent to the next life with two fine Bronze Age daggers, a whetstone (for sharpening the daggers), and a bronze pin or cloak fastener. Aubrey Burl has conjured up an imaginative but evocative backstory for this burial: "One can imagine this part-time warrior piping to his flock during the lazy hours of a Wessex summer, indolently watching the distant labours of sarsens being dragged and heaved upright at Stonehenge."[8]

BRYN CELLI DDU, BARCLODIAD Y GAWRES, AND THE CALDERSTONES

In terms of "prehistoric fame," only two other tombs in Wales find themselves on an equal footing with Pentre Ifan: the passage graves of Bryn Celli Ddu and Barclodiad y Gawres on the island of Anglesey (Ynys Môn, in Welsh), North Wales, a place rich in megalithic remains. Both monuments are more elaborate and later in date than the simple passage graves that were built in Wales in the Early Neolithic (e.g., the well-known Carreg Samson in Pembrokeshire) and represent the only two definite examples in Wales of the late passage grave tradition (ca. 3000–2500 BCE). Along with the now largely destroyed Calderstones monument in Liverpool, Bryn Celli Ddu and Barclodiad y Gawres boast important and unique (in Britain) assemblages of megalithic art, featuring motifs that are more commonly seen in passage graves in Ireland, Brittany, and Iberia. The similarities between the megalithic art and architecture of these three late passage graves, the renowned passage graves of the Boyne Valley area, and other passage graves in eastern Ireland strongly indicate that Late Neolithic communities from this region were in touch with their counterparts in northwestern Wales and England. It could perhaps even be the case that Late Neolithic settlers from Ireland built Bryn Celli Ddu, Barclodiad y Gawres, and the Calderstones. Whatever the truth, there can be little doubt that it is a rewarding experience to visit Bryn Celli Ddu or Barclodiad y Gawres and listen to the almost reverential hush descend as visitors enter their passages and dark chambers, in a way passing from the modern world into the Neolithic one. We can only imagine the feelings of the Late Neolithic people who entered Bryn Celli Ddu and Barclodiad y Gawres, but it seems likely that they felt a mixture of awe and fear as they passed from the world of the living to that of the dead.

Bryn Celli Ddu

Bryn Celli Ddu translates in English to "the mound in the dark grove" or "the dark grave-hill," and this renowned monument is located on the southern coast of Anglesey near the Menai Strait, a narrow stretch of tidal water that separates the island from mainland Wales. As with many of the megalithic tombs on Anglesey, the visitor to Bryn Celli Ddu is rewarded with a stunning view across the Menai Strait to the mountains of Snowdonia, which lie some 10 miles distant. About 140 meters to the northwest of Bryn Celli Ddu is a striking rock outcrop featuring some twenty-eight cupmarks on its upper surface, which somewhat surprisingly were only discovered as recently as 2005 by a team from the University of Bristol, England. This outcrop could perhaps have been of sacred significance and "may well have influenced the tomb builders in the selection of their site."[9] More recently, in 2015, a community-based archaeological research project discovered numerous cupmarks on four rock outcrops that lay on a ridge about half a mile north of Bryn Celli Ddu.

Various antiquarians explored Bryn Celli Ddu in the eighteenth and nineteenth centuries, but it is thanks largely to W. J. Hemp, who excavated and restored the monument between 1925 and 1929, that the prehistoric story of Bryn Celli Ddu was uncovered. Radiocarbon dates suggest that construction of Bryn Celli

Figure 9.5.   Entrance at Bryn Celli Ddu (image courtesy of Jensketch, CC BY-SA 4.0).

Ddu began around 3000 BCE, although there is debate as to whether it represents a single or a two-phase monument. Most archaeologists probably favor the latter and believe that an earlier circle henge comprising an outer ditch and inner stone circle was replaced by a later passage grave (perhaps around 2500 BCE).

Whatever the case, a ditch measuring around 21 meters in diameter and originally some 2 meters deep can still be seen surrounding the large mound of earth and stones covering the passage grave at Bryn Celli Ddu. Below the mound and within the area demarcated by the encircling ditch, Hemp uncovered evidence of a circle comprising fourteen or fifteen standing stones, finding stone sockets and three toppled stones that seem to have been deliberately broken by the passage grave builders. This evidence perhaps points to violent ideological conflict between two later Neolithic groups on Anglesey, with the destruction of the stone circle and its burial beneath the mound of the passage grave representing one group's extreme refusal to accept the new tradition of stone-circle building that emerged in Britain ca. 3000 BCE. Small deposits of cremated bone and quartz fragments and the almost complete cremation of a girl (about fifteen years old), who some archaeologists think may have been sacrificed, were also recovered from the sockets of some of the missing stones, which may have been subsequently incorporated into the passage grave.

Scatterings of quartz pebbles and traces of fires were found near the entrance to Bryn Celli Ddu, as were at least five postholes from an intriguing wooden structure that has been dated to the Late Mesolithic (Middle Stone

Age), ca. 6000 BCE. A small pit containing the bones of an ox was found just to the northeast of the postholes, and although it is not known whether the ox burial is contemporary with or later than the Mesolithic structure, the former seems more likely. From the entrance a narrow (about 1 meter wide) and relatively short (about 8 meters long) passage leads to the inner burial chamber, with the first 3 meters or so of the passage unroofed by capstones. In the inner, roofed part of the passage, there is a low stone shelf bench running along the northern wall, and the Welsh naturalist and antiquarian Thomas Pennant, who visited Bryn Celli Ddu in 1784, recorded that he found human bones on this bench but that they crumbled to dust when handled. The polygonal burial chamber at the end of the passage is roofed by two huge capstones. Near the center of the chamber there is a large, smoothly shaped standing stone nearly 2 meters high, which serves no structural purpose as it does not reach the roof. It is possible that this stone was removed from the earlier stone circle and set up to "watch" over the dead in the burial chamber. An early nineteenth-century account left by the Reverend John Skinner, a parish vicar with a passion for the past, recounts how this stone seriously spooked a local farmer who entered Bryn Celli Ddu hoping to find treasure: "He came to the mouth of a passage. . . . [A]nxious to reap the fruits of his discovery he procured a light and crept forward on his hands and knees along the dreary vault, when lo! In a chamber at the further end a figure in white seemed to forbid his approach. The poor man scarcely had the power to crawl backwards out of this den of spirits."[10]

The chance that treasure might be buried in the chamber helped the farmer to overcome his fear of its ghostly guardian, and he returned to Bryn Celli Ddu the next day. However, all he found were some large human bones near the standing stone that had previously caused his hasty exit from the monument. Hemp discovered this stone, which the farmer had dug under in his quest for treasure, still half fallen in the burial chamber and subsequently re-erected it. He also found small fragments of burnt and unburnt human bone, two flint arrowheads, a stone bead, limpet and mussel shells, and a shallow spiral motif lightly pecked or hammered into an upright on the southern side of the chamber.

Hemp's most interesting discoveries at Bryn Celli Ddu were found just outside the passage grave in the center of the henge. These consisted of an oval pit covered with a large stone slab and an adjacent standing stone, which were hidden when the mound was raised over the passage grave. Excavation of the pit showed that it had been scorched and hardened by the fire that had been lit in its base. A human ear bone was also found in the bottom of the pit, and although the significance of this curious deposit can only be speculated upon, "the ear bone, coming as it does from within the skull, may have been associated with the spirit of the deceased, perhaps even with his or her ability to hear."[11] The standing stone (known as the "pattern stone") only lay about 1 meter north of the pit, and Hemp must have been excited to discover that it had been

Figure 9.6. The Bryn Celli Ddu "pattern" stone (image courtesy of Wolfgang Sauber, CC BY-SA 3.0).

decorated with sinuous patterns and a spiral motif, although the true meaning of this abstract decoration lies forever hidden in the distant past. Today, the original can be seen in the National Museum of Wales in Cardiff, with a replica placed near the entrance to Bryn Celli Ddu.

Bryn Celli Ddu and the Midsummer Sunrise

In 1909, in his *Stonehenge and Other British Stone Monuments*, astronomer Sir Norman Lockyer (one of the pioneers of archaeoastronomy) was the first to propose that Bryn Celli Ddu had been deliberately aligned on the midsummer sunrise by its builders. However, Lockyer's theory found little truck with archaeologists and was largely forgotten until archaeologist Steve Burrow decided to test it by making his own observations at Bryn Celli Ddu. He was initially thwarted by bad weather in the summer of 2004 but returned to Bryn Celli Ddu the following year on the morning of the midsummer solstice, subsequently confirming that Lockyer had been right all along. "The effect of the solar alignment consists of a beam of light from the rising sun penetrating the passage and illuminating the rear wall of the chamber with a well-defined yellow box; this narrows to a thin strip as the sun climbs eastward over the course of about thirty minutes."[12]

Barclodiad y Gawres

Lying about 11 miles to the west of Bryn Celli Ddu and "spectacularly situated on a cliff-guarded promontory overlooking the Irish Sea"[13] is the equally well-known Barclodiad y Gawres ("the giantess's apronful")[14] passage grave. Barclodiad y Gawres is similar in size and appearance to Bryn Celli Ddu, although its passage is more complex, with three small side chambers forming a cross-like shape, therefore representing a fine example of what archaeologists refer to as a "cruciform" passage grave. Its builders also used the corbelling technique for the roof of the main chamber, using layers of overlapping stones topped by a small capstone.

Excavations undertaken at Barclodiad y Gawres in the early 1950s by Terence Powell and Glyn Daniel found the cremated bones of two men and two charred bone pins (that may have held shrouds together around the corpses of the two men) in its western chamber, with scraps of human bone also found in the eastern chamber. No bones were found in the central chamber, but evidence of a strange ceremony carried out here during the later Neolithic did come to light during the excavations at Barclodiad y Gawres. This evidence revealed that at some point people had entered the chamber and lit a fire, over which they poured a weird concoction "worthy of Macbeth's three witches."[15] The remains of this "witches brew" included the bones of creatures from both land and sea:

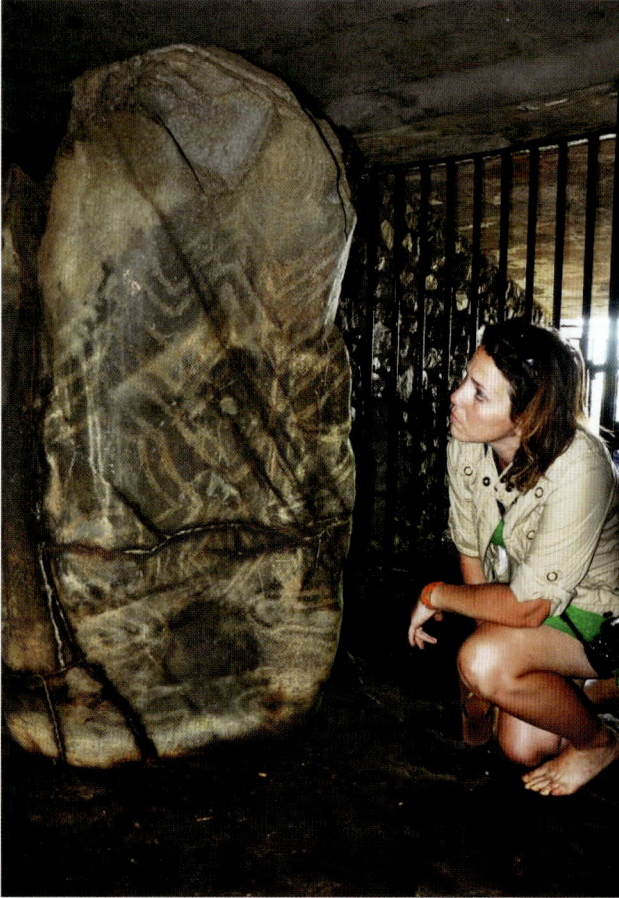

Figure 9.7. Decorated megalithic upright at Barclodiad y Gawres (image courtesy of Rich Mason, University of Liverpool Field School).

eel, whiting, wrasse, frog, toad, grass snake, mouse, shrew, and rabbit. Its meaning is unknown, but "it is a rare, almost unique glimpse of ritual that Barclodiad y Gawres gives us, one quite unsuspected today by the holiday makers as they take their children to paddle among the rocks beyond the cairn."[16] Megalithic art was also discovered on five of the megalithic uprights used in the construction of Barclodiad y Gawres. Three of these decorated stones were located at the end of the passage where it joins the burial chamber, with the other two located in the side chambers. The lightly pecked abstract motifs include diamond-shaped lozenges, zigzag lines, spirals, and sinuous, wavy lines that recall those seen on the Bryn Celli Ddu pattern stone.

The Calderstones

Little remains today of the Calderstones passage grave other than six sandstone slabs of varying sizes and shapes, which for many years were housed in a large greenhouse in a pleasant suburban park in Liverpool (Calderstones Park), having been moved here in 1954 from their previous location just outside the park gates. The stones were recently removed and sent to London for restoration work and are being re-erected under new protective housing in the courtyard of the park's nineteenth-century mansion house. The passage grave from which the Calderstones were removed was destroyed at some point in the nineteenth century, although it is thought to have been located near the park's present-day bowling green. The six remaining stones feature a rich collection of carvings dating from the later Neolithic to the twentieth century, with the prehistoric art (Late Neolithic to Early Bronze Age, ca. 3000–2000 BCE) including spirals, cupmarks, cup and ring motifs, concentric circles, parallel lines and arcs, a stylized metal dagger, and two footprints, which are very rare in megalithic art. Later carvings include a probable medieval church and cross, a bird (also probably medieval) that was only discovered in 2015 by a local schoolboy, and boot prints and graffiti carved in the nineteenth century by local farmworkers. These agricultural laborers are recorded as lying on the denuded mound of the passage grave, where they would soak up the sun after work during the week and on Sundays in the summertime, very probably unaware that their favorite sunbathing spot was some five thousand years old.

· 10 ·

Irish Megalithic Tombs

$\mathcal{O}$f the numerous megalithic monuments of the "Emerald Isle," there is one that stands out from all others: the Newgrange passage tomb in County Meath, southern Ireland. As has been said of this world-famous prehistoric monument, "Perhaps only Avebury, Stonehenge and the alignments of Carnac can take the breath away as Newgrange does. For visual splendour no other chambered mound in Europe can be compared with it."[1]

However, a large part of this "visual splendour" is due to a reconstruction of Newgrange's huge mound by Professor Michael O'Kelly after he had concluded his famous excavations at the site, which took place between 1962 and 1975. Today, as a result of O'Kelly's reconstruction, the huge number of visitors (about two hundred thousand people) who come to marvel at Newgrange every year are confronted by a passage tomb that has a spectacular steep facade on either side of its entrance, made from numerous quartz fragments and granite cobbles. In general, though, archaeologists were (and are) not particularly keen on O'Kelly's reconstruction of Newgrange's mound. For example, it has been said that "the vast green mound at Newgrange resembles a chirpy pill-box hat with a bright white headband—something Aer Lingus might one day adapt for its stewardesses."[2] Such scathing criticisms are probably justified to some extent. As many archaeologists have pointed out, the conservators who worked on the reconstruction of Newgrange's mound had to use concrete and metal pins to keep it from collapsing—building materials obviously not available to its builders some five thousand years ago when the passage tomb was built. Most archaeologists think that the striking steep-sided facade of Newgrange probably never existed, with the quartz fragments and granite cobbles of which it is constructed coming from a low platform that originally surrounded the base of its roughly circular mound.

Figure 10.1.   The spectacular but controversial mound of Newgrange (image courtesy of Tjp finn, CC BY-SA 4.0).

Leaving aside O'Kelly's controversial architectural "repair" work at New-grange, there can be little doubt that it is still an awe-inspiring monument that was constructed about 3200 BCE on top of a low ridge overlooking a bend in the famous River Boyne. In the native Gaelic, Newgrange is known as the Brugh na Bóinne (the palace/mansion of the Boyne), with the River Boyne a prominent feature of in the mythology of the ancient Irish and "their most sacred ground."[3] Its massive mound measures around 85 meters in diameter and 11 meters high and, somewhat remarkably, given its size, is composed mainly of water-rolled stones or cobbles that were taken from the bed of the nearby Boyne (it has been estimated that around 20,000 tons of material were used to construct the cairn). Intriguingly, some of the cobbles used to construct the Newgrange mound have been sourced to Dundalk Bay, which lies some 25 miles north of the passage tomb. Surrounding the mound are ninety-seven huge stones that form a massive curb around its perimeter, with many of these curbstones richly decorated with enigmatic carvings. The most impressive example is the one that stands directly in front of the entrance to the passage, with this 3-meter-long stone intricately carved with closely set swirling spirals and lozenge shapes. Spirals are a common feature of the megalithic art at Newgrange, and it has been speculated that they symbolized the eyes of a great Neolithic goddess who watched over the dead. An

Figure 10.2.   Early 1900s photograph of the entrance and decorated curbstone at New-grange (image courtesy of the National Library of Ireland on the Commons–Newgrange).

alternative suggestion is that "they represented the journey the dead must take before they reached their home in the Other-World."[4]

Twelve large standing stones can also be seen around the perimeter of the Newgrange mound, probably representing the remains of a huge stone circle (about 110 meters in diameter) consisting of some thirty-eight stones, that were raised in the Copper Age or Early Bronze Age ca. 2500–2000 BCE. One of these stones stands directly in front of the entrance at Newgrange, and at the winter solstice, it casts a shadow that "passes through" the triple-spiral carving on the superbly decorated curbstone in front of the entrance.

From the entrance, a long megalithic passage measuring some 19 meters long leads to a large central "cruciform" chamber, off which open three smaller side chambers or cells. The central chamber is roofed with a lofty and superbly constructed corbelled vault, its top rising 6 meters above the floor. Many of the megalithic orthostats, or uprights, used in the construction of the passage tomb, which came from sources several miles from Newgrange, are decorated with megalithic art, as are some of the capstones that form the roof of the passage, with the carved abstract motifs concentrated on the inner stones of the passage and the burial chamber. It is interesting to note that some of the slabs used for the capstones also have carved channels or grooves in their upper surfaces, which were probably made to carry off rain water seeping down through the stones of

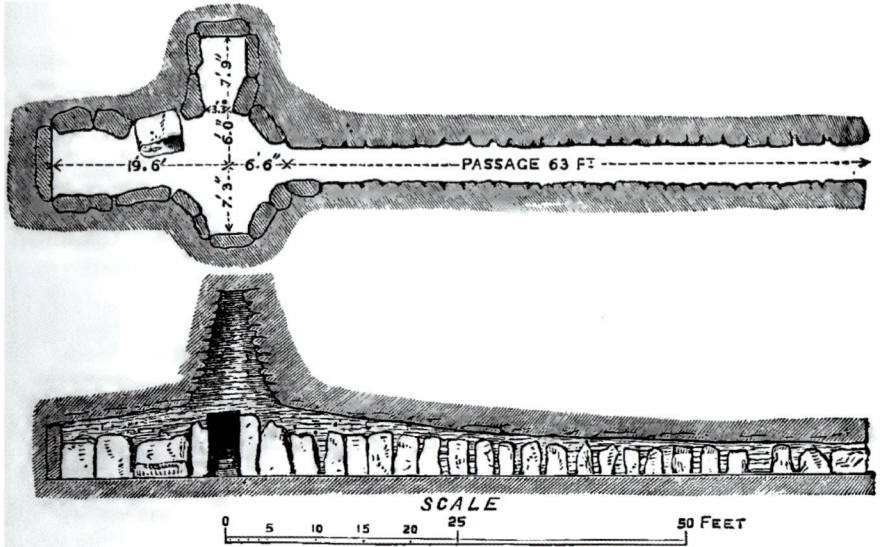

Figure 10.3.   Sketch of plan and cross section of Newgrange from *Wakeman's Handbook of Irish Antiquities*, 1903 (CC public domain).

the covering mound. Such inconsequential details somehow make the builders of Newgrange "more human" and bring us closer to them.

The most striking artifacts that came to light during O'Kelly's excavations at Newgrange were four large "basin stones" recovered from the smaller chambers, with two found, one inside the other, in the northern chamber. It seems likely that they had originally been used as containers for human bones and other artifacts, although it is hardly surprising that O'Kelly found these basin stones empty when he came across them, as many treasure seekers had plundered Newgrange since its discovery in 1699. Although few artifacts were recovered during O'Kelly's excavations in the passage and chambers of Newgrange, the remains of around five people were found mixed into the floor of the tomb, along with a small assemblage of artifacts such as small, carved chalk balls, or "marbles," a bone chisel, and stone beads and pendants.

NEWGRANGE AND THE MIDWINTER SUNRISE

It is damp and chill in the passage grave as the small group huddles together. Waiting . . . Watching . . . Outside the throng had grown past hundreds into the thousands. Men, women and children standing in the bitter pre-dawn air. White hoarfrost clings to grass blades, tree limbs, bushes. And yet the cold was welcomed. Still frigid air means no clouds would mar the celebrations. Finally a murmur went up from those highest up the mound as a rim of light appeared on the horizon. It was time. Soon their offerings would be made, their faces filled with hope. The world had turned. Once again the sun would climb high into the sky.

—Dick Ahlstrom, "People of the Passage Tombs"

Professor O'Kelly's most significant discovery at Newgrange was made at its entrance, or, more specifically, above it. Long before he conducted his excavations at Newgrange, it was known that a decorated lintel stone was located above its entrance (first recorded by William Wilde in 1847), and "careful work by O'Kelly and his team revealed the stone was . . . part of what they subsequently called a 'roof box,' a window to let light into the passageway."[5] However, it was not just random rays of sunlight that shone through this stone-built, window-like aperture. It was subsequently discovered by O'Kelly that Newgrange's builders had incorporated this small architectural feature into their monument to "trap" the rays of the midwinter sunrise so that they shone down the passage to illuminate the backstone of the end chamber, where a finely carved triple-spiral motif can be seen. It must have been a rather remarkable moment for O'Kelly as, having suspected that its "roof-box" had been built for this very purpose, he witnessed this event on December 21, 1967, from inside the chamber at Newgrange; he was the first person to do so in some five thousand years. The true significance of the midwinter sunrise to the builders of Newgrange is lost in the shadows that shroud the prehistoric past, but it was probably a very important time of year for its builders and, indeed, for many of the megalith builders of Europe: "Midwinter is the dead time of year. It is the time when the sun rises and sets farthest to the south, when the days are short and the nights are long and bitter. It is the time that primitive people dreaded, fearing that the Summer would never return and that the sun might continue moving southwards until it vanished, leaving the world in everlasting darkness. Such fears led to midwinter rites to protect the people from disaster. At Newgrange, the sun was for the dead, not the living."[6]

THE KNOWTH AND DOWTH PASSAGE TOMBS

Also found near Newgrange are the passage tombs of Knowth and Dowth, with the three tombs constituting the Boyne Valley passage tomb cemetery or "complex." The Knowth passage tomb lies about half a mile northwest of Newgrange and, like the latter, seems to have been built around the end of the fourth millennium BCE. Although Newgrange may be more visually striking and famous than Knowth, in truth the latter is the more impressive of the two and has been referred to as "the mother of all sites."[7] The mound at Knowth measures about 85 meters in diameter and 9 meters high and covers not one but two finely constructed passage tombs that face almost back-to-back, with their entrances in the western and eastern sides of the monument; the former comprises a simple square burial chamber and the latter, a cruciform chamber with a superb corbelled vault. The eastern tomb is the larger of the two and measures about 40 meters long, with the western one measuring some 34 meters in length. Immediately surrounding the mound at Knowth is a remarkable cluster of seventeen smaller passage tombs representing a dense concentration of these monuments that is unique in megalithic Europe (there were probably originally at least nineteen tombs). Knowth also has one of the densest concentrations of megalithic art in Europe, and at least 250 of the stones used in its construction were carved with the enigmatic motifs that characterize this art, with both the great boulder curbstones that surround its mound and the megalithic slabs used in its chambers and passages decorated. One of the curbstones features a motif that is almost identical to the early medieval sundials found in the walls of Anglo-Saxon churches and consists of eighteen rays spreading outward from a central hole, with two spirals and other carvings also seen on this stone. It is thought that Knowth's builders oriented the entrances of the eastern and western passage tombs on sunrise and sunset around the time of the spring and fall equinoxes, respectively.

It was in June 1962 that the Irish archaeologist George Eogan began his archaeological investigation of Knowth, with his annual excavations at the passage tomb continuing for some forty years until 2000. As a result of the work that represented a large part of his life, Eogan discovered the cremated and unburnt bones of more than 170 people in Knowth's two passage tombs, as well as numerous artifacts, such as miniature mace-head pendants made from stone and clay, stone and antler beads, mushroom-headed bone and antler pins, a broken stone mace head, basin stone fragments, and flint tools. The standout objects recovered by Eogan from Knowth were undoubtedly the exquisitely decorated, small flint mace head, which now resides in the National Museum of Ireland in Dublin, and a superbly decorated basin stone. This ornately carved and substantial object, measuring more than 1 meter in diameter and weighing about a third of a ton, is decorated with carved parallel grooves and concentric circles on its outer surface, with arcs and sun-like rays covering its curved inner one. However, although the basin stone is undoubtedly an impressive object that is strikingly and enigmatically decorated, in terms of artistic skill and finesse, it is no match for the mace head, which is undoubtedly one of the finest artifacts surviving from Neolithic Europe. This small object only measures about 8 centimeters long, and its maker selected an attractive creamy-white flint module with darker reddish-brown veins and patches as the raw material from which it was fashioned. The exquisitely carved decoration on the mace head comprises diamond-shaped facets and spirals, and on one side the highly talented Neolithic artisan who made it carved two interconnecting spirals above the hole that had held its long-since-decayed shaft. These spirals combine with the shaft hole to suggest two wide, staring eyes and a gaping mouth, and this was very probably what the unknown individual who made this small but superb memento of the later Irish Neolithic intended.

Dowth

The Dowth passage tomb is comparable in size to Newgrange and Knowth but unfortunately has so far not been the subject of a modern archaeological investigation. It was, however, subjected to antiquarian excavations in the nineteenth century that, although badly damaging the mound, did reveal two passage tombs opening off its southwestern side. The northern tomb comprises a passage measuring some 15 meters long, which leads to a cruciform chamber, while the southern one has a shorter passage leading to a broad chamber with a smaller cell or chamber on one side. More than thirty years ago, Jack Roberts and Martin Brennan recorded the rays of the midwinter sunset shining into the chamber of the southern passage tomb at Knowth. As has been noted, it is fitting that "the cairn known as the 'house of darkness' [has] a chamber oriented towards the time when the sun dies into the western horizon."[8] Fifteen of the hundred or so curbstones surrounding Dowth's mound are decorated with megalithic art, with motifs that look like rayed suns the most common.

In 2017, Irish archaeologists from University College Dublin (UCL) made a hugely important discovery when they unearthed the remains of an-

Figure 10.4.   Aerial view of Knowth and its "satellite" tombs (image courtesy of Raemond Carolan, CC BY-SA4.0).

other major passage tomb near Dowth while working on an excavation at the eighteenth-century Dowth Hall. Although the tomb had been badly damaged by the building of Dowth Hall (a servant's tunnel actually cuts through part of its mound), which it lies alongside, the archaeologists were able to ascertain that it comprised two burial chambers underneath a huge covering cairn measuring about 40 meters in diameter. The most significant find was a substantial curbstone that is richly decorated with a series of spiral motifs, and two other possible "satellite" tombs were found nearby. Dr. Steve Davis of UCL has said that the Dowth Hall passage tomb represents "the most significant megalithic find in Ireland in the last 50 years."[9]

THE LOUGHCREW, CARROWKEEL, AND
CARROWMORE PASSAGE TOMB COMPLEXES

Three other major passage tomb cemeteries or complexes can be found in Ireland: Loughcrew, Carrowkeel, and Carrowmore. The Loughcrew passage tombs are located on a ridge of high land comprising four hills that cover an area of around two miles in County Meath, with visitors to these monuments rewarded with stunning views of southern Irish farmland and distant hills. Approximately twenty-five passage tombs survive in the Loughcrew complex, most of which are

Figure 10.5.   Passage tomb at Loughcrew (image courtesy of Stephen Keavney, CC BY-SA 4.0).

located on the two highest hills, Carnbane West and Carnbane East. Most of the passage tombs were excavated in the nineteenth century, with human bones and artifacts such as bone pins, pendants, and pottery found inside their chambers. Several small balls made from chalk and stone and hundreds of water-rounded pebbles were also recovered from inside and around the tombs, and these enigmatic stones perhaps played a part in the religious rites performed here.

Many of the Loughcrew passage tombs are decorated with a striking and significant collection of megalithic art, and the monuments also vary in size, with Cairn D the largest and measuring an impressive 55 meters or so in diameter. It is also suspected that some of the tombs have their entrances oriented on astronomical events, with perhaps the strongest evidence for this idea found at Cairn T, on Carnbane East, which is probably aligned on the rising sun at the equinoxes.

Carrowkeel

The monuments of the Carrowkeel passage tomb complex (also known as the Carrowkeel-Keshcorran complex) are found above Lough Arrow in the Bricklieve Mountains in County Sligo, Northern Ireland, a range of high limestone ridges that overlook a glorious panorama of Northern Irish countryside. The central core of the complex is marked by a cluster of fourteen passage tombs, eight of which were excavated in April and June 1911 by the Irish archaeologist Robert Alexander Stewart Macalister and his colleagues, who believed the monuments were Bronze Age in date. Macalister later recounted, "On the very first day we discovered the hidden entrances to two of the intact cairns. . . . I had the privilege of being first to crawl down the entrance passage and did so with no little awe. I lit three candles and stood awhile, to let my eyes accustom themselves to the dim light. There was everything, just as the last Bronze Age man had left it, three to four thousand years before."[10]

Although it is now known that the excavated Carrowkeel passage tombs were built in the later Neolithic (ca. 3200–2900 BCE) rather than the Bronze Age, the 1911 excavations represent the only large-scale archaeological investigation of these important prehistoric monuments. Unfortunately, the tombs were excavated rather hastily, and many small artifacts and organic remains were likely missed as a result. Nevertheless, Macalister and his colleagues recovered cremated and unburnt human bones and various objects such as bone pins, stone balls, a boar tusk, bone beads and pendants, and twenty flat stones that were interpreted as "trays" on which human remains had been carried into the chambers of the passage tombs.

Seven passage tombs also lie about 2.5 miles to the west of the Carrowkeel complex on Keshcorran, the highest peak in the Bricklieve Mountains, and at the northern end of the nearby Lough Arrow is the Heapstown cairn. This huge monument measures some 60 meters in diameter, and although it remains unexcavated, it is probably a passage tomb, as is the Seelewey cairn, which lies about 2 miles to the east. This latter monument was dug into in the later nineteenth century by Lady Louisa Tennison and her party, with the 2-meter-wide trench that can still be seen running through the cairn to its center remaining as a testament to this unscientific excavation.

Carrowmore

The Carrowmore passage tomb cemetery, located above Lough Gill on the Cúil Ira peninsula on the northern coast of County Sligo in northwestern Ireland, "is dominated by the great cairn, traditionally known as Miosgán Meabha ('Queen Maeve's Heap'), on the summit of Knocknarea."[11] This enormous stone mound measures around 60 meters wide and 10 meters high, and although it has never been excavated, archaeologists strongly suspect that it contains passage tomb. Several smaller passage tombs surround Miosgán Meabha on the summit of Knocknarea, a dramatic flat-topped limestone peak that is the most prominent landmark in the whole of the Cúil Ira peninsula.

Miosgán Meabha overlooks and provides the focal point for the Carrowmore cemetery proper, which lies below Knocknarea to the east. Today, about thirty megalithic monuments in varying states of preservation, traditionally classified as simple passage tombs, can be found at Carrowmore. These monuments consist of single-chambered dolmen-like structures with short unroofed

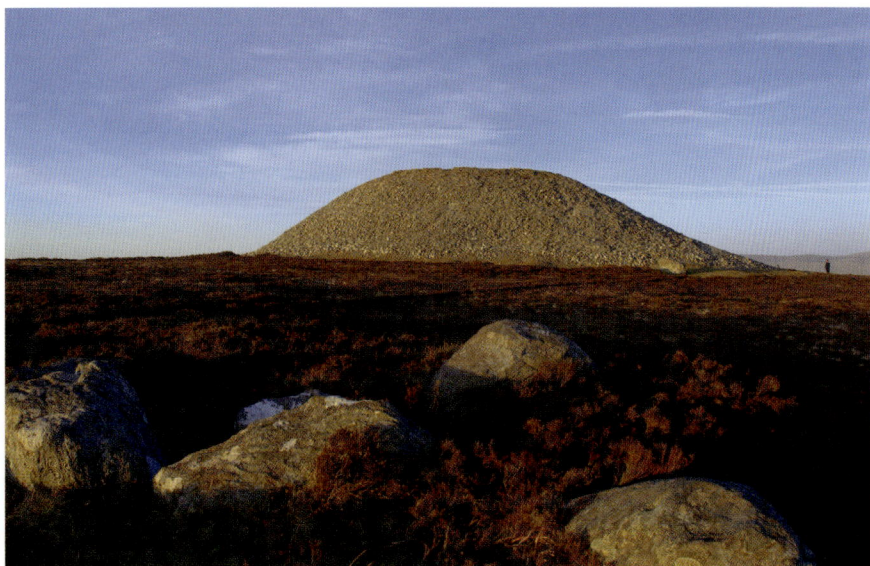

Figure 10.6.   Miosgán Meabha (Maeve's Heap) on the summit of Knocknarea (image courtesy of Bennybulb, CC BY-SA 4.0).

passages surrounded by substantial boulder circles, although it is probable that they were never covered by cairns. Near the center of the cemetery is the largest tomb in the Carrowmore complex, Listoghil, or Tomb 51, which consists of a large (reconstructed) cairn about 35 meters in diameter, featuring a small burial chamber of six uprights near its center, although no evidence of an adjoining passage survives. The Swedish archaeologist Göran Burenhult partly excavated Listoghil (about one-third of the monument) between 1996 and 1998, uncovering the cremated and unburnt bones of several children and adults from within and outside the burial chamber. Included among this skeletal material was an intriguing skull fragment displaying clear cut marks that could be related to the defleshing of the corpse or perhaps even scalping.

Based on radiocarbon dates provided by charcoal samples recovered from various tombs at the site, Burenhult proposed that the passage tombs at the Carrowmore cemetery were built between ca. 4300 and 3500 BCE, with the first monuments being built by late hunter-gatherer communities at the end of the Mesolithic (Middle Stone Age). However, most archaeologists have rejected this theory, pointing out that no artifacts diagnostic of final Mesolithic hunter-gatherer communities have been recovered from the Carrowmore complex and arguing that the early radiocarbon dates probably relate to Late Mesolithic activity preceding the building of its passage tombs. A recent dating program carried out on fragments of bone and antler pins found by Burenhult at some of the tombs in the Carrowmore complex suggests that it is perhaps more likely that the first examples began to be constructed around 3700 BCE.

IRISH PORTAL, WEDGE, AND ALTAR TOMBS

In addition to passage tombs, three other distinctive types of megalithic tomb are found in Ireland: portal tombs, court tombs, and wedge tombs. The portal tombs found in Ireland share the same architectural characteristics as the portal dolmens of Britain, and like their megalithic cousins across the Irish Sea, they consist of simple boxlike chambers (perhaps lacking a covering mound) with massive capstones, fronted by an H-shaped arrangement of two flanking uprights, often with a blocking slab between them. The court tombs essentially consist of long trapezoidal or rectangular cairns with unroofed oval or U-shaped open forecourts, presumably where rituals and ceremonies were held, which lead to two or more burial chambers set in the main body of the cairns. A typical wedge tomb comprises a relatively narrow, wedge-shaped or trapezoidal chamber formed of several uprights that decreases in height and width toward the rear, and rows of megalithic slabs often also flank chamber entrances, forming megalithic facades. Archaeological evidence found at wedge tombs indicates that they are the latest megalithic tomb type in Ireland and that the earliest examples were constructed around 2500 BCE, with the portal and court tombs built in the fourth millennium BCE. Some archaeologists see the similarities between wedge tombs and the *allées couvertes*, or gallery graves, of Brittany as evidence of prehistoric migration from northwestern France to Ireland, with immigrant Beaker communities searching for copper ore deposits responsible for their construction.

Creevykeel Court Tomb

One of the best-preserved and largest of the Irish court tombs is Creevykeel, County Sligo, which was excavated in 1935 by H. O'Neil Hencken and the Fourth Harvard Archaeological Expedition to Ireland. This impressive monument consists of a long trapezoidal cairn measuring about 55 meters long, with a narrow entrance passage at its wider eastern end leading to a large oval forecourt measuring 15 by 9 meters wide. At the rear of the Creevykeel forecourt, a megalithic entrance comprising two uprights and a lintel leads to a rectangular gallery (9 by 3 meters) divided into two chambers, with three smaller chambers set behind in the narrower western end, or "tail," of the cairn, two in the northern side and one in the southern side. The capstones of the chambers have long since disappeared, probably having been recycled by local farmers in more recent times.

The archaeological team from Harvard found evidence of fires in Creevykeel's forecourt and small deposits of cremated bone (probably human) in its main burial chambers. Among the prehistoric artifacts that came to light during the 1935 excavation were a finely made oval-shaped flint knife, a leaf-shaped arrowhead, flint scrapers, sherds from Neolithic and Early Bronze pottery vessels, quartz crystals, a perforated circular stone bead, two polished stone axes, and two small ball-like objects made from clay.

The excavation also uncovered a good deal of evidence of early Christian "squatters" at Creevykeel, who left behind such things as iron knives, blue glass beads, a bronze brooch, a whetstone, part of a bone comb, various animal bones (e.g., sheep, horse, rabbit, dog), and numerous periwinkle, limpet, oyster, and cockle shells. They also constructed an enigmatic small, circular stone chamber at the rear of Creevykeel's forecourt. Although the purpose of this structure is not clear,[12] it was discovered that it had been used as a burial place in more recent times, with the bones of at least two babies approximately seven months old found here, along with the skeleton of a cat, pieces of china crockery, and a few cattle, frog, and pig bones. This strange and rather sad evidence probably reveals that Creevykeel had been used as a *cíllin* by local people. As has been noted, "Cíllini, or children's burial grounds, were the designated resting places for stillborn and unbaptized children who were considered unsuitable for burial in consecrated ground by the Roman Catholic Church in Ireland."[13] A wide range of sites were used as *cíllini*, and, in addition to megalithic tombs, places such as ruined castles, deserted churches, and boundary ditches were used as burial sites for unbaptized children and other "marginal" members of Catholic society, such as criminals and people who had committed suicide.

The Labbacallee and Altar Wedge Tombs

One of the best-known and most impressive Irish wedge tombs is the well-preserved example known as Labbacallee or Leaba Caillighe (the bed of the witch or hag) in County Cork, with the tomb measuring around 13 meters long by 6 meters wide and featuring two burial chambers topped by three hefty capstones. Labbacallee was first described by John Aubrey in 1693 (apparently this was the earliest account of an Irish megalithic tomb) and excavated in 1934 by H. G. Leask and L. Price, marking the first scientific excavation of an Irish megalithic tomb.

In the smaller eastern chamber of the "bed of the witch," Leask and Price found cremated human bone, coarse pottery sherds, and, somewhat macabrely, a headless female skeleton, with the bone pin found alongside probably once pining together a long-decayed burial shroud. The western chamber contained numerous animal bones, more pottery sherds, the partial skeletons of a young male adult and child, and a skull that once sat on the shoulders of the woman whose skeleton lay in the smaller chamber. It is unclear how the skull became separated from the skeleton, although, given the name of the tomb in which she was laid to rest, it is tempting to see the woman as an actual prehistoric witch who was beheaded, perhaps because she was believed to have carried out a malevolent act of some sort. However, we might wonder why such a person would be privileged with burial in a megalithic tomb. In any case, it is not uncommon in Irish folklore for megalithic tombs to be associated with witches, although this does not preclude the woman having being viewed as somehow special when she was alive. Examination of the skeleton showed that one of her legs had been deformed, and perhaps the woman was viewed as "touched by the gods" because of this deformity. Of course, all this is mere speculation, and the role that the "headless woman" of Labbacallee played in life will remain forever unknown. Radiocarbon dates obtained on the human remains from the Labbacallee wedge tomb some fifty years after its excavation revealed that the burials in its two chambers date from the end of the Copper Age, about 2300 BCE.

Altar Wedge Tomb.   This small but fascinating tomb stands on the shores of Toormore Bay on the beautiful coast of West Cork in the Republic of Ireland. The entrance to its approximately 4-meter-long chamber faces directly toward Mizen Peak, a pyramid-shaped hill that lies 8 miles away across the bay, which was probably a deliberate design choice on the part of its builders rather than a coincidental orientation. It is interesting to note that the sun sets behind Mizen

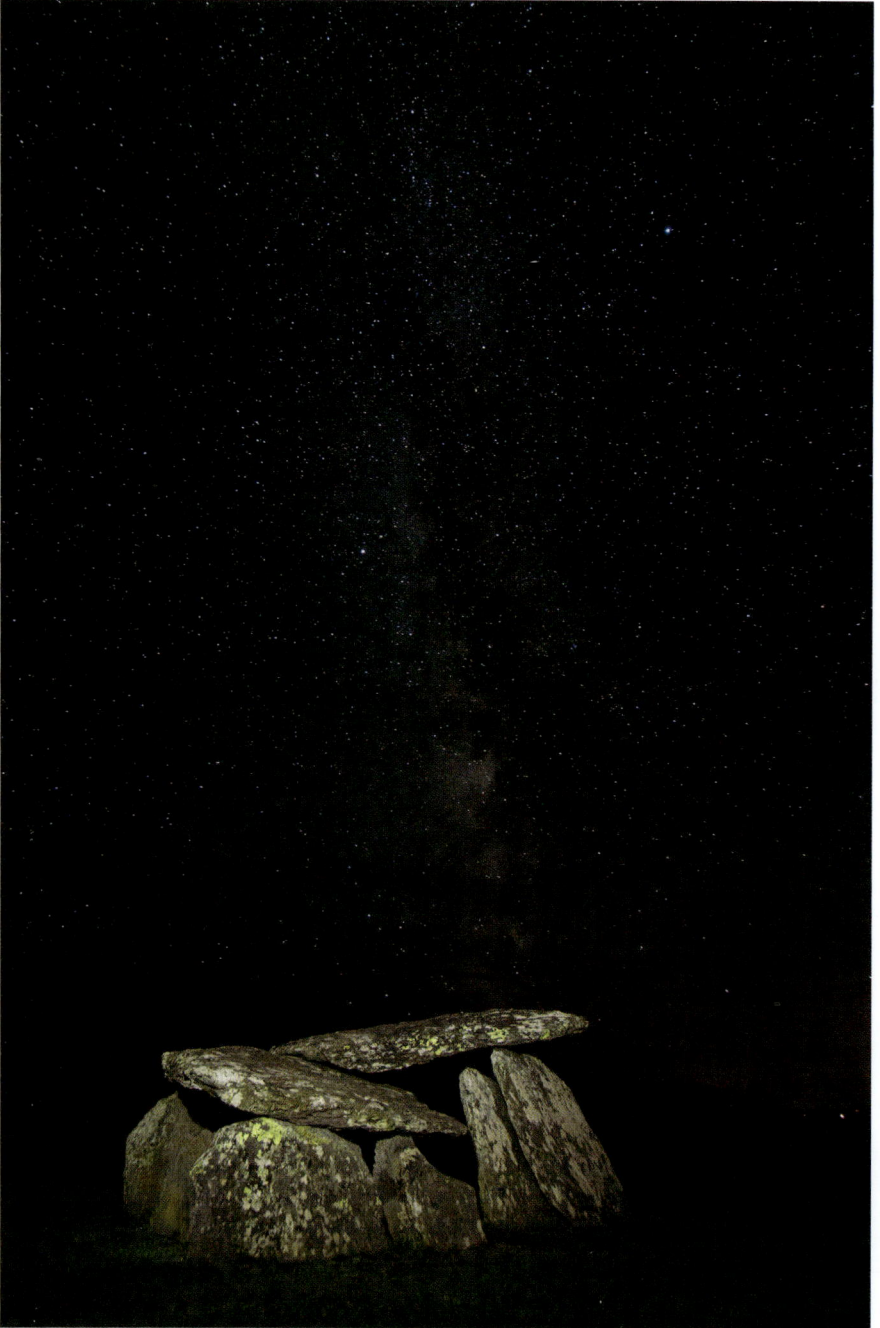

Figure 10.7.   The Altar wedge tomb and the Milky Way (image courtesy of Lukeoc88, CC BY-SA 4.0).

Peak in early February and November, with the latter marking Samhain, the ancient Celtic festival that celebrated the dead and marked the beginning of winter, or the "darker" half of the year (today's Halloween). Whether this festival dates back more than six thousand years to the time of the wedge tomb builders is debatable, but it seems likely that Mizen Peak had some sort of sacred significance to the people who built the Altar wedge tomb.

Finds were few and far between when the Irish archaeologist William O'Brien excavated the Altar wedge tomb in 1989, but he did uncover a small deposit of cremated bone dating to ca. 2000 BCE near its entrance, as well as two pits that had been dug inside the chamber. One dated to the Late Bronze Age, ca. 1000 BCE, and perhaps originally contained material (e.g., food offerings) that had long since perished; the other, dug in the Late Iron Age about 200 BCE, contained fish bones and periwinkle and limpet shells. As has been noted, this pit "may be evidence of the wedge tomb's incorporation into the larger mythological landscape centered around Mizen Peak."[14] In early Celtic mythology, Mizen Peak was the sacred mountain Carn Ui Néit and the place where the tyrant king Balor, leader of the demonic Fomorians, was beheaded by the sun god Lugh, a heroic warrior of the Fomorians' supernatural rivals, the Tuatha Dé Dannan ("the people/folk of the goddess Danu").

Poulnabrone

Many fine portal tombs can be found in both the Republic of Ireland and Northern Ireland,[15] but perhaps the best-known and most striking example is Poulnabrone in County Clare, Northern Ireland. This rather elegant monument, which has an "air of timeless durability,"[16] stands isolated on the famous "Burren," a starkly beautiful, high plateau characterized by striking karstic limestone formations, or "pavements," with a somewhat otherworldly quality.

Constructed and used from ca. 3800–3200 BCE, Poulnabrone consists of a soaring table-like capstone (about 2 meters from the ground) measuring about 3.5 meters long and supported on two sets of slender megalithic slabs that form the burial chamber, with a low "sill" stone set in a "gryke" (a natural crevice in the limestone pavement) in the tomb's north-facing entrance. This stone fractured at some point in antiquity, and although its original height is unknown, it may originally have reached the underside of the capstone, closing off the burial chamber. Three slabs were set on edge just outside the entrance, forming a smaller antechamber or portico, which had been filled with earth and stones shortly after the tomb was built. The purpose and date of this small structure are unclear; however, the skeleton of a newborn baby dating to the second millennium BCE was found in the antechamber, having been inserted into one of the grykes near the sill stone. The low, roughly oval cairn (about 55 centimeters high) surrounding the monument extends about 3 meters from the tomb and

Figure 10.8.   Sunset at Poulnabrone portal dolmen (image courtesy of Frank Chandler, CC BY-SA 4.0).

was constructed with large limestone slabs that were laid against the chamber uprights, with these slabs then covered with smaller flat stones. The cairn has probably not changed much in appearance since its construction and never completely covered the uprights and capstone.

Ann Lynch conducted excavations at Poulnabrone in 1986 and 1988, uncovering fascinating information about Ireland's early Neolithic tomb builders in the process. Somewhat remarkably, given that the tomb is such a prominent feature of the Burren, the burial deposit in the chamber was basically untouched. This contained the bones of about twenty adults and six children, with many of the bones deliberately jammed into the crevices, or grykes, in the chamber, showing that they had been brought to the tomb from bodies that had already decayed. Later analysis of the bones revealed the tip of a flint or chert arrowhead embedded in a probable male hipbone, with no signs of healing or infection evident on the bone, revealing that this individual had died around the same time that he or she was struck by the arrow. Two healed fractures were also found on an adult male skull and an upper-right rib bone.

Only a small number of individuals were interred at Poulnabrone over a period of some six centuries, indicating that they were somehow "special" members of their communities who were afforded a prestigious burial here in the Neolithic (as was the case with many of Europe's Neolithic tombs). Nevertheless, it seems that these people had not been spared the rigors of daily life, as their bones suggest that they were no strangers to hard physical labor. The people at Poulnabrone had been buried with an interesting collection of artifacts, among which were part of a "mushroom-headed" bone pin, a polished stone axe, two stone disc beads, two large pieces of quartz crystal, and flint and chert arrowheads. The most notable artifact, however, was a triangular perforated-bone pendant that is similar in appearance to a small slice of Swiss cheese.

As with many other megalithic tombs in Europe, the builders of the Poulnabrone dolmen are unlikely to have randomly chosen the location of their monument, and, interestingly, the entrance of the tomb faces a striking ravine nearby, where there is also a natural spring. We can never prove one way or the other whether the orientation of the tomb's entrance toward the ravine is coincidental or represents a deliberate choice on the part of the community that built the Poulnabrone dolmen. However, the possibility remains that this rather dramatic part of the Burren landscape was associated with supernatural forces and was perhaps viewed as a portal to a subterranean otherworld, where the spirits of the dead or Neolithic deities dwelt.

Scottish Megalithic Tombs

*T*here can be little doubt that of all the many megalithic tombs still surviving in Scotland, the Maeshowe passage tomb is the most celebrated, and justifiably so, as this is a superbly constructed and spectacular monument that belongs in the "top rank" of the European megaliths. As has been said of Maeshowe, which was built around five thousand years ago in the Late Neolithic, "The masonry ... is as near perfect as it's possible to get without the use of mortar. If one did not know that the passage had been constructed five thousand years ago, one could easily imagine it be the work of Victorian masons working with modern tools and lifting equipment. The burial chamber rivals anything in Neolithic Europe."[1]

Maeshowe is situated near the southeastern end of Loch Harray/Loch Stenness on Mainland, the main island of the Orkney archipelago. Like the other famous megalithic monuments in this area (e.g., the Stones of Stenness and Ring of Brodgar stone circles), Maeshowe is surrounded by a great natural amphitheater of hills that lends it a dramatic air. The huge grassy mound of Maeshowe measures nearly 8 meters high and 35 meters in diameter, making it a conspicuous feature of the landscape that can be seen from miles around. Uniquely for Orkney, it is surrounded by a circular henge, or rock-cut ditch and inner bank (in its original form, the bank was a stone wall measuring about 2 meters wide and high). Maeshowe's long and impressive passage is situated on the southwestern side of the mound, and research has shown that it was aligned on the setting sun at the time of the midwinter solstice.[2] The passage is also aligned on the 3-meter-high menhir known as the Barnhouse Stone, which stands some 700 meters to the southwest of Maeshowe, with the sun setting over its top behind the Hills of Hoy on the midwinter solstice.[3] It is unclear, however, whether the Barnhouse Stone was contemporary with Maeshowe or was raised some time after the passage grave was constructed.

Figure 11.1.   Maeshowe in winter (image courtesy of Sigurd Towrie).

Maeshowe's passage measures some 15 meters long and 1 meter wide; its outer (reconstructed) half is unroofed and has dry-stone walls, with its inner section comprising two enormous wall slabs (about 7 meters long) set on edge and topped by a single capstone of similar size. At the point where the passage becomes roofed, a square recess cut into the wall now contains a large square block that was found in the passage. It may be that this block was used to seal off the passage when rituals and ceremonies were taking place within the burial chamber, with only a privileged few allowed access to the "inner sanctum" of Maeshowe. The roofed part of the passage only measures around a meter high, and therefore anyone progressing along it must do so on hands and knees or awkwardly bent over. However, the effort of negotiating the passage is worth it, as the corbelled chamber is a breathtaking architectural space that clearly reveals the great skill of its Neolithic builders; three smaller chambers or cells, with almost perfectly square openings, open off its walls and are set nearly a meter above its floor. Finely shaped, huge stone slabs laid on top of each other were used for the walls of the burial chamber, with many courses of this impeccable dry-stone masonry being single huge slabs that almost span its whole width. The chamber measures about 4.6 meters square and some 3 meters high, being capped by a modern concrete slab due to its top half having been destroyed at some point in the past, with Viking tomb raiders perhaps the most likely suspects in this regard. The chamber's original height is unclear, but it may have reached as high as 6 meters. Built into each of its corners are four large dry-stone buttresses (designed to support the weight of the corbelled roof), each of which is flanked by a huge stone slab, with the tallest almost 3 meters in height. These narrow pillars clearly have no structural purpose, as they support nothing, and therefore they probably played a symbolic role. Whatever the purpose of these corner stones, it is suspected that they (and perhaps also the huge slabs forming the walls of the inner passage) came from an earlier, dismantled stone circle that once stood inside the bank and ditch surrounding the Maeshowe mound. Recent excavations undertaken at Maeshowe uncovered the socket of a large standing

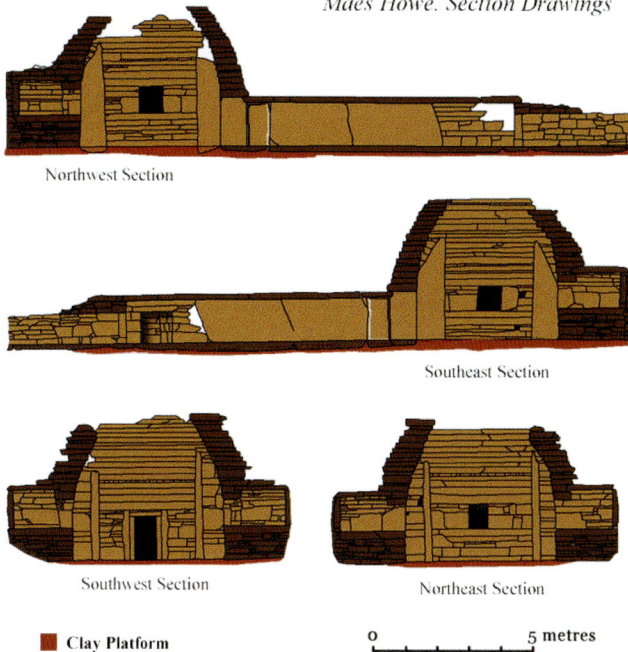

Figure 11.2.   Cross sections of Maeshowe's passage and chamber (image courtesy of Fantoman400, CC BY-SA 3.0).

stone at the rear of the mound, as well as stone paving and a drain, probably from an earlier Neolithic house, in front of the entrance.

The antiquarian James Farrer explored Maeshowe in July 1861, with his workmen digging down through the top of the mound after being thwarted by the debris that blocked the entrance passage, only to find that the chamber was basically empty of any Neolithic burials and artifacts. Farrer found only some horse bones and teeth and a human skull fragment, the dates of which are uncertain, as they are now lost. However, they perhaps provide "simple evidence that the traditional rites of ancestors and of totemism were practiced here in this late prodigy of megalithic tomb-building."[4]

Farrer did discover, however, the largest and most significant collection of Viking runes (thought to date to the mid-twelfth century) outside Scandinavia carved into the wall of Maeshowe's chamber. These included inscriptions such as "Tholfir carved these runes high up" and "Ingigerth is the most beautiful of all women."[5] We might doubt the sincerity of this latter inscription, given that it was carved alongside a crude depiction of a slavering dog. More finely executed were the depictions of a walrus, serpent, and lion or dragon carved into one of the chamber buttresses, and several Christian crosses can also be seen on the chamber walls. Some of this Viking graffiti may even have been carved during an episode mentioned in the Orkneyinga saga,[6] which recounts that Earl Harald and his men took shelter inside Maeshowe during a fierce winter snowstorm in 1153 CE: "On the thirteenth day of Christmas they travelled on foot over to Firth. During a snowstorm they took shelter in Maeshowe and two them [his men] went insane which slowed them down badly so that by the time they reached Firth it was night time" (Orkneyinga saga, chapter 93).[7]

Whether Earl Harald's men carved some of the runic inscriptions into the walls of Maeshowe's chamber, and whether this account even records a real event, can never be known for sure. However, it does seem likely that several of the runic inscriptions (which number around thirty) carved into the walls of Maeshowe's chamber were made by individuals sheltering from storms, which frequently sweep across Mainland Orkney. Interestingly, some of the inscriptions also refer to mysterious treasure within Maeshowe's chamber: for example, "To the north-west is a great treasure hidden. Happy is he who might find the great treasure" and "It is long ago that a great treasure lay hidden here."[8] Other inscriptions refer to the looting of this treasure, with one recording, "Hakon alone bore the treasure out of this mound,"[9] and another insisting, "It is certain and true as I say, that the treasure has been moved from here. The treasure was taken away three nights before they broke into his mound."[10] While these references to looted treasure may simply be related to a Viking myth, it is interesting to note that archaeological excavations at Maeshowe in the 1970s found evidence that the bank encircling the mound had been rebuilt in the ninth century CE. Therefore, "it now seems possible that the tomb was re-used, and its external appearance improved for the burial of a Viking chieftain, whose rich grave-goods were stolen three centuries later."[11] With this idea in mind, we might speculate that the original Neolithic burials in Maeshowe's chamber were cleared out to make way for the burial of the chieftain, helping to explain why Farrer found it empty in 1861.

In local folklore, Maeshowe was said to be the home of a feared supernatural creature known as the "Hugboy." Maeshowe's scary resident was undoubtedly a "Hogboon" or "Haugbi," with many of the Neolithic tombs of the Orkney Islands once believed to house one. The origin of this belief seems to lie with the Viking communities who settled on the islands, with "Hogboon" coming from the Old Norse *haug-bi* or *haug-buinn*, which roughly translates as "mound-dweller/farmer." The Norse settlers "believed that after death a person's spirit continued to live on, or near, the family farm. This particularly applied to the 'founding father' of the estate, over whose body a large 'haugr' or burial mound was constructed. This revered ancestor's spirit remained 'living' in his mound, usually becoming the family, or farm, guardian."[12]

QUOYNESS AND QUANTERNESS

Maeshowe gives its name to the small and unique group of Orkney passage graves (only ten in total) characterized by their long and low passages and square or rectangular burial chambers with adjacent smaller chambers or cells. After Maeshowe itself, the most notable of these Maeshowe-type passage graves are Quoyness and Quanterness, with the former located on the island of Sanday, the largest of the northern isles in the Orkney archipelago, and the latter on Mainland Orkney. Quoyness stands in a rather isolated but striking location near the coast on the peninsula of Elsness, which was probably a small island in the Neolithic, with the distinctively shaped cairn of the passage grave silhouetted against the sky when seen from a distance. James Farrer investigated Quoyness six years after his excavation of Maeshowe, discovering the bones of around ten adults and five children (dated to about five thousand years ago) in its chambers. Farrer also found artifacts such as a large bone pin (about 18 centimeters long), flint knives, and two curious ground-stone objects, one T-shaped and the other X-shaped. These stone artifacts of unknown purpose resemble similar objects found at the famous Skara Brae Neolithic village on Mainland Orkney. Unfortunately, as at Maeshowe, Farrer's excavation methods basically involved digging into the Quoyness cairn, and much valuable archaeological information was lost because of his unscientific approach to excavation.

The striking drum-shaped cairn (about 20 by 17 meters in width) and wide stone platform (about 41 by 32 meters) that confront visitors to Quoyness today represent a reconstruction of the monument directed by Vere Gordon Childe after his reinvestigation of the passage grave in the early 1950s, with both probably hidden below a covering mound in the Neolithic. As at Maeshowe, the low and narrow passage (less than a meter wide and high) at Quoyness is on the southeastern side of the cairn and measures around 8 meters long, leading to a rectangular burial chamber (about 4 by 2 meters) made from large water-worn slabs taken from the nearby shore. Although the Quoyness burial chamber is not as finely made as Maeshowe's, it is still an impressive feat of Neolithic funerary architecture, its dry-stone walls reaching upward to form a towering chimney-like space. Four smaller side chambers and two end ones also open off the inner walls of the chamber.

Second in size only to Maeshowe, Quanterness passage grave is located on the lower slopes of Wideford Hill, just above the Bay of Firth, and today stands behind a farmhouse, its grass-grown mound (about 30 meters in diameter by 3 meters high) hidden by a surrounding belt of trees. As has been noted, "The Quanterness chambered tomb is a key site for the Orcadian Neolithic. This stems from its excavation in 1972–4 to modern standards, its comparatively undisturbed state, and the sheer size of its human bone assemblage."[13] The approximately 9-meter-long, low-entrance passage lies on the east side of the mound (although it has been somewhat damaged by the later Iron Age roundhouse built in front of Quanterness) and leads to a main rectangular burial chamber that has six smaller outer chambers opening off its walls. When Quanterness was briefly excavated in the early 1800s by George Barry, the corbelled roof of the chamber was still intact and stood at a height of about 4 meters. Colin Renfrew's excavations at Quanterness in the early 1970s uncovered the remains of at least 157 men, women, and children in its chambers, representing one of the largest human bone assemblages from Neolithic Britain. Given that Renfrew left some parts of the chambers at Quanterness unexcavated, it is thought that, in total, the remains of around four hundred people were in fact interred in the tomb. Numerous pottery sherds from about thirty-seven distinctive Grooved Ware vessels[14] were also recovered, along with various artifacts such as a rubbing stone used for grinding grain, a bone point made from the wing bone of a cormorant, flint scrapers and blades, and a solitary but unique bead made from lead ore.

STALLED CAIRNS

The majority of the eighty or so megalithic tombs found on the Orkney Islands are of the Orkney-Cromarty type, which are also known as "stalled cairns" because their burial chambers are divided into small compartments, or stalls, by projecting upright stone slabs. Circular, oval, or rectangular cairns cover the chambers and are normally accessed by short passages leading from one end or side of the cairn. These unique Scottish monuments are found not only on most of the islands of the Orkney archipelago but also on the Scottish mainland, being concentrated in clusters in the northern and central Highlands.

One of the best-preserved Scottish stalled cairns is Midhowe on the island of Rousay, which was investigated in 1932 by whiskey magnate Walter

Figure 11.3.   Interior of Midhowe stalled cairn (image courtesy of Michael Maggs, CC BY-SA 4.0).

Figure 11.4.   Camster Long cairn and entrances (image courtesy of Orikrin1988, CC BY-SA 3.0).

Grant. Thought to have been built around 3500 BCE, Midhowe comprises a substantial rectangular cairn measuring some 32 meters long by 13 meters wide, with the walls of its chamber surviving to a height of about 2.5 meters. Twelve stone slabs run down each side of the chamber, creating twenty-four stalls, some of which feature low stone shelves or benches. When Grant entered the chamber, he discovered that human skeletons had been laid on some of the benches, which may perhaps have given him something of a shock when he entered this ancient burial place. The strange collection of fish and animal bones that Grant uncovered in the chamber perhaps hinted that the people buried here had animal totems:

> One could perhaps explain away as the remains of funeral feasts the ox and sheep bones found at Mid Howe, even perhaps the bream, wrasse and heap of limpet shells for bait, but it would have been a desperate community that chewed the oily and tough skua, cormorant and guillemot, and only the starving could have fancied the scrawny flesh of buzzard, eagle, gannet and crow whose bones also lay in the tomb. . . . The most likely explanation for such a variety of bones is that people named each other after animals as American

Indians did—Swift Running Horse, White Eagle, He Who Swims Like a Fish—each person with his own totem that was taken with him to the grave.[15]

Of course, it is possible that some of the above birds flew into Midhowe by accident and subsequently became trapped and died, but harder to explain is the pigeon's egg that was found carefully placed underneath the armpit of one of the skeletons in the burial chamber.

THE GREY CAIRNS OF CAMSTER

The most spectacular examples of the Orkney-Cromarty stalled cairns are not found on the Orkney Islands, however, but rather in Caithness in the far north of mainland Scotland. Representing two of the best-preserved megalithic tombs in Britain, these two monuments, Camster Long and Camster Round, stand about 200 meters apart in an open area of moorland. Camster Long is the more spectacular and architecturally complex of the two monuments but basically consists of an enormous trapezoidal cairn measuring nearly 70 meters. It has two separate burial chambers (now fitted with modern fiberglass domes) in its northeastern end, with their entrance passages on the southeastern side of the cairn (which still reaches about 4.5 meters high above the chambers). Excavations at the site in the 1970s revealed that the two burial chambers had originally been two smaller, separate monuments and that the monumental stone mound covering them was added later. Short "horns" project from each end of the cairn to form forecourt areas at the northeastern and southwestern ends of the cairn (measuring about 20 and 10 meters wide, respectively), and an unusual, low stone platform juts out from its front, perhaps being used by Neolithic "religious specialists" for rituals and ceremonies. The antiquarian Joseph Anderson explored Camster Long in 1886 but only found a meager collection of human and animal remains in the southern burial chamber: "there were found on the floor a few fragments of human skulls and other bones of the skeleton, unburnt and mingled with broken bones of the horse, ox, deer, and swine."[16]

Camster Round is very well preserved and virtually intact, its covering mound of stones nearly 4 meters high and about 18 meters in diameter, with its fine burial chamber, which has a corbelled roof, reached by a passage on the southeastern side of the cairn. Joseph Anderson investigated the burial chamber in 1865, uncovering many human skull fragments and bones on its floor, along with many fragments from pottery vessels and a finely made flint knife. In the rubble that had been deliberately used to block the passage, the remains of two skeletons were also found, perhaps belonging to bodies that had been placed there in an upright, sitting position. Strangely, the leg bones were missing from the two individuals.

CAIRNHOLY I AND II

Another two well-known Scottish megalithic tombs are Cairnholy I and II, two visually striking monuments located in a beautiful hillside setting overlooking Wigtown Bay in Galloway, in southwestern Scotland. Cairnholy I and II belong to a group of megalithic tombs known as Clyde/Clyde-Carlingford cairns, which resemble the court tombs found in parts of Ireland and are thought to be among the earliest in Scotland, having been built around six thousand years ago.

Cairnholy I is the larger and better preserved of the two monuments, comprising an imposing, curved megalithic facade of eight tall standing stones, which stand at the rear of the forecourt in front of the tomb's entrance, behind which are two inner chambers set in a now denuded cairn measuring about 50 meters long by 15 meters wide. Cairnholy II was much robbed for building stone in the more recent past, but its two entrance or portal stones remain standing, behind which are the remains of two chambers, located in a long cairn much reduced in height (about 60 centimeters) and measuring about 20 by 12 meters.

Figure 11.5.   The megalithic facade at Cairnholy I (image courtesy of Scotstarvit, CC BY-SA 3.0).

Both monuments were excavated in 1949 by Stuart Piggott and Terence Powell, who uncovered a rich collection of grave goods from Cairnholy I, among which were a fragment from a jadeite axehead (imported from continental Europe), a leaf-shaped flint arrowhead, sherds of Early Neolithic pottery, a "plano-convex" flint knife, a jet bead, scraps of cremated bone, and a small lozenge-shaped slab decorated with a cupmark surrounded by six concentric circles. The excavation also uncovered evidence underneath the fill of earth and stone that blocked the entrance to the tomb, showing that six fires had been lit by Neolithic people in the forecourt area of Cairnholy I. Numerous sherds of Neolithic pottery, a piece of pitchstone imported from the Isle of Arran off the western coast of Scotland, and a mass of shells belonging to mussels, limpets, winkles, and whelks were also found in association with the remains of these fires. This evidence likely represents the remains of rituals or ceremonies carried out in the forecourt area prior to the blocking of the tomb's entrance, and although not spectacular, it provides us with a rather remarkable snapshot of the religious practices of Scotland's Neolithic communities.

The archaeological evidence found at Cairnholy II was less impressive, but numerous pottery sherds from both Neolithic and later Beaker vessels, a flint scraper, a leaf-shaped flint arrowhead, and a plano-convex flint knife were nevertheless found during the excavation of its chambers. A patch of burnt earth in the outer chamber marked the place where somebody had lit a fire, probably in the Early Bronze Age.

Figure 11.6.   Cairnholy II (image courtesy of Scotstarvit, CC BY-SA 3.0).

THE TOMB OF THE EAGLES

One of the most famous Scottish megalithic tombs is the Isbister cairn, which is more popularly known as the "Tomb of the Eagles." Located dramatically above precipitous cliffs on the east coast of South Ronaldsay Island, Orkney, Isbister is a "hybrid" monument that comprises a long chamber containing both the stalls that are characteristic of the Orkney-Cromarty tombs and three smaller side cells or chambers, which are more commonly found in the Maeshowe-type passage graves. The Tomb of the Eagles was discovered by chance in 1958 by local farmer Ronnie Simison, who had noticed a wall-like section of stones poking out of a large mound in one of his fields. Excited about what might lie beneath the mound, this Orcadian farmer subsequently carried out a three-day partial excavation of the cairn, initially finding a fine cache of objects comprising an oval-shaped stone mace head, three stone axes, a small stone knife, and a button made from jet. Returning to the site after his initial discovery, he continued digging down into the mound, eventually reaching the interior, where "by the flickering light of a cigarette lighter, Ronnie Simison saw the 30 human skulls that filled the chamber—his first encounter with the long-dead occupants of the Tomb of the Eagles."[17]

Shortly after Simison's discovery of this approximately five-thousand-year-old tomb, it was closed up with the idea that professional archaeologists would return in the future to carry out a more thorough excavation of the site. However, after almost twenty years this excavation had still not happened, and Simison decided to return to the Tomb of the Eagles in 1976 to resume his excavation of the monument himself, having been inspired and learning from the archaeologists who had worked on the Bronze Age "burnt mound"[18] also discovered on his land. He subsequently recovered some 16,000 human bones (representing at least 324 individuals) and many human skulls from inside the tomb. Large numbers of fish and animal bones (mainly belonging to calves and lambs) were also found both inside and outside the tomb, with some of the young cows and sheep perhaps being sacrificed as offerings to the ancestral dead who were believed to dwell within its walls. Curiously, bones and talons belonging to the magnificent bird that gave its name to this Late Neolithic tomb—the white-tailed sea eagle—were also found scattered in large numbers throughout the tomb, with these avian remains representing at least eight and perhaps as many as twenty birds. The popular theory is that the sea eagle had been the totem animal of the Neolithic tribe who had built the Isbister chambered cairn, but a radiocarbon carbon dating program carried out on the sea eagle bones in 2006 showed that they had been deposited in the tomb between ca. 2500 and 2000 BCE, in the Copper Age or Early Bronze Age. The significance of the sea eagle to the people who did this remains a mystery, but it reveals that the Tomb of the Eagles was still a focus of ritual activity many hundreds of years after its construction. A recent reexamination of the human bones by researchers from the University of Bradford and Orkney Museum has also provided graphic evidence of the darker side of Neolithic life. At least 20 percent of the eighty-five skulls from the tomb display violent injuries; some have been caved in or even split in two, with wooden clubs and stone axes very probably behind this shocking evidence. Clearly, the exchanges between the Orkney Islands' first farming communities were far from amicable and sometimes extremely violent.

ACHNACREEBEAG: A "FRENCH" MEGALITHIC TOMB IN SCOTLAND?

Although not particularly well known—at least outside academia—the megalithic tomb of Achnacreebeag, in the county of Argyll, has provided fascinating evidence to suggest that a Neolithic community from Brittany undertook a long and dangerous journey from their homeland and settled on the western coast of Scotland. Achnacreebeag was excavated from 1968 to 1970 by Graham Ritchie of the Royal Commission on the Ancient and Historical Monuments of Scotland, who uncovered two periods of construction, the first of which was represented by a small, closed megalithic chamber underneath a circular cairn measuring around 18 meters in diameter. In the second phase, a small passage grave was added to the southeastern side of the cairn, which was extended to a length of about 21 meters to form an oval-shaped stone mound.

No finds were made in the chamber of the earlier megalithic tomb, which had been cleared out at some point in the distant past. At first sight, the meager finds from the passage tomb hardly seem to be anything to write home about: the remains of one nearly complete Early Neolithic pot, sherds from two others, and a flint knife in the chamber; a few flint tools and sherds of Beaker pottery mixed in with the later deposit of earth and stones used to block the passage. However, the unspectacular Neolithic pottery assumed a greater significance when it was later realized that it bore a striking resemblance to that found in early megalithic tombs built ca. 4000 BCE in Brittany: "At Achnacreebeag, Graham Ritchie excavated a two-phase monument featuring a closed chamber that had a simple passage tomb added to it. . . . [I]n the passage tomb he found fragments of three distinctive pots, which the current author has identified (with verification from Breton pottery specialists) as being of Breton Middle Neolithic types."[19]

Furthermore, two-phase monuments comprising earlier small megalithic chambers and later simple passage tombs were also built in the Morbihan area of Brittany in the Early Neolithic. Not all archaeologists agree with the idea that

Achnacreebeag was built by an immigrant group from Early Neolithic Brittany, but when considered together, the artifactual and architectural evidence points more strongly in this direction, with this group perhaps forced to leave their home because they were "running from trouble."

THE CAIRNS AT BALNUARAN OF CLAVA

In the countryside of Inverness-shire in northeast Scotland, there is a group of distinctive monuments known as the Clava Cairns, named for the three well-known and well-preserved examples located alongside each other on the southern side of the valley of the River Nairn at Balnuaran of Clava. These monuments are only located about a mile from the famous Culloden battlefield, where the House of Stuart's attempts to reclaim the British throne were effectively ended. Although thousands of visitors flock to Culloden every year, not many realize that only a short walk away "lies a very different link with the past, every bit as evocative as Culloden, and in many ways more tangible despite dating back to around 2000 BC."[20]

There are two distinct types of Clava Cairn, passage graves and ring cairns, which roughly date from 2500–2000 BCE. The former consist of circular, corbelled chambers and short passages set in mounds of stone or cairns, which have a ring or curb of low boulders running around their outer edges. The latter somewhat resemble a giant donut and consist of low, circular stone banks or cairns that are set within an inner and outer boulder curb, with the open central area of the cairn not accessed by a passage. Both types of monument are also surrounded by stone circles, which stand a short distance from their outer curbs. In both the passage graves and the ring cairns, the stones in the outer curbs are graded in height, with the tallest at the southwest and the shortest at the northeast. The stone circles surrounding both types of monument are also arranged in this way, suggesting that the southwest had some special significance to their builders.

Both types of Clava Cairn are represented at Balnuaran of Clava, where two passage graves and a ring cairn are placed close together in a lovely woodland setting. The builders of the cairns arranged their monuments in a diagonal line running northeast to southwest, with the passage graves at either end and the ring cairn in the middle. An interesting feature of the ring cairn is the four enigmatic stone paths or causeways (now overgrown with grass) that radiate outward like rays from the edge of the low stone platform on which the cairn was built to join up with the bases of four of the stones of the surrounding circle. One of these paths is on the western side, with the other three on the eastern one; their meaning remains elusive.

The most notable aspect of the cairns at Balnuaran of Clava is that the entrances of the two passage graves "are aligned exactly on the midwinter solstice: a phenomenon that can still be observed today."[21] Excavations undertaken at the site in 1994 and 1995 also discovered an intriguing aspect of the covering cairns of the two passage graves: on their southwestern sides, the majority of the stones used were of a "red" type (e.g., sandstone, pegmatite), while on their northeastern sides, "white" types of stone, such as gneiss and a quartz-rich granite, predominated. It has been noted, "This would make the front of the cairns glow red in the reflected sunlight of the setting sun at and around Midwinter. The northeastern side would also flash white around Midsummer sunrise, but the focus of the site on the Winter Solstice made this less instantly apparent."[22]

In fact, all the entrances of the Clava Cairn passage graves face the southwestern arc of the horizon where the midwinter sun sets, although "the orientations of these sites cover too wide an arc for all the sites to have been directed towards the sun."[23] Archaeologists have thus suggested that many of the passage graves of the Clava Cairn group were oriented on the rising summer moon. It is therefore possible that the scatterings of white quartz found at other Clava Cairn examples (e.g., Corrimony, where thousands of pieces were found in association with the outer curb and passage) may be related to religious beliefs about the moon.

Evidence of such beliefs was perhaps also found during a nineteenth-century excavation conducted at the earlier passage grave of Achnacree in Argyll, which is located near the Achnacreebeag passage grave. Like its near neighbor, Achnacree was perhaps built by Neolithic settlers from France, although the Neolithic pottery found here suggests that they may have hailed

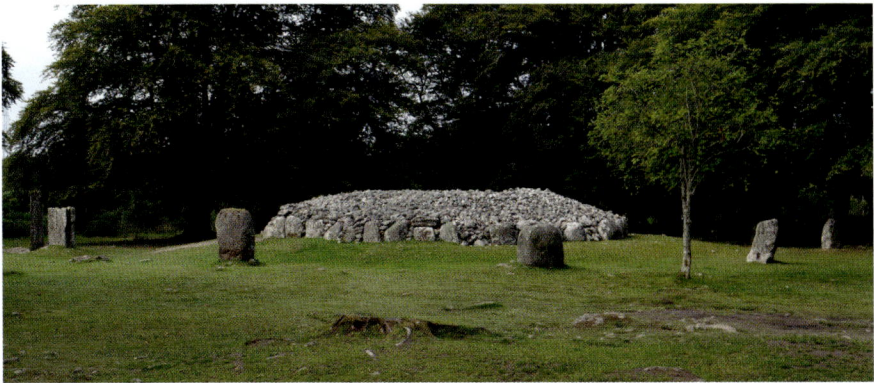

Figure 11.7. The northeastern passage grave at Balnuaran of Clava (image courtesy of Sir Gawain, CC BY-SA 4.0).

from Normandy rather than Brittany. Two smaller chambers lay off the main one (which was devoid of human remains), and in one of them there were two stone shelves or ledges on which the nineteenth-century diggers found eight quartz pebbles still in place some fifty-five hundred years after the building of the tomb (ca. 3600 BCE). An intact pottery vessel was found among the rubble and earth on the floor of this side chamber, and this contained four quartz pebbles, while the broken pots found here also appear to have originally contained one each. As has been remarked, a possible but unproveable idea is that these "white stones were soul-stones symbolizing the moons to which the spirits of the dead had gone."[24] We will never know whether this theory is true, but it does seem likely that the cold, white face of the moon hanging in the prehistoric night sky would have meant something very different to the megalith builders of Europe than it does to us today.

· *12* ·

Megalithic Germany and Holland

$\mathcal{T}$here may be no world-famous megalithic monuments in Germany and Holland to match the likes of Stonehenge, the Carnac alignments, or Newgrange passage tomb. However, both countries can nevertheless lay claim to possessing some superb megaliths, which are probably not as well known as they ought to be. One of the best known is the Gollenstein ("golden stone") menhir, which stands majestically on the high ridge known as the Blieskastler mountain, near the pretty town of Blieskastel in the Saarland region of southwestern Germany. Measuring nearly 7 meters in height, this huge standing stone is the tallest in Germany and probably also in central Europe. It is thought that the stone was raised in the Early Bronze Age ca. 2000 BCE, although there is a possibility that it is many hundreds of years older than this.

The Gollenstein menhir also has something of an interesting history. At the start of World War II in 1939, soldiers of the German Wehrmacht decided that it needed to be destroyed, as they feared that French artillery spotters would be able to use it as a reference point for the shelling of a series of underground bunkers located nearby. This great standing stone, which had remained standing for at least four thousand years, was subsequently shattered into four parts after it was toppled to the ground by the German soldiers, although it was reconstructed (with the aid of concrete) and re-erected in 1951, with further restoration work taking place on the menhir in 2002.

This Gollenstein menhir was also "Christianized" at some point in the more recent past, probably in the nineteenth century (or possibly much earlier in the medieval period), as revealed by the small, window-like niche that was carved into one side of the standing stone, at the back of which there is inscribed a cross and the initials "IHS." Objects such as small statues of Christian saints and wooden crosses would have been placed in the niche, along with the candles that left black soot marks on its walls. Just below the niche there are the faint

181

Figure 12.1.   The Gollenstein menhir (image courtesy of Oliver Herold, CC BY-SA 30).

traces of a carved human figure, which may possibly be a representation of the Iron Age Celtic weather god Taranis, although it is perhaps more likely that this carving was made in the nineteenth century.

Another impressive German standing stone from the Saarland region is the Spellenstein menhir, which today stands oddly out of place in the front garden of a modern house in a suburb of the town of Saint Ingbert. This tall and narrow sandstone megalith measures just over 5 meters in height and shows clear signs of having been shaped by stone tools. The original location of the Spellenstein menhir is unknown, but it is thought to have been erected in its present location at the end of the nineteenth century, having survived the construction of the later houses that now surround it. When the Spellenstein menhir was raised in the landscape is unclear, but an Early Bronze Age date is probably likely.

The German menhir that perhaps possesses the most powerful prehistoric presence is the Riesentein ("giant's stone") megalith, found near the village of Wolfershausen in the central state of Hesse. This huge, rectangular slab reaches nearly 5 meters high, has a maximum width of 5.5 meters, is about a meter thick, and weighs well over 40 tons. The Riesenstein menhir was probably erected in the later Neolithic around 3000 BCE, with human bones dating to this time found by German archaeologists at the base of this tremendous standing stone.

Figure 12.2.   The Spellenstein menhir (image courtesy of Kh80, CC GFDC).

GRAVES OF THE GIANTS

In the provinces of Mecklenberg and Lower Saxony in northern Germany, there are two dense concentrations of striking megalithic tombs, which are known alternatively as *hünenbetten* ("giants' beds"), *hünengrabben* ("giants' graves"), and *Großsteingräber* ("large stone tombs"). Very similar monuments can be found in the Netherlands, where they are also known as "giants' beds," or *hunebedden*, and, like their German counterparts, were built by communities of the Late Neolithic Funnel Beaker culture.[1] These German and Dutch megalithic tombs typically comprise low rectangular chambers formed from a row of juxtaposed trilithons (i.e., two uprights and a capstone), with massive glacial boulders used for the capstones, and a mixture of dry-stone walling and earth once filling the gaps between the chamber uprights. It is also not uncommon to find oval or circular arrangements of standing stones surrounding the burial chambers. These are thought to represent megalithic curbs or revetments that bordered now denuded earthen mounds in which the chambers were set, which may only have reached to the top of the chamber uprights, with the capstones deliberately left visible by the builders of the German and Dutch giants' tombs. However, it is quite possible that some examples had no covering mound at all. Short entrance passages (on the southern or eastern side) can also be seen at many of these monuments, and thus, technically speaking, the German and Dutch giants' tombs belong to the passage grave family.

German Hünengrabben

There are many fine *hünengrabben* still surviving in Germany, but one of the best-preserved and most spectacular examples is the Hüven *hünengrab* (Hünengrab 842), which stands in idyllic woodland near Hüven. This superb monument has survived virtually intact for some five thousand years, comprising an oval ring of fifty curbstones surrounding a long chamber, which is roofed by nine capstones (originally there were elven). Though less well preserved, the Thuine *hünengrab* (Hünengrab 847) is still impressive, its approximately 27-meter-long chamber roofed by seventeen capstones (three are missing) and surrounded by an unusual and almost complete double ring of curbstones. French officers of Napoleon's army are thought to have plundered the tomb in the early nineteenth century, though antiquarian excavations in 1820 and 1878 uncovered some stone tools, pottery vessels, amber beads, charcoal, and human bones. Like Hüven, Thuine is located just across the Dutch border in an area of countryside between the Ems and Weser rivers in northwest Germany, where there is a notable concentration of *hünengrabben*. It seems likely that the builders of these and other *hünengrabben* in the area were in touch with their "Dutch" neighbors.

Figure 12.3. The Hüven *hünengrab* (image courtesy of Franck Vincentz, CC BY-SA 3.0).

The most renowned *hünengrabben* in Germany are probably the Visbek Bride and Bridegroom (Visbeker Braut and Bräutigam),[2] which lie close together in oak woodland in the beautiful Wildeshauser Geest nature reserve of Lower Saxony in northeastern Germany.[3] Both of these somewhat atypical monuments consist of huge, rectangular enclosures comprising hundreds of standing stones that border the now denuded earthen mounds that once probably contained the burial chambers. The Bridegroom measures nearly 105 meters long by 9 meters wide, and the Bride is about 80 meters long by 7 meters wide. The latter monument is trapezoidal in shape, being broader at its southwestern end, which is marked by four standing stones. The stones in its two longer sides decrease in size as they run away to the narrower northeastern end of the monument, where there are two large menhirs. The southwest/northeast orientation of the Visbeker Braut suggests that it could have been aligned toward the midwinter sunset and sunrise by its builders. A sunken burial chamber (about 10 meters long) is located roughly in the middle of the monument toward its broader southeastern end, although its capstones are missing, presumably having been recycled for building material in later times. The Visbeker Bräutigam is aligned east/west (perhaps indicating an interest in sunrise or sunset at the equinoxes) and also features a single burial chamber sunk into the earth, with its five hefty capstones sitting on top of a sunken rectangular burial chamber that measures around 9 by 3 meters.

Figure 12.4.   The Visbek "Bridegroom" (image courtesy of Einsamer Schütze, CC GNU).

Four other *hünenbetten* can be found in the woods near the Visbek Bride and Bridegroom, among which is the well-known Heidenopfertisch ("offering table"), a monument that inspired many nineteenth-century painters, with one of its two remaining capstones measuring about 5 meters long and 3 meters wide. This capstone was originally around 7 meters long, but a piece was dynamited off it in the nineteenth century. There is also the Visbek Brautwagen ("bridal coach"), with its four huge, rounded capstones sitting on top of a sunken rectangular burial chamber measuring around 9 by 3 meters.

German Steinkisten

Also found in Germany are the *Steinkisten* ("stone cists"). These megalithic tombs are found in the states of Westphalia and Hesse (northwestern and central Germany, respectively) and were constructed by people of the Late Neolithic Wartberg culture.[4] They resemble the *allées couvertes* of France and Belgium, comprising long rectangular chambers (often sunk into the floor) roofed by megalithic slabs or, in some cases, wooden beams. The Steinkiste von Züschen, near Fritzlar in northern Hesse, is probably the best-known example; it was accidentally discovered in 1894, after a local farmer decided to remove the large sandstone blocks that he had repeatedly come across while plowing one of his fields. Subsequent archaeological excavation by German archaeologist Johannes Boehlau uncovered a sunken rectangular chamber

Figure 12.5. The Züschen *Steinkiste* (image courtesy of Einsamer Schütze, CC BY-SA 3.0).

built of rectangular sandstone slabs that measured 20 meters long and about 3.5 meters wide, with a "porthole" slab separating the main chamber from a small antechamber at the front. The almost perfectly circular hole cut in this slab measures 50 centimeters in diameter and in German is known as a *Seelenloch* ("soul hole"). These circular openings are found at other examples of German *Steinkisten* and may have been used to make offerings to the spirits of the dead in the chambers, perhaps also allowing them to visit the world of the living.

The Lohra Steinkiste was also discovered accidentally (in 1931) by a farmer plowing one of his fields. However, the ensuing archaeological investigation of the monument by Professor Otto Uenze from the nearby University of Marburg (Hesse) unearthed the cremated remains of around twenty people and a significant collection of grave goods. Among these artifacts were twenty virtually intact pots that had been placed in a line on the chamber floor, a fine greenstone axe made from serpentine, and a slate blade or knife.

Dutch Hunebedden

Only fifty-four *hunebedden* survive in Holland today, nearly all of which are found in the picturesque province of Drenthe in northeastern Holland, with about another thirty or so known to have been destroyed here in more recent times. The fact that the Scandinavian glacier known as the Hondsrug ("dog's back") left behind many "erratics," or boulders, in this region helps to explain why there is a concentration of *hunebedden* in this part of Holland, as the Dutch landscape otherwise lacks the huge stones needed for megalith building. The *hunebedden* have been nicely described as "looking like great reptiles in the gentle Dutch countryside, often oddly disarming, like a child's drawing of a dinosaur."[5]

Two of the best-known *hunebedden* are found close together in the parkland behind the fine medieval church in the village of Rolde. These monuments have long been a source of fascination, with Antonius Schonhovious, the canon of Saint Donation's Cathedral in the city of Bruges, the first to write about them in a manuscript of 1547, speculating that they were built by demons. In the nineteenth century, members of the Dutch royal family even visited the two monuments, known as D17 and D18 by Dutch archaeologists, with all the Dutch *hunebedden* labeled this way.

Another pair of *hunebedden* (D19 and D20) can be seen in the pretty village of Drouwen, a popular summer resort for Dutch holidaymakers. These two monuments lie virtually alongside each other, being only 14 meters apart, and were excavated in 1912 with human bones and an exceptional array of objects recovered from *hunebed* D19. Included among the grave goods were more than four hundred Funnel Beaker pottery vessels, twelve axes made from flint, nine

Figure 12.6.   *Hunebed* **D18 at Rolde, with** *hunebed* **D17 visible in the background (image courtesy of Michael Perryman CC BY-SA 3.0).**

amber beads, and six copper strips that may have been used as jewelry (the oldest metal objects yet known from Holland). Other flint tools were found in the chamber of D19, and under modern microscopic analysis, it was found that some of these had been used for harvesting cereal crops, with another tool displaying traces of hide-working.

Included among the grave goods were some four hundred pottery vessels, thirteen polished stone axes, nine amber beads, and six copper bands that had been used as jewelry.

Several *hunebedden* also can be found in the countryside surrounding the town of Emmen, with the most notable, the Schimmer Es *hunebed* (D43), somewhat resembling the Visbek monuments in Germany. Measuring some 40 meters long by 5–6 meters wide, it was partially restored in the twentieth century and consists of a low, rectangular mound of earth with rounded ends that is bordered by large standing stones interspersed with dry-stone walling. Two separate rectangular chambers are located within the mound, one near its wider northeastern end and the other near the middle, with the former accessed by a short passage, although the middle chamber seems to have lacked one. This magnificent megalithic monument has a powerful boatlike appearance, looking almost like a Viking longship adorned along its sides with the shields of the warriors who sit within.

The most famous *hunebed*, however, is the example found near the village of Borger. This monument was explored by Titia Brongersma[6] in June 1685, marking the first serious investigation of a *hunebed* and dispelling the myth that they were built by giants, given that Brongserma found normal-sized human bones (cremated) and pottery vessels in its burial chamber. The Borger *hunebed*

Figure 12.7. **The Schimmer Es** *hunebed* (image courtesy of Holidayineurope, CC BY-SA 3.0).

Figure 12.8.   Aerial view of the Borger *hunebed* (image courtesy of Wdejager, CC BY-SA 4.0).

(D27) is the largest of the Dutch giants' tombs and is visited by thousands of tourists each year.[7] It measures nearly 23 meters long and some 4 meters wide, with the nine massive capstones that cover its burial chamber looking rather like giant tortoise shells. On its southern side is a short entrance passage comprising two pairs of opposed uprights, with the inner two covered by a bulky capstone. Given that Titia Brongserma only dug out a small part of the burial chamber and that the monument has not yet been the subject of a modern and thorough archaeological investigation, it seems likely that the Borger *hunebed* has not yet yielded all its Neolithic secrets.

• 13 •

Megalithic Scandinavia

$\mathcal{E}$ven though it is a small country in the far north of Europe, Denmark has one of the densest distributions of megalithic tombs on the European continent, with around twenty-five hundred examples surviving today and some four thousand others thought to have been destroyed in more recent times. The first Danish megalithic tombs were constructed about 3800 BCE by Funnel Beaker communities and are classified into three types by Scandinavian archaeologists: round dolmens (*rundysse*), long dolmens (*langdysse*), and passage graves (*jættestue*). Around 10 percent of Danish passage graves contain unusual twin passages and chambers within their covering mounds. Claus Clausen has carried out a detailed analysis of the orientation of the Danish passage grave entrances, with his research suggesting that "they could have been inspired by the behavior of the rising full moon during the summer."[1] Traditionally, the megalithic capstones of all the dolmens are thought to have been hidden by covering mounds of earth and stone, although at some examples there is no visible evidence of these. As in other parts of Europe, the builders of some Danish megalithic tombs may have wanted to display the magnificent monumental stones that they used as capstones for the burial chambers of the dolmens rather than hide them under covering mounds of earth and stone.

The best-known Danish round dolmen is probably Poskær Stenhus ("stone house"), which stands in lovely rolling countryside on the Djursland peninsula in eastern Jutland. This is the largest example in Denmark, and the capstone of its burial chamber weighs some 12–15 tons, with the chamber enclosed in an equally impressive stone circle or curb about 13 meters in diameter, consisting of twenty-three huge granite boulders. This renowned Danish megalithic tomb had a "close shave" in 1859, when a local landowner, Ole Hansen, decided that it would provide a convenient source of building material and set about blowing it up with dynamite. He managed to destroy at least one of its standing stones

Figure 13.1.   The Poskær Stenhus round dolmen (© Villy Fink Isaksen, CC BY-SA 3.0).

but, fortunately, was stopped in his tracks by a local priest before he destroyed the monument. Poskær Stenhus subsequently came under the official protection of the Danish authorities in 1860.

One of the most notable Danish passage graves is Grønhøj (also in eastern Jutland), which was excavated and restored in 1940, showing that World War II did not stop Danish archaeologists from enjoying their work. The excavation uncovered a remarkable deposit of more than seven thousand pottery sherds piled in a layer (0.3 meters deep) just outside the entrance to Grønhøj, among which were twenty intact pots. This collection of pottery opened a small but fascinating window onto the long-lost religious rites of Denmark's passage grave builders, as painstaking archaeological detective work revealed that the sherds had come from whole vessels deliberately smashed at its entrance by Neolithic people. Some of these pots perhaps contained libations to the spirits or deities who lingered within the dark interior of Grønhøj passage grave.

The Hulbjerg passage grave on the island of Langeland is also worth mentioning. This monument comprises a circular mound (about 20 meters in diameter) edged with a ring of low, slab-like menhirs, which covers a short passage (5 meters long) leading to a rectangular burial chamber measuring some 6 by 2 meters. Hulbjerg was excavated in 1960 by Håkon Berg, who uncovered the remains of around fifty-five adults and children laid to rest with objects such as flint axes, daggers, arrowheads, amber beads, and decorated pottery. Intriguingly, a skull found in the passage bore possible evidence that a prehistoric "dentist"

Figure 13.2.   The Hulbjerg passage grave (image courtesy of Praeceptor, CC BY-SA 3.0).

had tried to remove a painful abscess on a molar tooth with a flint drill. If so, this cannot have been a particularly pleasant experience for his "patient."

Some of the best preserved and most impressive Danish passage graves are found on the small but beautiful island of Møn in southeastern Denmark, with the finest examples being the Kong Asgers Høj ("King Asger's mound") and Klekkende Høj (*høj* means "mound") passage graves. Beneath the huge mound of Kong Asgers Høj there is an 8-meter-long passage leading to a substantial burial chamber measuring some 10 meters long by 2 meters wide. Klekkende Høj is even more striking, as, unusually, it has two parallel entrance passages measuring around 7 meters long, which are entered from the eastern side of its massive mound. The passages lead to a single central chamber, measuring about 9 meters long and 1.5 meters high and divided by two large megalithic slabs, with each passage thus entering a separate chamber measuring around 4.5 meters long. Klekkende Høj was investigated in the later eighteenth century by the governor of Møn, the grandly titled Antione de Bosc de la Calmette, whose laborers dug down through the mound and removed some of the capstones of its chambers to discover many human bones and artifacts such as flint axes, pottery vessels, and amber beads.

Also found on the island is Grønjaegers Høj ("the green huntsman's mound"), with this outstanding megalithic monument one of the largest *langdysse* found in Denmark. Its rectangular, low earthen mound or platform measures about 100 meters long by 10 meters wide and is surrounded by around 140 large standing stones about 1.5 meters in height. Grønjaegers Høj contains three burial chambers, with the largest located toward the western end of the monument and roofed by an enormous boulder. At the western end is a facade of

Figure 13.3.   Klekkende Høj passage grave (image courtesy of Sandpiper, CC public domain).

three standing stones measuring about twice the height of those surrounding the mound, and it has been pointed out that these "tall . . . red stones contrast dramatically with the white capstone covering the [main] burial chamber."[2] Other Danish megalithic tombs feature different colored stones in their architecture, with grey and reddish granite boulders used in the facade at Kong Svends Høj passage grave, for example. This is a phenomenon common to many other European megalithic tombs, and it has been noted that "the significance of colours in the Neolithic is difficult to ascertain [but] clearly there was a mythical and symbolic relationship between the colour and architecture of the tombs."[3] Even larger than Grønjaegers Høj is the Lindeskov long dolmen on Funen, the third-largest island of Denmark. The mound of this massive Neolithic monument is bordered by 126 standing stones and measures nearly 170 meters long, although it contains only one burial chamber.

Another well-known Danish long mound is Troldkirken (the troll church), which is located on a hill near the village of Sønderholm in a very scenic area of northern Jutland. Measuring some 50 meters long by 7 meters wide, forty-seven standing stones surround its now denuded mound, which measures about 1 meter high. The largest of these stones (about 2.5 meters high) stands at the northeastern end of the mound, which is oriented northeast/southwest, the direction of the midwinter sunrise and sunset, respectively. Roughly in the center of the mound is a single burial chamber or dolmen with a huge capstone. Troldkirken came under the protection of Danish law in 1809, the first prehistoric site in Denmark to do so.

THE TUSTRUP MEGALITHIC CEMETERY

The most famous Danish megalithic monuments are probably those found at the site of Tustrup, also on the Djursland peninsula. This megalithic necropolis dates to ca. 3200 BCE and contains three Neolithic tombs: one round dolmen and two passage graves. One of these is much larger than the other (one of the largest passage graves in Denmark in fact) and consists of a 6-meter-long passage leading to a main chamber measuring 10 meters long and about 2 meters high, with a smaller side chamber (unusual in Danish passage graves) opening off its southwest corner; these are covered by a mound that measures around 27 meters in diameter.

The three megalithic monuments at Tustrup cluster in an arc or semicircle around a "mortuary" or "cult house" that was excavated between 1954 and 1957 by Poul Kjærum.[4] This structure was found to comprise an outer U-shaped enclosure of small standing stones (about 1 meter high) open to the northeast and surrounding a square room or chamber measuring about 5 by 5 meters. The rear wall of this room was faced with four megalithic slabs of about 1.5 meters, with its side walls originally boarded with oak tree trunks split in two, forming wooden walls measuring about 2 meters high that had burnt down (radiocarbon dates obtained from the burnt timbers suggested that this event occurred around 2500 BCE). Evidence was also found to suggest that these walls had supported a roof comprising a lower layer of birch bark sheets, over which grass turfs were laid, although whether it had been flat or angled could not be determined. The broken half of a standing stone (probably around 1.5 meters high originally) was also discovered in the middle of the entrance to the mortuary house on its northeastern side, and it may be that this was set up to mark the midwinter sunrise.

Figure 13.4.   The larger of the Tustrup passage graves (image courtesy of Ajepbah, CC SA-BY 3.0).

A fine collection of pottery was also unearthed during the excavation, and this had been buried in two groups on either side of an oval pit filled with sand that had been dug in the middle of the timber-lined chamber. This ceramic assemblage included fourteen bowls, eight of which were accompanied by a ceramic spoon or ladle, and six funnel beakers, with the bowls and beakers ornately decorated. No burials were found during the excavation of the Tustrup mortuary house, but it may be that the dead were laid here during the funeral rites that preceded their subsequent interment in one of the nearby megalithic tombs, with the flesh left to decompose from their bodies. Danish archaeologists now think that this small but intriguing structure had at least two phases of construction and was deliberately destroyed, with its wooden and stone walls perhaps burned down and toppled in an act of prehistoric iconoclasm by a later Neolithic group following different religious traditions.

SWEDISH MEGALITHS

The northern limits, or "border," of the European megalithic phenomenon are marked by the dolmens and passage and gallery graves of Sweden. About 450 passage graves and dolmens survive in the Swedish landscape today, although many examples have since been destroyed, with some fifteen hundred gallery graves remaining. One of the core areas of the Swedish megalithic tombs is Falbygden in the province of Västergötland, southern Sweden, with a notable concentration of passage graves found in a short stretch of countryside around the village of Karleby. The megalithic passage and chamber of one of these eleven passage graves (Ragnvald's Grave) has a chamber measuring 17 meters long and a passage measuring 13 meters, making it the largest example found in Sweden, if not the whole of Scandinavia. Analysis of the orientation of the passage graves found in the Falbygden region has suggested that their builders were concerned with positioning their monuments so that the rays of the midwinter sunrise shone into them.

As in neighboring Denmark, the builders of Sweden's megalithic tombs also appear to have deliberately incorporated different colored stones in their architecture, as revealed by an analysis of some thirty examples from the western coastal region of Bohuslän. For instance, at the Naseröd South round dolmen, stones of contrasting red and white colors stand opposite each other in the circle or curb that surrounds its burial chamber, while at the Hjälteby passage grave, white stones were used for the megalithic uprights of its short passage, with darker ones used for its burial chamber. Differently textured rocks and rocks with striking natural inclusions also seem to have been deliberately chosen for the architectural components of some of these Swedish megalithic tombs.

Figure 13.5.   The remains of "Ragnvald's Grave" (image courtesy of Gunnar Creutz, CC BY-SA 3.0).

ALES STENAR: A RECYCLED NEOLITHIC LONG DOLMEN OR A BRONZE AGE MEGALITHIC MONUMENT?

Sweden is also home to the renowned and controversial Ales Stenar (Ale's Stones), with this superb monument stunningly located on a clifftop overlooking the Baltic Sea, high up above the fishing village of Kåseberga in the province of Scania. Ales Stenar comprises fifty-nine huge standing stones of granite and quartzite that form a ship-like arrangement measuring 67 meters in length and 19 meters in width at its widest point. Its standing stones average about 2–3 tons in weight and mostly stand about 2–2.5 meters high, although the single stones at either end of the monument are taller (about 3 and 4.5 meters high). The quartzite stones used for Ales Stenar are thought to have been quarried from a source on the coast about 20 miles to the east. In the nineteenth century, the Swedish antiquarian Magnus Bruzelius recorded smaller "ship settings" of standing stones on either side of Ales Stenar, but these have since been destroyed.

Excavations were undertaken at Ales Stenar between 1989 and 2004 by Professor Märta Strömberg and her team, and the organic material they recovered (e.g., birch charcoal and fragments of human bone) provided a series of radiocarbon dates. Most of these dates fall between ca. 600 and 1050 CE and strongly suggest—if not prove—that Ales Stenar was built during the early Viking era around fourteen hundred years ago. An Early Neolithic hearth (ca. 3450 BCE) was discovered about 1.5 meters away from the monument, with a fragment from a later Neolithic stone "battle axe" also found within its interior. At the least, this evidence revealed much earlier prehistoric activity on the clifftop that was to later provide the dramatic setting for the Ales Stenar megalithic "ship."

Intriguingly, many cupmarks were found on several of the standing stones at Ales Stenar, and as these can often be seen at other Swedish passage graves and dolmens, this led Strömberg to plausibly suggest that the monument may well have been built from recycled stones gathered from a much older megalithic one located nearby. Therefore, in 2006 a geophysical survey was undertaken by Sweden's National Heritage Board, and an underground "anomaly" was identified just to the northeast of Ales Stenar, showing up as a large circular structure (50 meters in diameter) that had a smaller but still substantial rectangular structure (22 by 10 meters) at its center. This latter structure bore a resemblance to the well-known Skogsdala long dolmen, located about 9 miles northwest of Ales Stenar.

When archaeologists returned to Ales Stenar six years later to undertake a small-scale excavation of the anomaly, no human remains or objects were found, but investigation of the circular structure uncovered likely evidence of a disman-

Figure 13.6.   Ales Stenar (image courtesy of Jorchr, CC BY-SA 3.0).

tled long dolmen (surrounded by a ditch of uncertain date). This consisted of depressions in the ground and foundation pits, seemingly marking the presence of a former burial chamber, with further depressions around the chamber probably marking the location of large standing stones that had once edged the mound or platform in which it was set. It is hard to disagree with the lead archaeologist on the dig, Bengst Söderberg's, reading of this evidence: "All of the stones had been taken away. And I would say, most probably they are standing 40 meters away from the dolmen where the ship setting is situated."[5]

Not all scholars, however, are prepared to accept that Ales Stenar is a Viking age monument. For example, Nils-Axel Mörner and Bob G. Lind have argued that Ales Stenar was erected in the Late Bronze Age ca. 700 BCE and that its basic geometry or layout mirrors that of Stonehenge, with its builders incorporating several astronomical alignments into their monument.[6] Most Swedish archaeologists would probably disagree with this theory, as the radiocarbon evidence points more strongly toward a Viking age date for the construction of Ales Stenar, regardless of whether its stones came from an earlier Neolithic dolmen.[7] However, it does seem likely that these dissenters would nevertheless agree that Ales Stenar is a monument "so remarkable both in beauty and scientific value that it deserves to become incorporated on the World Heritage list."[8] This is a statement that could be applied to many other of the megalithic monuments of Europe, with these remarkable structures, arguably the most compelling remnants of Europe's prehistoric past, no doubt continuing to be a great source of awe and wonder long into the future.

Epilogue

Megalithic Websites

*T*he great fascination that people have with Europe's megalithic monuments means that there is an abundance of websites devoted to the subject, some of which (to put it politely) feature "questionable" theories. However, there are many fine websites that are well worth a look, and the more notable examples are included here, along with some other fine sites dealing with megalithic matters. "Megalithomaniacs" can also find some great groups on Facebook that are all about megalithic monuments—for example, Standing with Stones, Prehistoric Explorers Club, Silent Earth: Messages from Our Ancestors, Irish Stones–Megalithic Research Group, and Megalítico Portugal. Countless videos on European megalithic monuments can likewise be found on YouTube.

THE MEGALITHIC PORTAL

Founded in 2001 and run by Andy Burnham, this site is probably the best in terms of the sheer scale and scope of its content, with searchable maps allowing visitors to search for a mind-boggling collection of megalithic monuments not only in Europe but also around the world. There is much more to this rather remarkable megalithic resource, but, in short, it is a veritable treasure trove of megaliths and is thoroughly recommended. Burnham is also the author of the recently published *The Old Stones: A Field Guide to the Megalithic Sites of Britain and Ireland* (2018), a book that should be on the shelf of any megalith enthusiast.

STONE PAGES

This website represents the work of two megalithomaniacs from Italy, Paola and Diego, a husband-and-wife team who have been visiting and photographing megalithic monuments in Europe for more than thirty years. The couple started Stone Pages in 1996, which, as they tell us, was "the very first guide about European megalithic sites" to appear on the web. There are six sections on megalithic monuments in England, France, Ireland, Italy, Scotland, and Wales, as well as a "Tours" section that deals with the couple's various "megalithic journeys" in Europe. The most useful feature of Stone Pages is the "Megalinks" section, which, among other things, provides links to a range of websites dealing with megalithic and other prehistoric matters in Europe and around the world.

THE MODERN ANTIQUARIAN

This fine website based on Julian Cope's popular and entertaining books, *The Modern Antiquarian* and *The Megalithic European*, provides another invaluable and wide-ranging resource on the megaliths of Europe. As the blurb on the homepage says, "Since launching in March 2000ce, the site has grown to be a massive resource for news, information, images, folklore & weblinks on the ancient sites across the UK, Ireland and Europe, thanks to the remarkable efforts of all those who contribute."

VOICES FROM THE DAWN: THE FOLKLORE OF IRELAND'S PREHISTORIC MONUMENTS

This wonderful website is highly recommended and provides a huge amount of fascinating information on both the archaeology and the folklore of numerous Irish megalithic monuments; it also covers Iron Age and early Christian sites and monuments. Voices from the Dawn is obviously a labor of love for its author, Howard Goldbaum, who writes on the site, "To put my hands on a stone touched by the hands of a Neolithic Irish architect thousands of years ago brought a sense of communion with human history. To simulate this sense of connection for visitors to Voices from the Dawn, the site contains media, such as audio, video, and virtual reality panoramas, designed to create a digital verisimilitude."

MEGALITHOMANIA

This is another very useful site for those wishing to explore the megalithic monuments of Ireland; it also covers early Christian and medieval monuments. Visitors to the site are provided with many useful snippets of information on the megalithic monuments of Ireland, which are arranged by type and county.

WAKEMAN'S HANDBOOK OF IRISH ANTIQUITIES

Readers with a keen interest in Irish megaliths might also like to look at the online version of John Cooke's *Wakeman's Handbook of Irish Antiquities*, which has been made available online by Boston College Libraries, Massachusetts. Although published in 1903, and thus now rather dated, this book is filled with interesting information on Irish megaliths (and other ancient sites and monuments in Ireland), several of which have since been destroyed; the text is also accompanied by many fine illustrations.

ORKNEYJAR: THE HERITAGE OF THE ORKNEY ISLANDS

This splendid website is the work of Orcadian journalist Sigurd Towrie and has been up and running since 1997. Many short articles on the megalithic and later ancient monuments of the Orkney Islands can found on this visually attractive site, along with numerous other articles dealing with the rich heritage of this fascinating archipelago, which is probably more Viking than Scottish.

THE EUROPEAN ROUTE OF MEGALITHIC CULTURE

This site was produced by the Council of Europe as part of its Cultural Routes program, which was launched in 1987. The homepage states, "The goal of the Association Megalithic Routes is to link together a selection of the oldest monuments of Europe by cultural routes which not only lead to the megalithic monuments but also highlight the manifold features of the surrounding landscape." This nicely produced site has many excellent photographs and is a useful resource for anyone wishing to visit the more famous megalithic monuments of

Europe, although, at the time of this writing, only those found in Germany, the Netherlands, Denmark, Sweden, and Great Britain were included.

AENIGMATIS

Created by astronomer Martin J. Powell, this is another good site that features brief but informative sections on megalithic monuments in Wales, England, and Scotland. It includes the detailed results of a field survey carried out by the author at megalithic monuments in South Wales, which investigated possible astronomical alignments at these megaliths. Recommended books on megalithic monuments are also included on the site.

SILENT EARTH

Among other things, this interesting website covers both megalithic and later sites and monuments in various parts of England, Wales, Scotland, and Ireland, with many nice photographs, providing added visual appeal.

THE JOURNAL OF ANTIQUITIES

Created by Ray Spencer, this excellent website features numerous megalithic monuments in Britain and Ireland and much more besides. As Spencer tells us, "The journal will include the following: Prehistoric, Celtic, Roman, Anglo-Saxon, Viking and Medieval sites but, also I will put some more recent curiosities on the blog, as well. Included on here will be burial chambers, standing stones, stone circles, inscribed stones, ancient crosses, holy wells/springs, ancient churches, hillforts, earthworks, rock-art, glacial erratics and other stuff! Oh, and myths, legends and folklore, too."

MEGALITHIA

This nice little site mainly focuses on megalithic monuments in Britain and Ireland but also has a section on Carnac. A useful feature is the inclusion of location maps for each separate monument, and there is also a bibliography detailing recommended books on megaliths.

MEGALITHIC PAGES

Although there is not that much actual written information about megalithic monuments on this site, it has a great photographic gallery, which allows visitors to look at hundreds of pictures of megaliths not only in Europe but also elsewhere in the world.

MEGALITHICS

This website is similar to the above Megalithic Pages and features "an archive of over 5000 photos of stone circles and other megalithic monuments in the British Isles, Ireland and Europe." Many of the monuments included on the site are also accompanied by "full spherical VR panoramas and infrared photography, plus ten figure map references measured on site using GPS [global positioning satellites]."

STONE-CIRCLES.ORG.UK

The blurb on the homepage of this excellent website tells us that it is "an ongoing investigation into the prehistory of Great Britain encompassing the stone circles, standing stones, henges, hillforts, burial chambers and barrows that scatter the countryside of these islands." Created by Chris Collyer in the late 1990s, this site is jam-packed with hundreds of great photographs of numerous megalithic monuments, with useful information about each monument also included.

Notes

CHAPTER 1: AN INTRODUCTION TO MEGALITHIC EUROPE

1. Evan Hadingham, *Early Man and the Cosmos* (London: William Heinemann, 1983), 115.

2. Hadingham, *Early Man and the Cosmos*, 115.

3. Viki Cummings, "Formalizing the Sacred? The Late Mesolithic and Early Neolithic Monumental Landscapes of Britain and Ireland," in *Landscapes in Transition*, edited by Bill Finlayson and Graeme Warren (Oxford: Oxbow, 2010), 120.

4. Quoted in Chris Scarre, "Stones with Character: Animism, Agency and Megalithic Monuments," in *Materialitas: Working Stone, Carving Identity*, ed. Blaze O'Connor, Gabriel Cooney, and John Chapman (Oxford: Oxbow, 2009), 15.

5. George W. Oesterdiekhoff, "Magic and Animism in Old Religions: The Relevance of Sun Cults in the World-view of Traditional Societies," *Croatian Journal of Ethnology* 45 (2008), 44.

6. Chris Catling, "Invasion, Colonisation or Imitation?" *British Archaeology* 290 (2014), 18.

7. In fact, Neolithic Europe was not the prehistoric idyll envisaged by some scholars, and there is a considerable (and growing) body of archaeological evidence indicating that violence and warfare were not uncommon among its early farming communities, as famously revealed at the Talheim "death-pit" in southern Germany. Here, in 1983, a local man digging in his garden uncovered human bones in what subsequently turned out to be a Neolithic mass grave from the time of the later Linear Pottery culture (ca. 4900 BCE). A confused mass of bone was excavated by archaeologists, representing the bodies of at least thirty-four adults and children who had been thrown haphazardly into a shallow pit. The subsequent scientific examination of the bones revealed that twenty people had been brutally clubbed to death by stone axes, and it seems likely that the other people in the pit had also died violently, even though they displayed no lethal wounds on their skulls. In short, the evidence uncovered from the Talheim death-pit points strongly toward the massacre of a small Linear Pottery community. There is even evidence of Neolithic battles involving hundreds of combatants. For example, at Crickley Hill in Gloucestershire, Southwest England, a large force of archers assaulted the Neolithic settlement that was located on the hilltop, subsequently overrunning it and burning down its houses and defensive palisade.

8. It was not just copper that came into use during the Copper Age but also gold. In contrast to copper, which was extracted from rudimentary mines, most gold was panned from river and stream beds (placer deposits) and cold-hammered into shape to produce various items of jewelry, such as gold pendants, beads, pins, and large discs. The most spectacular collection of Copper Age gold was found with the "Varna Chieftain," who was laid to rest with nearly one thousand gold artifacts in a grave uncovered at the famous prehistoric cemetery of Varna, on Bulgaria's Black Sea coast.

9. Alasdair Whittle, *Europe in the Neolithic: The Creation of New Worlds* (Cambridge: Cambridge University Press, 1996), 253.

10. Morgan Stirling Saletta, "The Arles-Fontvieille Megalithic Monuments: Astronomy and Cosmology in the European Neolithic" (unpublished PhD diss., University of Melbourne, 2014), 4.

11. Hayden, *Shamans, Sorcerers, and Saints: A Prehistory of Religion* (Washington, DC: Smithsonian Books, 2003), 252.

12. Janet Alison Hopkins, "So My Name Shall Live: Stone-Dragging and Grave-Building in Kodi, West Sumba," *Journal of the Humanities and Social Sciences of Southeast Asia* 142 (1986), 32, doi: https//doi.org/10.1163/22134379-900003367.

13. Quoted in Colin Renfrew, *Before Civilization: The Radiocarbon Revolution and Prehistoric Europe* (London: Pimilico, 1999), 153–54.

14. Manuel Calado, "The Role of Ritual Monuments in the Neolithic Transition of the Central Alentejo," in *Monuments and Landscape in Atlantic Europe: Perception and Society during the Neolithic and Early Bronze Age*, ed. Chris Scarre (London: Routledge, 2002), 26.

15. Barry Cunliffe, *Facing the Ocean: The Atlantic and Its Peoples, 8000 BC to AD 1500* (Oxford: Oxford University Press, 2001), 198.

16. From Old Welsh and translating as "stone with a bent/crooked back." In Wales, "cromlech" is often used when referring to megalithic tombs.

17. Calado, "The Role of Ritual Monuments," 25.

18. Emmanuele Lodolo and Zvi Ben-Avraham, "A Submerged Monolith in the Sicilian Channel: Evidence for Mesolithic Human Activity," *Journal of Archaeological Science: Reports* 3 (2015), 403.

19. Both Téveic and Hoedic were excavated in the 1930s by the husband-and-wife team of Marthe and Saint-Just Péquart, and they found an abundance of grave goods that were indicative of Late Mesolithic "complex" hunter-gatherer societies in Europe (e.g., bone pins, flint blades, and many hundreds of small perforated shells from necklaces, bracelets, and headdresses). In some graves, small, tentlike structures made from red deer antlers had been placed over the dead, perhaps marking out people of higher status, and there was also evidence of violence at the former site, such as the fragments of a flint projectile found embedded in the spine of one individual.

20. John Michell, *Megalithomania: Artists and Antiquarians at the Old Stone Monuments* (Glastonbury, UK: Squeeze Press, 2007), 10.

21. Jean-Pierre Mohen, *Standing Stones: Stonehenge, Carnac and the World of Megaliths* (London: Thames & Hudson, 1999), 37.

22. Some of these American antiquarians produced important early archaeological works recording monuments that no longer exist. For example, the first book on North American archaeology, *Ancient Monuments of the Mississippi Valley* by Ephraim George Squier and Edward Hamilton Davis (1848), contains fine engravings illustrating native burial mounds that have long since been destroyed.

23. Mohen, *Standing Stones*, 35.

24. For example, *Antiquities of Cornwall* (1872) by William Copeland Borlase or the *Antigüedades prehistóricas de Andalucía* (Prehistoric antiquities of Andalucia, 1868) by M. de Góngora y Martínez.

25. Stuart Piggott, "A Saint in a Stone Circle," *Antiquity* (Notes & News) 57 (1973), 293.

26. L. V. Grinsell, "Folk-lore of Prehistoric Monuments," *Folklore* 48 (1937), 248.

27. De Garis quoted in Peter Goodall, "Revealing Guernsey's Ancient History in Fact and Fiction," *Shima* 10 (2016), 120, doi:10.21463/shima.10.2.12.

28. Stirling Saletta, *The Arles-Fontveille Megalithic Monuments*, 60.

29. Lewis Thorpe, trans., *Gerald of Wales: The Journey through Wales/the Description of Wales* (London: Penguin, 1978), 187.

30. Mohen, *Standing Stones*, 17.

CHAPTER 2: THE HEARTLAND OF MEGALITHIC EUROPE

1. Brittany was known as "Armorica" by the ancient Romans, who are famously lampooned in the much-loved *Asterix* comic books, which hint at the remarkable megalithic heritage of this region, with Asterix's great friend, Obelix, employed as a menhir delivery man.

2. Aubrey Burl, *Prehistoric Avebury* (New Haven, CT: Yale University Press, 2002), 2.

3. Thom's famous "megalithic yard" equaled a remarkably precise 0.829 meters. However, its existence finds little support among today's archaeologists, who argue that it is more likely that the megalith builders set out their monuments by simpler methods such as pacing out the distances between the stones used in their construction. Thom was nevertheless a hugely influential figure in the development of "astroarchaeology," which is concerned with the study of astronomical alignments at megalithic monuments.

4. Chris Scarre, *Landscapes of Neolithic Brittany* (Oxford: Oxford University Press, 2011), 120, doi:10.1093/acprof:osobl/9780199281626.001.0001.

5. Le Rouzic was a local Breton and a prolific excavator who investigated many megalithic monuments in the Carnac region. He started his archaeological career working as a field assistant for James Miln, a wealthy Scotsman and notable figure in Breton archaeology, who became fascinated with Brittany's megaliths after he first visited there, subsequently excavating many megalithic (and other Roman and medieval) sites in Brittany until his death in 1881.

6. Quoted in Morgan Sterling Saletta, "The Arles-Fontvieille Megalithic Monuments: Astronomy and Cosmology in the European Neolithic" (PhD diss., University of Melbourne, 2014), 67.

7. Scarre, *Landscapes of Neolithic Brittany*, 84.

8. Charles-Tanguy Le Roux, "New Excavations at Gavrinis," *Antiquity* 59 (1985), 184.

9. Le Roux, "New Excavations at Gavrinis," 185.

10. The Beaker culture emerged ca. 2800 BCE, probably in Iberia, and subsequently spread across many parts of Europe. It is named for the striking decorated pottery, or "bell beakers," that are often found in its graves. Other characteristic objects found in Beaker graves are flint "barbed and tanged" arrowheads; archer's stone wrist guards, or "bracers" (which may actually have been ornamental rather than functional items designed to protect the wrist from the lash of the bowstring); copper daggers; and small pieces of sheet-gold jewelry such as basket "earrings" (it may be more likely that these delicate objects were worn as ornaments in braided

hair). Most significantly, metalworking spread through Europe during the time of the Beaker culture. Traditionally, the distinctive artifacts of the Beaker culture were viewed as proof of an actual ethnic group (the famous "Beaker folk") whose communities migrated across Europe, but this idea became unpopular in the later twentieth century. More recently, however, this idea has started to gain favor again among archaeologists as ancient DNA analysis has suggested that the traditional view of the Beaker folk is closer to the truth.

11. Scarre, *Landscapes of Neolithic Brittany*, 69.

12. Richard Hornsey, "The Grand Menhir Brise: Megalithic Success or Failure?" *Oxford Journal of Archaeology* 6 (1989), 189.

13. Hornsey, "The Grand Menhir Brise," 209.

CHAPTER 3: MEGALITHS OF FRANCE, SWITZERLAND, AND ITALY

1. Roger Joussaume, *Dolmens for the Dead: Megalith Building throughout the World* (London: B. T. Batsford, 1987), 97–98.

2. Quoted in Jennifer Pinkowski, "Neolithic France," *Archaeology* 58, no. 3 (May/June 2005), https://archive.archaeology.org/0505/abstracts/france.html.

3. The LBK roughly dates from 5500 to 4500 BCE, and archaeologists think that it emerged first on the Hungarian Plain, subsequently spreading rapidly westward across central Europe and beyond, probably through the migration of LBK farming groups.

4. Joussaume, *Dolmens for the Dead*, 135.

5. Simon Kaner, "La Chaussée Tirancourt," in *Tombs, Graves and Mummies*, ed. Paul Bahn (London: Phoenix Illustrated, 1996), 46.

6. Kaner, "La Chaussée Tirancourt," 47.

7. Joussaume, *Dolmens for the Dead*, 146.

8. The Remedello culture dates from ca. 3300 to 2500 BCE, with its archaeological traces primarily concentrated in the Po Valley, where it is first thought to have emerged.

9. Richard Osgood and Sarah Monks, *Bronze Age Warfare* (Stroud, UK: Sutton, 2000), 83. The battle of Omdurman was fought on September 2, 1898, with the British forces of Major General Herbert Kitchener defeating the Mahdist army of Abdullah al-Taashi.

10. Marie Besse, "Sion Petit Chasseur," in *Ancient Europe 8000 B.C.–A.D. 1000: Encyclopedia of the Barbarian World*, ed. Peter Bogucki and Jan Crabtree (New York: Thomson Gale, 2004), 1:448.

CHAPTER 4: MEGALITHIC IBERIA

1. José E. Márquez Romero and Juan Fernandez Ruiz, *The Dolmens of Antequera: Official Guide to the Archaeological Complex* (Seville: Consejeria de Cultura, 2009), 70.

2. Examples of prehistoric ritual shafts have been discovered by archaeologists in various parts of Europe. For example, there is the well-known Wilsford Shaft in Wiltshire, southern England, which was dug in the later Bronze Age, ca. 1300 BCE. Bronze Age people deliberately deposited objects such as amber beads, bone needles, and an ox skull in this 30-meter-deep shaft, probably as offerings to the supernatural forces that were believed to live below ground in an underworld.

3. Leonardo Garciá Sanjuán and David W. Wheatley, "Natural Substances, Landscape Forms, Symbols and Funerary Monuments: Elements of Cultural Memory among the Neolithic and Copper Age Societies of Southern Spain," in *Material Mnemonics: Everyday Memory in Prehistoric Europe*, ed. Katina T. Lillios and Vasileios Tsamis (Oxford: Oxbow, 2010), 26.

4. In fact, where this line passes through the mountain, there is a prehistoric rock shelter containing painted abstract animal and humanlike motifs. The date of these motifs is uncertain, but it is possible that they are contemporary with the use of Menga.

5. Garciá Sanjuán and Wheatley, "Natural Substances, Landscape Forms, Symbols and Funerary Monuments," 30.

6. Some archaeologists have questioned the defensive nature of the Los Millares settlement, but its architecture does strongly suggest that its inhabitants were concerned with defending themselves from some unknown external threat. For example, the outer wall measures more than 300 meters in length and incorporates several semicircular towers and a "barbican" entrance comprising two projecting hornlike stone walls, which feature narrow openings that look very much like the archer's arrow slits seen in the walls of medieval castles. Thirteen circular structures that have been interpreted as small forts or lookout posts were also built on the ridges surrounding Los Millares.

7. Antonio Margado et al., "The Allure of Rock Crystal in Copper Age Southern Iberia: Technical Skill and Distinguished Objects from Valencina de la Concepcion," *Quaternary International* 30 (2015), 5.

8. Roger Joussaume, *Dolmens for the Dead: Megalith Building throughout the World* (London: B. T. Batsford, 1988), 196.

9. Simon Broughton, "Midsummer Monument: The Sacred Stones of Portugal's Stonehenge," *Independent*, June 17, 2016, https://www.independent.co.uk/travel/europe/portugal-evora-stonehenge-cromlech-midsummer-solstice-almendres-zambujeiro-stone-circle-a7085496.html.

10. Fernando Pimenta, Luís Tirapicos, and Andrew Smith, "A Bayesian Approach to the Orientations of Central Alentejo Megalithic Enclosures," *Archaeoastronomy* 22 (2009), 3.

11. Curt Roslund, Yasmine Kristiansen, and Birgitta Hårdh, "Portuguese Passage Graves in the Light of the Easter Moon," *Fornvännen* 95 (2000), 1.

12. Roslund, Kristiansen, and Hårdh, "Portuguese Passage Graves in the Light of the Easter Moon," 1.

13. Fabio Silva, "A Tomb with a View: New Methods for Bridging the Gap between Land and Sky in Megalithic Archaeology," *Advances in Archaeological Practice* (2014), 31.

14. Silva, "A Tomb with a View," 32.

15. Linea Sundstrom, "Mirror of Heaven: Cross-Cultural Transference of the Sacred Geography of the Black Hills," *World Archaeology* 28 (1996), 181–82.

16. Alice C. Fletcher, "Star Cult among the Pawnee—a Preliminary Report," *American Anthropologist* 4 (1902), 732–33.

CHAPTER 5: MEGALITHS OF THE MEDITERRANEAN ISLANDS

1. Not all archaeologists are comfortable with describing these Maltese megalithic monuments as "temples," but the archaeological evidence that has been found at them surely reveals that these were special buildings primarily reserved for religious rituals and ceremonies. It thus

seems reasonable to refer to them as "temples," and, in any case, nobody has come up with a better term for these remarkable structures.

2. David H. Trump, *Malta: Prehistory and Temples* (Malta: Midsea, 2002), 72.

3. Archaeological evidence does, however, strongly suggest that the first temples were built by the descendants of Early Neolithic people from Sicily who crossed the Mediterranean to the Maltese archipelago around 5500 BCE.

4. Anthony Pace, *The Tarxien Temples, Tarxien* (Malta: Heritage Books, 2010), 11.

5. Pace, *The Tarxien Temples, Tarxien*, 17.

6. Trump, *Malta*, 95.

7. Diane Woolner, "Graffiti of Ships at Tarxien, Malta," *Antiquity* 31 (1957), 67.

8. In 1988, a crude rock-cut tomb comprising two small chambers was discovered to the southeast of the caves, representing the earliest funerary activity on the Xagħra plateau. The tomb dated to ca. 4100–3700 BCE and contained the skeletal remains of about sixty-five adults and children who had been buried with an interesting collection of grave goods, such as sixteen miniature stone axes (some of which had been perforated to be worn as pendants), shell beads and pendants, two complete pottery cups, flint and obsidian tools, a very large sea snail shell (perhaps a conch-like wind instrument), twenty-six bone pendants that look like stylized human figures, and a small stone "idol" featuring a stylized human face that may perhaps have been the "guardian" of the tomb.

9. Caroline Malone et al., "The Death Cults of Prehistoric Malta," *Scientific American, Special Edition* 15 (2005), 21.

10. Paul Devereux, "A Ceiling Painting in the Hal-Saflieni Hypogeum as Acoustically-Related Imagery: A Preliminary Report," *Time and Mind* 2 (2009), 226.

11. Anthony Pace, *The Hal Saflieni Hypogeum, Paola* (Malta: Heritage Books, 2004), 30.

12. Trump, *Malta*, 100.

13. Alastair Service and Jean Bradbery, *A Guide to the Megaliths of Europe* (London: Granada, 1981), 129.

14. Michael Hoskin, Peter Hochsieder, and Doris Knösel, "The Orientations of the Taulas of Menorca (2): The Remaining Taulas," *Journal for the History of Astronomy* 31 (Archaeoastronomy Supplement 15) (1990), 37.

15. Hoskin, Hochsieder, and Knösel, "The Orientations of the Taulas of Menorca (2)," 37.

16. Service and Bradbery, *A Guide to the Megaliths of Europe*, 138.

CHAPTER 6: THE STONE CIRCLES OF BRITAIN AND IRELAND

1. Neil Oliver, *A History of Ancient Britain* (London: Weidenfeld & Nicolson, 2011), 103.

2. Aubrey Burl, *Prehistoric Stone Circles* (Princes Risborough, UK: Shire, 2005), 10.

3. Aubrey Burl, *Stonehenge: A Complete History and Archaeology of the World's Most Enigmatic Stone Circle* (London: Constable & Robinson, 2007), 130.

4. In 2002, archaeologists discovered the remarkable Ness of Brodgar ritual and ceremonial complex (dating from the Late Neolithic to the Early Bronze Age (ca. 3200–2200 BCE) on the narrow ridge of land (the Brodgar peninsula) that lies between the two circles. Excavations at this now famous site are ongoing, and readers can learn all about them on the Ness of Brodgar website (wwww.nessofbrodgar.com).

5. Oliver, *A History of Ancient Britain*, 113.

6. For those readers who wish to know more about this amazing prehistoric settlement, a quick search of the internet will bring up many sites about Skara Brae.

7. Colin Richards, "The Great Stone Circles Project," *British Archaeology* 81 (2005), 19.

8. Colin Richards, "Monuments as Landscape: Creating the Centre of the World in Late Neolithic Orkney," *World Archaeology* 28 (1996), 203.

9. Alistair Service and Jean Bradbery, *A Guide to the Megaliths of Europe* (London: Granada, 1981), 205.

10. The moon's major standstill occurs every 18.6 years, when moonrise changes from northeast to southeast and moonset from northwest to southwest.

11. Aubrey Burl, *Rites of the Gods* (London: J. M. Dent & Sons, 1981), 192.

12. In the summer of 1977, a young Washington artist named Anna Sofaer discovered two such Anasazi symbols carved in a rock face close to the summit of the impressive Fajada Butte in the famous Chaco Canyon, New Mexico. The carvings were located just behind three sandstone slabs that seemed to have been deliberately stacked vertically on one end, one behind the other, leaning at an angle against the rock face. Sofaer returned to the site around noon the next day, with her second visit taking place just one week after the summer solstice. She made the intriguing discovery that a narrow gap between the left and middle slabs caused a narrow sliver, or "dagger," of bright sunlight to pierce the larger of the spirals. Sofaer later made another intriguing discovery—one week before the winter solstice, this same spiral was framed between two slivers of sunlight cast by both gaps between the three slabs.

13. The same cannot be said for the Grey Croft stone circle, which has as its backdrop the Sellafield nuclear power station. Thankfully, this ugly blot on the Cumbrian landscape is now in the process of being decommissioned and dismantled.

14. "Castlerigg Stone Circle," English Heritage, www.english-heritage.org.uk/visit/places/castlerigg-stone-circle.

15. This is a word loaded with modern connotations, and it should be borne in mind that many Neolithic stone axes were never used functionally, seemingly having a deeper significance connected to their place of origin, and were also often carried across many hundreds of miles of land and sea to be deposited at numerous funerary and ritual monuments in Europe. It appears that axes made from rare Alpine rocks (i.e., jadeite/jade, omphacite, and eclogite) were particularly prized by Neolithic people in Europe and must have been used to cement bonds and alliances between individuals and communities. A French-led research project, Projet Jade, has tied down the source area of these rocks: the Mont Viso and Mont Beigua massifs of the Italian Alps. One of these Italian alpine axes was famously found beside the "Sweet Track," a Neolithic timber track-way that originally led across watery marshland in Somerset, southwestern England. It is likely that this axe began its journey to Somerset at Mont Viso, meaning it traveled almost a thousand miles to reach its final destination. We can only guess at what made these axes so sought after, but it is quite probable that they came from mountains that were deemed sacred or "magical" places.

16. Aubrey Burl, *The Stone Circles of the British Isles* (New Haven, CT: Yale University Press, 1976), 85.

17. Trevor Garnham, *Lines on the Landscape, Circles from the Sky: Monuments of Neolithic Orkney* (Stroud, UK: Tempus, 2004), 169.

18. Garnham, *Lines on the Landscape Circles from the Sky*, 169.

19. Burl, *Prehistoric Stone Circles*, 38.

20. Burl, *The Stone Circles of the British Isles*, 292.

21. Henry W. Taunt, *The Rollright Stones: The Stonehenge of Oxfordshire* (Oxford: Henry W. Taunt & Co., 1907), 24–25. Like many people in Edwardian Britain, Taunt and his

companions evidently believed in fairies, as revealed by the following passage from his book on the Rollright Stones: "We ourselves spent Midsummer night at Rollright last year. . . . We sat on the stile by the King-stone waiting for the fairies to reveal themselves, but beyond the glinting lights nothing appeared" (42).

22. Burl, *Prehistoric Stone Circles*, 20.

23. However, rather than the effects of many centuries of weathering, the appearance of this fine standing stone probably has more to do with the fact that nineteenth-century visitors often chipped pieces from it as souvenirs, as did many passing drovers from Wales, who used the pieces as lucky charms against the devil.

24. Arthur J. Evans, "The Rollright-Stones and Their Folk-lore," *Folklore* 6 (1895).

25. D. McCormick quoted in Burl, *The Stone Circles of the British Isles*, 297.

26. Burl, *The Stone Circles of the British Isles*, 237.

27. Captain (later Admiral) Henry Boyle Townshend Somerville came from a wealthy and well-known Anglo-Irish family. He was shot dead by the Irish Republican Army at home in 1936 for allegedly recruiting local men for the British navy and army, although it is more likely that he had simply supplied references for them.

28. Griffiths also excavated two other prehistoric monuments nearby, Circle 275 and Circle 278, with the former possibly a diminutive stone circle built by people who had traveled to Wales from southern Ireland and the latter an example of a ring cairn (i.e., a low circular stone ring with an open central space), which yielded a cremation and an Early Bronze Age pottery vessel.

29. Burl, *The Stone Circles of the British Isles*, 272.

CHAPTER 7: STONEHENGE AND AVEBURY

1. It is also worth mentioning that visitors are free to wander around both the exterior and the interior of Avebury and can "get up close and personal" with its impressive standing stones, even touching them if they wish. Contrastingly, at Stonehenge a low rope barrier surrounds the stones, and the visitor must be content with an exterior view of the monument, unless an expensive and oversubscribed special-access tour is booked, which allows you to walk freely among the stones (but not to touch them!).

2. Mark Gillings and Joshua Pollard, *Avebury* (London: Duckworth, 2004), 1. Stukeley originally interpreted Avebury as a monument built by the Iron Age druids, with its inner stone circles temples dedicated to worship of the sun and moon and a temple to Ertha, or the Earth (a former stone and timber circle known as the Sanctuary), lying at the end of the avenue of standing stones that ran from its southern entrance (the West Kennet Avenue), and a hypothetical temple to the Manes (spirits of the underworld) at the end of the one running from its western entrance (the Beckhampton Avenue). He later drastically revised his interpretation of the Avebury complex and came up with the theory that Avebury was a *Dracontium* (or serpent) temple, dedicated to God, with the whole complex laid out in the form of a colossal snake.

3. However, overexaggeration aside, the collection of notes and drawings that Stukeley made during his visits to Avebury between 1718 and 1725 have provided modern archaeologists with many invaluable insights into this extraordinary monument, which was literally being destroyed before Stukeley's eyes as he carried out his fieldwork.

4. Aubrey Burl, *The Stone Circles of the British Isles* (New Haven, CT: Yale University Press, 1976), 320–21. Like his successor, William Stukeley, John Aubrey was one of the founding fathers of British archaeology and "discovered" Avebury while out pursuing the very British (and very cruel) "sport" of foxhunting.

5. A "henge" is a Neolithic and Bronze Age religious monument comprising an outer bank and inner ditch that encloses a circular, flat inner area, where rituals and ceremonies must have been carried out, although at Stonehenge the bank atypically lies inside the encircling ditch.

6. Gillings and Pollard, *Avebury*, 43.

7. Alexander Kieller (1889–1955) was born in Scotland into great wealth, as he was the sole heir to the great fortune amassed by Kieller & Sons, a marmalade and confectionery business founded by mother and son James and Janet Kieller in the mid-eighteenth century, with the famous "Kieller's marmalade" exported around the world in the late nineteenth century. Kieller used his inherited wealth to pursue his passion for archaeology, excavating not only at Avebury but also at the nearby Neolithic enclosure on Windmill Hill (which he bought), with this site now one of the best-known monuments from prehistoric Britain. Kieller also collaborated with O. G. S Crawford on the first book on aerial photography to be published in Britain.

8. Gillings and Pollard, *Avebury*, 174.

9. Alisdair Whittle, *Sacred Mound Holy Rings: Silbury Hill and the West Kennet Palisade Enclosures: A Later Neolithic Complex in North Wiltshire* (Oxford: Oxbow, 2007), 107.

10. Alexander Kieller, "Avebury: Summary of Excavations, 1937 and 1938," *Antiquity* 50 (1939), 231.

11. Burl, *The Stone Circles of the British Isles*, 322.

12. In the wider area around Stonehenge, on Salisbury Plain (the so-called Stonehenge Region, which covers an area of land roughly measuring four miles long by two miles wide), there is a remarkable and diverse collection of numerous prehistoric sites and monuments. Among these monuments are many Early Bronze Age burial mounds and the famous Neolithic Cursus, an avenue-like earthwork monument consisting of low parallel banks and ditches that runs for nearly two miles across Salisbury Plain. William Stukeley coined the name Cursus from the Latin for racecourse, suggesting it had been used by ancient Britons for chariot racing! There is also the Durrington Walls "Super-henge," and recent archaeological work here has suggested that this huge site may well have been the settlement of the workers who raised Stonehenge's massive megaliths.

13. Timothy Darvill, "Houses of the Holy: Architecture and Meaning in the Structure of Stonehenge, Wiltshire, UK," *Time and Mind* 9 (2016), 91–92, doi:10.1080/17516 96X.2016.1171496.

14. Aubrey Burl, *A Brief History of Stonehenge* (London: Constable and Robinson, 2007), 235.

15. Darvill, "Houses of the Holy," 99.

16. George Nash, "Rare Examples of British Neolithic and Bronze Age Human Representations in Rock-Art: Expressions in Weapons and Warriorship," Congresso Internacional da IFRAO 2009, Piaui, Brasil, June 29–July 3, 2009.

17. M. Parker Pearson, J. Pollard, C. Richards, D. Schlee, and K. Welham, "In Search of the Stonehenge Quarries," *British Archaeology* 146 (2016), 18.

18. Parker Pearson et al., "In Search of the Stonehenge Quarries," 18.

19. H. H. Thomas, "The Source of the Stones of the Stonehenge," *Antiquaries Journal* (1923), 239–60.

20. For more on this subject, see Christopher P. Green, "Stonehenge: Geology and Prehistory," *Proceedings of the Geologists' Association* (108), 1–10.

21. Parker Pearson et al., "In Search of the Stonehenge Quarries," 23.

22. Mike Parker Pearson et al., "Megalith Quarries for Stonehenge's Bluestones," *Antiquity* 93 (2019), 56.

23. Brian John, Dyfed Ellis-Gruffyd, and John Downes, "Observations on the Supposed 'Neolithic Bluestone Quarry' at Craigy Rhosyfelin, Pembrokeshire," *Archaeology in Wales* 54 (2015), 139–48.

24. Christopher Catling, "Message in the Stones," *Current Archaeology* 212 (2007), 17.

25. Timothy Darvill quoted in Catling, "Message in the Stones," 17.

26. Mike Parker Pearson and Ramilisonina, "Stonehenge for the Ancestors: The Stones Pass on the Message," *Antiquity* 72 (1998), 308.

27. Darvill, "Houses of the Holy," 105.

28. Darvill, "Houses of the Holy," 105.

29. Mark Gillings and Joshua Pollard, "Non-portable Stone Artefacts and Contexts of Meaning: The Tale of Grey Wether (www.museums.ncl.ac.uk/Avebury/stone4.htm)," *World Archaeology* 31 (1999), 184.

30. Timothy Darvill and Geoff Wainwright, "Beyond Stonehenge: Carn Menyn Quarry and the Origin and Date of Bluestone Extraction in the Preseli Hills of South-west Wales," *Antiquity* 88 (2014), 1112.

31. Parker Pearson et al., "In Search of the Stonehenge Quarries," 18.

32. Catling, "Message in the Stones," 15.

33. Catling, "Message in the Stones," 15.

34. Timothy Darvill, "Afterworld: Dances beneath a Diamond Sky," in *Skyscapes: The Role and Importance of the Sky in Archaeology*, ed. Fabio Silva Nicholas Campion (Oxford: Oxbow), 142.

CHAPTER 8: ENGLISH MEGALITHIC TOMBS

1. Belas Knap's mound measures approximately 55 meters long and 18 meters at its wider northern end, which is about 4 meters high. There are four burial chambers in the mound, with two in its eastern side and one each in the western side and northern end of the mound. Excavations carried out at the long barrow in 1863 and 1929–1930 yielded the remains of about forty individuals, two of whom displayed lethal skull fractures that had been caused by stone axes or wooden clubs—providing further proof that southern England could be a very dangerous place to live in the Early Neolithic.

2. Quoted in Austin Kinsley, "West Kennet Long Barrow Wiltshire," Silent Earth: Messages from Our Ancestors, June 19, 2018, https://www.silentearth.org/west-kennet-long -barrow-wiltshire.

3. Neil Oliver, *A History of Ancient Britain* (London: Weidenfeld & Nicolson, 2011), 79.

4. Julian Thomas and Alasdair Whittle, "Anatomy of a Tomb—West Kennet Revisited," *Oxford Journal of Archaeology* 5 (1986), 153.

5. Stuart Piggott, "The Excavation of the West Kennet Long Barrow: 1955–56," *Antiquity* 32 (1958), 238.

6. Oliver, *A History of Ancient Britain*, 85.

7. Aubrey Burl, *Rites of the Gods* (London: J. M. Dent & Sons, 1981), 71.

8. For example, Avebury, Uffington Castle Iron Age hillfort, and the remarkable Uffington White Horse, an enormous stylized horse figure (approximately 110 meters long) carved into the chalk of Uffington Hill in the Vale of the White Horse, Oxfordshire, probably by a Late Bronze Age tribe some three thousand years ago. Wayland's Smithy only lies about one mile from this masterpiece of prehistoric art.

9. Meg Van Huygen, "Give My Body to the Birds: The Practice of Sky Burial," *Atlas Obscura*, March 11, 2014, https://www.atlasobscura.com/articles/sky-burial.

10. R. C. J. Atkinson, "Wayland's Smithy," *Antiquity* 39 (1965), 130.

11. Alasdair Whittle, Alex Bayliss, and Michael Wysocki, "Once in a Lifetime: The Dating of the Wayland's Smithy Long Barrow," *Cambridge Archaeological Journal* 17, no. 1 (2007), 114.

12. Paul Ashbee, "The Medway Megaliths in Perspective," *Archaeologia Cantiana* 111 (1993), 62.

13. The most common form of trophy taking in nonstate warfare was probably head-hunting, which is recorded in many cultures across the world, although it was not always enemy heads that were taken in warfare. For example, enemies could be scalped, which, of course, has become synonymous with the native Indians of North America, although it was carried out by other cultures in other parts of the world. In the sixteenth century, French artist Jacques Le Moyne de Morgues recorded that the Timucua Indians of Florida cut off the arms and legs of their defeated enemies, while in the nineteenth century Bishop Ioann Veniaminov described how the native Eskimo groups of the Aleutian Islands cut off the ears and other body parts of their defeated enemies. Trophy taking was not a practice carried out solely by "primitive" peoples, as American soldiers, for example, are known to have collected Japanese skulls during the brutal Pacific campaign of World War II. The Americans sometimes sent these skulls home as "souvenirs," often bearing autographs and inscriptions made by them. In one extreme case, a soldier collected twenty Japanese skulls on which he had marked the dates and locations of their owners' deaths.

14. Michael Wysocki et al., "Dates, Diets, and Dismemberment: Evidence from the Coldrum Megalithic Monument, Kent," *Proceedings of the Prehistoric Society* 79 (2013), 8.

15. Rick J. Schulting and Michael Wysocki, "'In This Chambered Tumulus Were Found Cleft Skulls . . .': An Assessment of the Evidence for Cranial Trauma in the British Neolithic," *Proceedings of the Prehistoric Society* 71 (2005), 113.

16. Schulting and Wysocki, "In This Chambered Tumulus."

17. George Nash, "Rare Examples of British Neolithic and Bronze Age Human Representations in Rock-Art: Expressions in Weapons and Warriorship," Congresso Internacional da IFRAO 2009, Piaui, Brasil, June 29–July 3, 2009.

CHAPTER 9: WELSH MEGALITHIC TOMBS

1. Chris Scarre, "Consolidation, Reconstruction and the Interpretation of Megalithic Monuments," *Arkeos* 16 (2006), 15.

2. George Nash, "Light at the End of the Tunnel: The Way Megalithic Art Was Viewed and Experienced," *Documenta Praehistorica* 33 (2006), 213.

3. Parc le Breos was an extensive medieval deer park that was probably established in the early thirteenth century by the De Breos lords of Gower, a powerful medieval Norman-Welsh dynasty.

4. Lubbock was a keen archaeologist, and his *Pre-historic Times, as Illustrated by the Ancient Remains, and the Manners and Customs of Modern Savages* was published in 1865. Its title is rather cumbersome, and it is now very dated, but Lubbock's book remains a classic of antiquarian scholarship.

5. Glyn Daniel, "The Chambered Barrow in Parc Le Breos Cwm, S. Wales," *Proceedings of the Prehistoric Society* 3 (1937), 76.

6. W. F. Grimes, "The Excavation of Ty-Isaf Long Cairn Brecknockshire," *Proceedings of the Prehistoric Society* 5 (1939), 119.

7. Grimes, "The Excavation of Ty-Isaf Long Cairn Brecknockshire," 126.

8. Aubrey Burl, *The Stonehenge People* (London: Barrie & Jenkins, 1989), 166.

9. Steve Burrow, "Bryn Celli Ddu Passage Tomb, Anglesey: Alignment, Construction, Date and Ritual," *Proceedings of the Prehistoric Society* 76 (2010), 249.

10. Nash, "Light at the End of the Tunnel," 209.

11. David Lewis-Williams and David Pearce, *Inside the Neolithic Mind* (London: Thames & Hudson, 2005), 185.

12. Burrow, "Bryn Celli Ddu Passage Tomb, Anglesey," 253.

13. Lewis-Williams and Pearce, *Inside the Neolithic Mind*, 187.

14. Barclodiad y Gawres derives its rather unusual name from the local legend that basically tells of a giantess who dropped her apronful of stones (for a house she was building with her husband) on the headland where the passage grave is situated.

15. John Sharkey, *The Meeting of the Tracks: Rock Art in Ancient Wales* (Llanrwst, UK: Gwasg Carreg Gwalch, 2004), 47.

16. Aubrey Burl, *Rites of the Gods* (London: J. M. Dent & Sons, 1981), 90.

CHAPTER 10: IRISH MEGALITHIC TOMBS

1. Alastair Service and Jean Bradbery, *A Guide to the Megaliths of Europe* (London: Granada, 1981), 218.

2. Francis Pryor, *Britain BC: Life in Britain and Ireland before the Romans* (London: HarperCollins, 2003), 215.

3. Jack Roberts, "The Brú na Boinne: The Great Passage Cairns and Prehistoric Art of the Boyne Valley," *Adoranten* (2015), 44. The Boyne Valley was also the scene of the famous Battle of the Boyne in 1690, a conflict that pitched the armies of the Protestant and Dutch King William III (William of Orange) and the Catholic King James II against one another as the latter sought to regain control of the British Crown, which he had lost to William only a year before. William won, and the ramifications of his victory are still being felt in Ireland today.

4. Aubrey Burl, *Rites of the Gods* (London: J. M. Dent & Sons, 1981), 86.

5. Neil Oliver, *A History of Ancient Britain* (London: Weidenfeld & Nicolson, 2011), 129.

6. Burl, *Rites of the Gods*, 87.

7. George Eogan quoted in Roberts, "The Brú na Boinne."

8. Roberts, "The Brú na Boinne," 57.

9. Quoted in "Bru na Boinne: Megalithic Tomb Discovered in Meath," *BBC News*, July 17, 2018, https://www.bbc.co.uk/news/world-europe-44850668.

10. Quoted in Robert Hensey et al., "A Century of Archaeology—Historical Excavation and Modern Research at the Carrowkeel Passage Tombs, County Sligo," *Proceedings of the Royal Irish Academy* 114C (2013), 1.

11. John Waddell, *The Prehistoric Archaeology of Ireland* (Bray, UK: Wordwell, 2000), 68.

12. This curious structure may perhaps have been a primitive metalworking foundry. However, the fact that no traces of fire were found on its stones argues against this theory, and thus it may have been used for some other purpose, with the drying of grain a possibility.

13. Eileen M. Murphy, "Children's Burial Grounds in Ireland (Cíllini) and Parental Emotions toward Infant Death," *International Journal of Historical Archaeology* 15 (2011), 409, doi:10.1007/s10761-011-0148-8.

14. William O'Brien, "Megaliths in a Mythologised Landscape: South-west Ireland in the Iron Age," in *Monuments and Landscape in Atlantic Europe: Perception and Society during the Neolithic and Early Bronze Age*, ed. Chris Scarre (London/New York: Routledge, 2002), 170.

15. The most impressive of Ireland's portal tombs—at least in terms of scale—is the Brownshill dolmen (also known as the Kernanstown Cromlech), in County Carlow, southern Ireland. This monument has an enormous, 1.5-meter-thick capstone weighing an estimated 100–150 tons.

16. Chris Catling, "Poulnabrone's Portal Tomb: Honouring the Neolithic Dead," *Current Archaeology* 298 (2015), 21.

CHAPTER 11: SCOTTISH MEGALITHIC TOMBS

1. Francis Pryor, *Britain BC: Life in Britain and Ireland before the Romans* (London: HarperCollins, 2003), 246.

2. In fact, this research has shown us that the rays of the setting sun shine down the passage of Maeshowe to illuminate its chamber not just on the midwinter solstice but also for three weeks on either side of midwinter's day.

3. As long ago as 1892, a local schoolmaster, Magnus Spence, realized that Maeshowe and the Barnhouse Stone were aligned on the midwinter sunset.

4. Aubrey Burl, *Rites of the Gods* (London: J. M. Dent & Sons, 1981), 124.

5. "Maeshowe's Runes—Viking Graffiti," Orkneyjar: The Heritage of the Orkney Islands, www.orkneyjar.com/history/maeshowe.html.

6. The Orkneyinga saga was written in the early 1200s and is basically a narrative of the lives and times of the various Viking leaders who ruled the Orkney Isles between the ninth and thirteenth centuries CE.

7. "Maeshowe's Runes—Viking Graffiti."

8. David Murray and Andrew Hollinrake, "Maes Howe Archaeology Notes," Canmore, 2006, https://canmore.org.uk/site/2094/maes-howe.

9. Murray and Hollinrake, "Maes Howe Archaeology Notes."

10. Murray and Hollinrake, "Maes Howe Archaeology Notes."

11. "The Hogboon—Orkney's Mound Dweller," Orkneyjar: The Heritage of the Orkney Islands, www.orkneyjar.com/folklore/hogboon/index.html.

12. "The Hogboon—Orkney's Mound Dweller."

13. Rick Schulting et al., "Revisiting Quanterness: New AMS Dates and Stable Isotope Data from an Orcadian Neolithic Tomb," *Proceedings of the Society of Antiquaries of Scotland* 140 (2010), 1.

14. Grooved Ware is a distinctive type of pottery that was widely used in prehistoric Britain and Ireland from the Late Neolithic to the Early Bronze Age from ca. 3000 to 2200 BCE. It first emerged in the Orkney Islands.

15. Burl, *Rites of the Gods*, 116.

16. Joseph Anderson, "On the Horned Cairns of Caithness: Their Structural Arrangement, Contents of Chmabers, &c," *Proceedings of the Society of Antiquaries of Scotland* 7 (1866), 498.

17. "The Isbister Cairn—the Tomb of the Eagles: The Discovery of the Cairn," Orkneyjar: The Heritage of the Orkney Islands, www.orkneyjar.com/history/isbister/index.html.

18. Although archaeologists cannot say for sure what the purpose of "burnt mounds" was, piles of shattered rock and charcoal are found in association with stone- or wood-lined troughs at these prehistoric sites. It seems likely from this evidence that stones were heated on fires and then dropped into the water-filled troughs, subsequently shattering through thermal shock and heating up the water at the same time. It has been suggested that the troughs were used for cooking or bathing or perhaps for the treatment of animal hides.

19. Alison Sheridan, "The Neolithization of Britain and Ireland: The 'Big Picture,'" in *Landscapes in Transition*, ed. Bill Finlayson and Graeme Warren (Oxford: Oxbow, 2010), 92.

20. "Clava Cairns," Undiscovered Scotland, https://www.undiscoveredscotland.co.uk/inverness/clavacairns/index.html.

21. Richard Bradley, "The Land, the Sky and the Scottish Stone Circle," in *Monuments and Landscape in Atlantic Europe: Perception and Society during the Neolithic and Bronze Age*, ed. Chris Scarre (London: Routledge, 2002), 125.

22. David Trevarthen, "Illuminating the Monuments: Observation and Speculation on the Structure and Function of the Cairns at Balnuaran of Clava," *Cambridge Archaeological Journal* 10 (2000), 297.

23. Bradley, "The Land, the Sky and the Scottish Stone Circle," 125.

24. Burl, *Rites of the Gods*, 93.

CHAPTER 12: MEGALITHIC GERMANY AND HOLLAND

1. The Funnel Beaker culture roughly dates from ca. 4200 to 2800 BCE and takes its name from the distinctive, finely decorated pottery vessels with funnel-shaped necks made by its communities. The Funnel Beaker culture was spread across northern Europe, occupying large parts of Holland, Germany, Poland, and Scandinavia.

2. In local folklore, the Visbek monuments are said to be the wedding parties of a bride and groom turned to stone, with the bride pleading to God that she would rather suffer this fate than be forced by her father to marry a rich man whom she did not love, her heart belonging instead to a poor shepherd she had loved since childhood.

3. The Wildeshauser Geest covers a huge area of land measuring nearly 950 square miles and is one of the largest nature reserves in Germany. It is rich in both ancient history and wildlife.

4. The Wartberg culture dates to 3600–2800 BCE, and its settlements and monuments are distributed in the German regions of northern Hesse, Lower Saxony, and Thuringia.

5. Alistair Service and Jean Bradbery, *A Guide to the Megaliths of Europe* (London: Granada, 1981), 159.

6. Titia Brongersma was a Frisian poet, and her excavation of the monument inspired her to write the poem "Ode on the Hunebed."

7. *Hunebed* D27 is located just outside the Hunebed Centrum, an excellent and popular museum devoted to the story of Holland's *hunebed* builders.

CHAPTER 13: MEGALITHIC SCANDINAVIA

1. Claus Clausen, "Neolithic Cosmology?" *Adoranten* (2014), 68.
2. Magdalena S. Midgley, "Monuments and Monumentality: The Cosmological Model of the World of the Megaliths," *Documenta Praehistorica* 37 (2010), 58.
3. Midgley, "Monuments and Monumentality," 58.
4. Since the discovery of the Tustrup Neolithic cult or mortuary house, at least ten other examples have been discovered in Denmark.
5. Quoted in Tia Ghose, "A Swedish Stonehenge? Stone Age Tomb May Predate English Site," *Live Science*, October 10, 2012, https://livescience.com/24157-ancient-tomb-ales-swedish-stonehenge.html.
6. Nils Axel-Mörner and Bob G. Lind, "Stonehenge Has Got a Younger Sister—Ales Stones in Sweden Decoded," *International Journal of Astronomy and Astrophysics* 2 (2012), 23–27.
7. Many other ancient ship settings can be found in Sweden (and Denmark) that date from the Bronze Age to the Viking period (ca. 1700 BCE–1050 CE), probably representing symbolic vessels that carried the dead into the afterlife. The most significant concentration of Bronze Age ship settings is found on Gotland, Sweden's largest island, with these monuments varying in length from approximately 10–40 meters. Several examples have yielded cremated human remains placed in pottery urns, which are accompanied by bronze objects such as razors, tweezers, and pins. The Askeberga or Ranstena ship setting in the southern Swedish province of Västergötland is another example that may possibly be prehistoric in date. This gargantuan monument comprises twenty-four massive boulders that have been estimated as weighing between 20 and 30 tons each, arranged in two slightly bowed rows measuring 53 meters in length. The general archaeological consensus is that the Ranstena ship setting was built in the Viking period, although some scholars have argued that it was raised in the Bronze Age, with its builders aligning their monument on the midwinter sunset.
8. Axel-Mörner and Lind, "Stonehenge Has Got a Younger Sister," 26.

Bibliography

Adams, Ron L., and Ayu Kusmawati. "The Social Life of Tombs in West Sumba, Indonesia." *Archaeological Papers of the American Anthropological Association* 20 (2011): 17–32.

Adamson, Tom. "Stonehenge: The Stone Mason and His Craft." *Antiquity* (News & Notes) 76 (2002): 41–42.

Ahlstrom, Dick. "People of the Passage Tombs." *Irish Times.* December 15, 2011. https://www .irishtimes.com/news/science/people-of-the-passage-tombs-1.11731.

Anderson, Joseph. "On the Horned Cairns of Caithness: Their Structural Arrangement, Contents of Chambers, &c." *Proceedings of the Society of Antiquaries of Scotland* 7 (1866): 480–512.

Armit, Ian, and David Reich. "Beakers: How Ancient DNA Is Changing the Way We Think about Prehistoric Britain." *British Archaeology* 160 (2018): 14–19.

Ashbee, Paul. "Coldrum Revisited and Reviewed." *Archaeologia Cantiana* 118 (1998): 1–43.

———. "The Medway Megaliths in Perspective." *Archaeologia Cantiana* 111 (1993): 57–111.

———. "The Wilsford Shaft." *Antiquity* 37 (1963): 116–20.

Atkinson, R. J. C. "Moonshine on Stonehenge." *Antiquity* 40 (1966): 212–16.

———. "Wayland's Smithy." *Antiquity* 39 (1965): 126–33.

Atursson, Magnus, Timothy Earle, and James Brown. "The Construction of Monumental Landscapes in Low-Density Societies: New Evidence from the Early Neolithic of Southern Scandinavia (4000–3300 BC) in Comparative Perspectives (November 5, 2015)." *Journal of Anthropological Archaeology* 41 (2016): 1–18.

Bahn, Paul, ed. *Tombs, Graves and Mummies.* London: Phoenix Illustrated, 1996.

Barnatt, John, and Mark Edmonds. "Places Apart? Caves and Monuments in Neolithic and Earlier Bronze Age Britain." *Cambridge Archaeological Journal* 12 (2002): 113–29.

Barnes, Gina L., and Guo Dashun. "The Ritual Landscape of 'Boar Mountain' Basin: The Niuheliang Site Complex of North-Eastern China." *World Archaeology* 28 (1996): 161–76.

Barrett, John C., and Ilhong Ko. "A Phenomenology of Landscape: A Crisis in British Landscape Archaeology?" *Journal of Social Archaeology* 9 (2009): 275–94.

Baxter, Mary. "Dancing with the Dead in a Mass Grave." *British Archaeology* 50 (1999): 6–7.

Bayliss, Alex, Alasdair Whittle, and Michael Wysocki. "Talking about My Generation: The Date of the West Kennet Long Barrow." *Cambridge Archaeological Journal* 17 (2007): 85–101.

Berg, Stefan. "Knocknarea: The Ultimate Monument." *In Monuments and Landscape: Perception and Society during the Neolithic and Early Bronze Age*, edited by Chris Scarre, 139–51. London: Routledge, 2002.

Berg, Stefan, and Robert Hensey. "Unpicking the Chronology of Carrowmore." *Oxford Journal of Archaeology* 32 (2013): 343–66.

Blake, Emma. "Identity-Mapping in the Sardinian Bronze Age." *European Journal of Archaeology* 2 (1999): 35–55.

Bogucki, Peter, and Pam Crabtree. *Ancient Europe 8000 B.C.–A.D. 1000: Encyclopedia of the Barbarian World.* Vol. 1. New York: Thomson Gale, 2004.

Bonanno, A., T. Gouder, C. Malone, and S. Stoddart. "Monuments in an Island Society: The Maltese Context." *World Archaeology* 22 (1990): 190–205.

Bradley, Richard. "Darkness and Light in the Design of Megalithic Tombs." *Oxford Journal of Archaeology* 8 (1989): 251–59.

———. "Deaths and Entrances: A Contextual Analysis of Megalithic Art." *Current Anthropology* 30 (1989): 68–75.

———. "Long Houses, Long Mounds and Neolithic Enclosures." *Journal of Material Culture* 1 (1996): 239–56.

———. "Ruined Buildings, Ruined Stones: Enclosures, Tombs and Natural Places in the Neolithic of South-West England." *World Archaeology* 30 (1998): 13–22.

———. *The Significance of Monuments: On the Shaping of Human Experience in Neolithic and Bronze Age Europe.* London: Routledge, 1998.

Bradley, Richard, and Tim Phillips. "Display, Disclosure, and Concealment: The Organization of Raw Materials in the Chambered Tombs of Bohuslän." *Oxford Journal of Archaeology* 27 (2008): 1–13.

Bradley, Richard, Peter Skoglund, and Joakim Wehlin. "Imaginary Vessels in the Late Bronze Age of Gotland and South Scandinavia: Ship Settings, Rock Carvings and Decorated Metalwork." *Current Swedish Archaeology* 18 (2010): 79–103.

Burl, Aubrey. *Prehistoric Astronomy and Ritual.* Princes Risborough, UK: Shire, 1983.

———. *Prehistoric Avebury.* New Haven, CT: Yale University Press, 2002.

———. *Prehistoric Henges.* Princes Risborough, UK: Shire, 1991.

———. *Prehistoric Stone Circles.* Princes Risborough, UK: Shire, 2005.

———. *Rites of the Gods.* London: J. M. Dent & Sons, 1981.

———. *The Stone Circles of the British Isles.* New Haven, CT: Yale University Press, 1976.

———. *Stonehenge: A Complete History and Archaeology of the World's Most Enigmatic Stone Circle.* London: Constable & Robinson, 2007.

———. *The Stonehenge People.* London: Barrie & Jenkins, 1989.

Burnham, Andy. *The Old Stones: A Field Guide to the Megalithic Sites of Britain and Ireland.* London: Watkins, 2018.

Burrow, Steve. "Bryn Celli Ddu Passage Tomb Anglesey: Alignment, Construction, Date and Ritual." *Proceedings of the Prehistoric Society* 76 (2010): 249–70.

Card, Nick. "The Heart of Neolithic Orkney." *Current Archaeology* 199 (2005): 342–47.

———. "Neolithic Temples of the Northern Isles: Stunning New Discoveries in Orkney." *Current Archaeology* 241 (2010): 12–19.

Cassen, Serge. "Stelae Reused in the Passage Graves of Western France: History of Research and the Sexualization of the Carvings." In *Neolithic Orkney in Its European Context*, edited by A. Ritchie, 233–46. Cambridge, UK: McDonald Institute Monographs, 2000.

Cassen, Serge, Laurent Lescop, Valentin Grimaud, and Guilaume Robin. "Complementarity of Acquisition Techniques for the Documentation of Neolithic Engravings: Lasergrammetric and Photographic Recording in Gavrinis Passage Tomb." *Journal of Archaeological Science* 45 (2014): 126–40.

Catling, Chris. "Bluestonehenge." *Current Archaeology* 237 (2009): 22–28.

———. "Great Stone Circles." *Current Archaeology* 294 (2014): 20–27.

———. "Invasion, Colonisation or Imitation?" *Current Archaeology* 290 (2014): 18–25.

———. "Message in the Stones." *Current Archaeology* 212 (2007): 12–19.

———. "Poulnabrone's Portal Tomb: Honouring the Neolithic Dead." *Current Archaeology* 298 (2015): 20–27.

Chesson, Meredith S., ed. "Social Memory, Identity and Death: Anthropological Perspectives on Mortuary Rituals." *Archaeological Papers of the American Anthropological Association* 10 (2001): 1–133.

Cicciloni, Ricardo, and Marco Cabras. "GIS-Based Landscape Analysis of Megalithic Graves in the Island of Sardinia (Italy)." *Journal of Lithic Studies* 4 (2015): 1–23.

Clark, Geoffrey, and Christian Reepmeyer. "Stone Architecture, Monumentality and the Rise of the Early Tongan Chiefdom." *Antiquity* 88 (2014): 1244–60.

Clausen, Claus. "Neolithic Cosmology?" *Adoranten* (2014): 68–75.

Clifford, Elsie M. "The Excavation of Nympsfield Long Barrow, Gloucestershire." *Proceedings of the Prehistoric Society* 8 (1938): 188–213.

Cooijmans, Christian. "Between the Cracks: A Socio-historical Context of the Runic Inscriptions of Maes Howe, Orkney." BA thesis, Utrecht University, 2012.

Cooney, Gabriel. "Newgrange—a View from the Platform." *Antiquity* 80 (2006): 697–710.

———. "The Place of Megalithic Tomb Cemeteries in Ireland." *Antiquity* 64 (1990): 741–53.

Cummings, Vicki. "All Cultural Things: Actual and Conceptual Monuments in the Neolithic of Western Britain." In *Monuments and Landscape in Atlantic Europe: Perception and Society during the Neolithic and Early Bronze Age*, edited by Chris Scarre, 107–21. London: Routledge, 2002.

———. "Experiencing Texture and Transformation in the British Neolithic." *Oxford Journal of Archaeology* 21 (2002): 249–61.

Cummings, Vicki, and Chris Fowler, eds. *The Neolithic of the Irish Sea: Materiality and Traditions of Practice*. Oxford: Oxbow, 2004.

Cummings, Vicki, and Robert Johnson, eds. *Prehistoric Journeys*. Oxford: Oxbow Books, 2007.

Cummings, Vicki, Andrew Jones, and Aaron Watson. "Phenomenology and Asymmetry in the Monuments of the Black Mountains, Southeast Wales." *Cambridge Archaeological Journal* 12 (2002): 57–70.

Cummings, Vicki, and Alasdair Whittle. *Places of Special Virtue: Megaliths in the Neolithic Landscapes of Wales*. Oxford: Oxbow, 2004.

———. "Tombs with a View: Landscape, Monuments and Trees." *Antiquity* 77 (2003): 255–66.

Cummins, W. A. "The Neolithic Stone Axe Trade in Britain." *Antiquity* 48 (1974): 201–5.

Cunliffe, Barry. *Facing the Ocean: The Atlantic and Its Peoples, 8000 BC to AD 1500*. Oxford: Oxford University Press, 2004.

———, ed. *Prehistoric Europe: An Illustrated History*. Oxford: Oxford University Press, 1997.

Curt, Roslund. "Portuguese Passage Graves in the Light of the Easter Moon." *Fornvännen* 95 (2000): 1–12.

Daniel, Glyn. "The Chambered Barrow in Parc le Breos Cwm, S. Wales." *Proceedings of the Prehistoric Society* 3 (1937): 71–86.

Darvill, Timothy. "Afterworld: Dances beneath a Diamond Sky." In *Skyscapes: The Role and Importance of the Sky in Archaeology*, edited by Fabio Silva and Nicholas Campion, 140–48. Oxford: Oxbow, 2015.

———. "Houses of the Holy: Architecture and Meaning in the Structure of Stonehenge, Wiltshire, UK." *Time and Mind* 9 (2016): 89–121.

Darvill, Timothy, Peter Marshall, Mike Parker Pearson, and Geoff Wainwright. "Stonehenge Remodelled." *Antiquity* 86 (2012): 1021–40.

Darvill, Timothy, and Geoff Wainwright. "Beyond Stonehenge: Carn Menyn Quarry and the Origin and Date of Bluestone Extraction in the Preseli Hills of South-West Wales." *Antiquity* 88 (2014): 1099–114.

———. "SPACES—Exploring Neolithic Landscapes in the Strumble-Preseli Area of South-west Wales." *Antiquity* 76 (2002): 623–24.

Deguilloux, Marie-France, Ludovic Soler, Marie-Hélène Permonge, Chris Scarre, Roger Joussaume, and Luc Laporte. "News from the West: Ancient DNA from a French Megalithic Burial Chamber." *American Journal of Physical Anthropology* 144 (2011): 108–18.

Devereux Paul. "A Ceiling Painting in the Hal-Saflieni Hypogeum as Acoustically-Related Imagery: A Preliminary Report." *Time and Mind* 2 (2009): 225–32.

———. "Interview with Professor Timothy Darvill: The Magical Stones of Preseli." *Time and Mind* 1 (2008): 187–94.

Dronfield, Jeremy. "Entering Alternative Realties: Cognition, Art and Architecture in Irish Passage-Tombs." *Cambridge Archaeological Journal* 6 (1996): 37–72.

———. "Subjective Vision and the Source of Irish Megalithic Art." *Antiquity* 69 (1995): 539–49.

Edmonds, Mark, and Colin Richards. *Understanding the Neolithic in North-Western Europe*. Glasgow: Cruithne Press, 1998.

Eogan, George. "Megalithic Art and Society." *Proceedings of the Prehistoric Society* 65 (1999): 415–46.

Evans, John H. "Notes on the Folklore and Legends Associated with the Kentish Megaliths." *Folklore* 57 (1946): 36–43.

Fleming, Andrew. "Megaliths and Post-modernism: The Case of Wales." *Antiquity* 79 (2005): 921–32.

———. "The Myth of the Mother Goddess." *World Archaeology* 1 (1969): 247–61.

Forde-Johnston, J. L. "Megalithic Art in the North-West of Britain: The Calderstones: Liverpool." *Proceedings of the Prehistoric Society* 23 (1958): 20–39.

Fowler, Chris, and Vicki Cummings. "Places of Transformation: Building Monuments from Water and Stone in the Neolithic of the Irish Sea." *Journal of the Royal Anthropological Institute* 9 (2003): 1–20.

Gaffney, Vince, and Chris Gaffney. "Stonehenge's Hidden Landscape." *Current Archaeology* 296 (2014): 10–13.

García Sanjuan, Leonardo, Chris Scarre, and David W. Wheatley. "The Mega-site of Valencina de la Concepción (Seville, Spain): Debating Settlement Form, Monumentality and Aggregation in Southern Iberian Copper Age Societies." *Journal of World Prehistory* 30 (2017): 239–57.

Garnham, Trevor. *Lines on the Landscape, Circles from the Sky: Monuments of Neolithic Orkney*. Stroud, UK: Tempus, 2004.

Gillings, Mark, and Joshua Pollard. *Avebury*. London: Duckworth, 2004.

Gillings, Mark, Josh Pollard, and Rick Peterson. "Avebury." *British Archaeology* 103 (2008): 29–33.

Giot, P.-R. "The Chambered Barrow at Barnenez in Finistère." *Antiquity* 32 (1958): 233–46.

Gonzalez, Cesar A., and Lourdes Costa Ferrer. "Orientation of Megalithic Monuments in Germany and the Netherlands." *Mediterranean Archaeology and Archaeometry Special Issue* 6 (2006): 201–8.

Goodall, Peter. "Revealing Guernsey's Ancient History in Fact and Fiction." *Shima* 10 (2016): 118–28.

Green, Martin J., and Michael J. Allen. "An Early Prehistoric Shaft on Cranborne Chase." *Oxford Journal of Archaeology* 16 (1997): 121–32.

Griffiths, W. E. "The Excavation of Stone Circles near Penmaenmawr in North Wales." *Proceedings of the Prehistoric Society* 26 (1960): 303–40.

Grima, Reuben. "An Iconography of Insularity: A Cosmological Interpretation of Some Images and Spaces in the Late Neolithic Temples of Malta." *Papers from the Institute of Archaeology* 12 (2001): 48–65.

———. "Landscape, Territories, and the Life-Histories of Monuments in Temple Period Malta." *Journal of Mediterranean Archaeology* 21 (2008): 35–56.

Grimes, W. F. "The Excavation of Ty-Isaf Long Cairn Brecknockshire." *Proceedings of the Prehistoric Society* 5 (1939): 119–42.

———. "The Megalithic Monuments of Wales." *Proceedings of the Prehistoric Society* 2 (1936): 106–39.

Grinsell, L. V. "Folk-lore of Prehistoric Monuments: A Paper Read before the Society on March 17th, 1937." *Folklore* 48 (1937): 248–59.

Grinsell, Leslie. "The Naveta of El Tudons (Menorca)." *Antiquity* 55 (1981): 196–99.

Guilane, Jean, and Jean Zammit. *The Origins of War: Violence in Prehistory*. Oxford: Wiley-Blackwell, 2005.

Hadingham, Evan. *Early Man and the Cosmos*. London: William Heinemann, 1983.

Hall, S. C., and A. M. Hall, *Ireland: Its Scenery, Character, &c*. Vol. 3. London, 1841.

Harding, A. F. *European Societies in the Bronze Age*. Cambridge: Cambridge University Press, 2000.

Hawkes, Jaquetta. "God in the Machine." *Antiquity* 41 (1967): 174–80.

Hawkins, Gerald. "Stonehenge Computer." *British Archaeology* 74 (2004): 20–21.

Hayden, Brian. *Shamans, Sorcerers, and Saints: A Prehistory of Religion*. Washington, DC: Smithsonian Books, 2003.

Heath, Julian. *Sacred Circles: Prehistoric Stone Circles of Wales*. Pwllheli: Llygad Gwalch, 2010.

———. *Warfare in Neolithic Europe: An Archaeological and Anthropological Analysis*. Barnsley, UK: Pen & Sword, 2017.

Hencken, H. O' Neil. "A Long Cairn at Creevykeel, Co. Sligo." *Journal of the Royal Society of Antiquaries of Ireland* 9 (1939): 53–98.

Hensey, Robert. "The Observance of Light: A Ritualistic Perspective on 'Imperfectly Aligned' Passage Tombs." *Time and Mind* 1 (2008): 319–29. doi: 10.2752/175169708X329363.

Hensey, Robert, Pádraig Meehan, Marion Dowd, and Sam Moore. "A Century of Archaeology—Historical Excavation and Modern Research at the Carrowkeel Passage Tombs, County Sligo." *Proceedings of the Royal Irish Academy* 114C (2013): 1–31.

Holtorf, Cornelius. "The Life-Histories of Megaliths in Mecklenburg-Vorpommern (Germany)." *World Archaeology* 30 (1998): 28–38.

Hornsey, Richard. "The Grand Menhir Brisé: Megalithic Success or Failure?" *Oxford Journal of Archaeology* 6 (1987): 185–217.

Hoskin, Michael. "Orientations of Dolmens of Western Europe: Summary and Conclusions." *Journal for the History of Astronomy* 39 (2008): 507–14.

———. "Orientations of Neolithic Monuments of Brittany: The *Allées Couvertes*." *Journal for the History of Astronomy* 38 (2007): 493–501.

———. "Orientations of Neolithic Monuments of Brittany: The Early Dolmens." *Journal for the History of Astronomy* 38 (2007): 487–92.

Hoskin, Michael, Peter Hochsieder, and Doris Knösel, "The Orientations of the Taulas of Menorca (2): The Remaining Taulas." *Journal for the History of Astronomy* 31 (Archaeo-astronomy Supplement 15) (1990): 37–48.

Hutton, Ronald. *The Pagan Religions of the British Isles: Their Nature and Legacy.* London: Book Club Associates, 1991.

Insoll, Timothy. "Shrine Franchising and the Neolithic in the British Isles: Some Observations Based upon the Tallensi, Northern Ghana." *Cambridge Journal of Archaeology* 16 (2006): 223–38.

Jelly, Kevin, and George Nash. "New over Old: An Image-Based Reassessment of Le Dehus Passage Grave's 'Le Gardien Tombeau,' Guernsey." *Time and Mind* 9 (2016): 245–65.

John, Brian, Dyfed Ellis-Gruffydd, and John Downes. "Observations of the Supposed 'Neolithic Bluestone Quarry' at Craig Rhoysyfelin, Pembrokeshire." *Archaeology in Wales* 54 (2015): 139–48.

Jones, Andy M., and Graeme Kirkham. "From Landscape to Portable Art: The Changing Settings of Simple Rock Art in South-West Britain and Its Wider Context." *European Journal of Archaeology* 16 (2013): 636–59.

Jones, N. W. *The Neolithic Chambered Cairns of Breconshire.* Clwyd-Powys Archaeological Report No. 1126 (2012): 1–25.

Jorge, Ana. "Reconnecting the Late Neolithic Social Landscape: A Micro-Regional Study of Objects, Settlements and Tombs from Iberia." *European Journal of Archaeology* 17 (2014): 434–67.

Joussaume, Roger. *Dolmens for the Dead; Megalith Building throughout the World.* London: B. T. Batsford, 1988.

Kahn, Miriam. "Stone-Faced Ancestors: The Spatial Anchoring of Myth in Wamira, Papua New Guinea." *Ethnology* 29 (1990): 51–66.

Kalb, Philine. "Megalith-Building, Stone Transport and Territorial Markers: Evidence from Vale de Rodrigo, Evora, South Portugal." *Antiquity* 70 (1996): 683–85.

Keeley, Lawrence. *War before Civilization.* Oxford: Oxford University Press, 1996.

Kent, E. J. "Ancient Memories: Standing Stones and Ritual Landscapes." *Australian Folklore* 30 (2015): 37–47.

Killick, Sean. "Neolithic Landscapes and Experience: The Medway Megaliths." *Archaeologia Cantiana* 130 (2010): 339–49.

Kinnes, Ian. "Les Fouaillages and Megalithic Origins." *Antiquity* 56 (1982): 24–29.

———. "Monumental Function in British Neolithic Burial Practices." *World Archaeology* 7 (1975): 16–29.

Kinnes, Ian, and James Hobbs. "Le Gardien du Tombeau: Further Reflections on the Initial Neolithic." *Oxford Journal of Archaeology* 8 (1989): 159–66.

Kirch, P. V. "Monumental Architecture and Power in Polynesian Chiefdoms: A Comparison of Tonga and Hawaii." *World Archaeology* 22 (1990): 206–22.

Kjærum, Poul. "Mortuary Houses and Funeral Rites in Denmark." *Antiquity* 25 (1967): 190–96.

Kohring, Shiela. "Materiality, Technology, and Constructing Social Knowledge through Bodily Representation: A View from Prehistoric Guernsey." *European Journal of Archaeology* 17 (2014): 248–63.

Kolb, Michael J. "The Genesis of Monuments among the Mediterranean Islands." In *The Archaeology of Mediterranean Prehistory*, edited by Emma Blake and A. Bernard Knapp, 156–79. Oxford: Blackwell, 2005.

Laporte, Luc, and Chris Scare, eds. *The Megalithic Architectures of Europe*. Oxford: Oxbow, 2016.

Laporte, Luc, and Jean-Yves Tinévez. "Neolithic Houses and Chambered Tombs of Western France." *Cambridge Archaeological Journal* 14 (2004): 217–34.

Large, Jean-Marc, and Emmanuel Mens. "The Douet Alignment on the Island of Hoedic (Morbihan, France): New Insights into Standing Stone Alignments in Brittany." *Oxford Journal of Archaeology* 28 (2009): 239–54.

Le Cont, David. "Orientations of Channel Islands Megalithic Tombs." *Journal for the History of Astronomy* 34 (2008): 497–506.

Le Roux, Charles-Tanguy. "New Excavations at Gavrinis." *Antiquity* 59 (1985): 183–87.

Lewis, A. L. "On Some Rude Stone Monuments in Wales." *Journal of the Anthropological Institute of Great Britain and Ireland* 7 (1878): 118–23.

Lewis-Williams, David, and David Pearce. *Inside the Neolithic Mind*. London: Thames & Hudson, 2005.

Lillios, Katina, ed. *Comparative Archaeologies: The American Southwest (AD 900–600) and the Iberian Peninsula (3000–1500 BC)*. Oxford: Oxbow, 2011.

———. "Lives of Stone, Lives of People: Re-viewing the Engraved Plaques of Late Neolithic and Copper Age Iberia." *European Journal of Archaeology* 7 (2004): 125–28.

Lillios, Katina T., and Vasileios Tsamis, eds. *Material Mnemonics: Everyday Memory in Prehistoric Europe*. Oxford: Oxbow, 2010.

Lodolo, Emanuele, and Zvi Ben-Avraham. "A Submerged Monolith in the Sicilian Channel: Evidence for Mesolithic Human Activity." *Journal of Archaeological Science: Reports* 3 (2015): 398–407.

Lozano, José Antonio, Gerardo Luiz-Puertas, Manuel Hódar-Correa, Fernando Pérez-Valera, and Antonio Morgado. "Prehistoric Engineering and Astronomy of the Great Menga Dolmen (Málaga, Spain): A Geometric and Geoarchaeological Analysis." *Journal of Archaeological Science* 41 (2014): 759–71.

Lynch, Ann. "Poulnabrone: A Stone in Time . . . " *Archaeology Ireland* 2 (1998): 105–7.

Lynch, Frances. *Megalithic Tombs and Long Barrows in Britain*. Princes Risborough, UK: Shire, 1997.

Lynch, Frances, Stephen Aldhouse-Green, and Jeffrey L. Davies. *Prehistoric Wales*. Stroud, UK: Sutton, 2000.

Mackie, Euan W. "Maeshowe and the Winter Solstice: Ceremonial Aspects of the Grooved Ware Culture." *Antiquity* 71 (1997): 338–59.

———. *The Megalith Builders*. London: Book Club Associates, 1977.

Malone, Caroline. "Metaphor and Maltese Art: Explorations in the Temple Period." *Journal of Mediterranean Archaeology* 21 (2008): 81–109.

Malone, Caroline, Anthony Bonanno, Tancred Gouder, Simon Stoddart, and David Trump. "The Death Cults of Prehistoric Malta." *Scientific American* 269 (1993): 110–17.

———. "The Death Cults of Prehistoric Malta." *Scientific American, Special Edition* 15 (2005): 21.

Malone, Caroline, and Simon Stoddart. "Excavations in Gozo, 1987–94." *Malta Archaeological Review* 1 (1996): 2–5.

Malone, Caroline, Simon Stoddart, Anthony Bonanno, Tancred Gouder, and David Trump. "Mortuary Ritual of 4th Millennium BC Malta: The Zeebug Period Chambered Tomb from the Brochtorff Circle, Xaghra." *Proceedings of the Prehistoric Society* 61 (1995): 303–45.

Márquez Romero, José, and Juan Fernández Ruiz. *The Dolmens of Antequera: Official Guide to the Archaeological Complex*. Seville: Junta de Andalucía Consejeria de Cultura, 2009.

Marshall, Steve. "Acoustics of the West Kennet Long Barrow, Avebury, Wiltshire." *Time and Mind* 9 (2016): 43–56.

Masset, Claude. "The Megalithic Tomb of La-Chaussée Tirancourt." *Antiquity* 46 (1972): 297–300.

Masters, Lionel. "The Excavation and Restoration of the Camster Long Chambered Cairn, Caithness, Highland, 1967–80." *Proceedings of the Society of Antiquaries of Scotland* 127 (1997): 123–83.

McGuiness, David. "Druids' Altars, Carrowmore and the Birth of Irish Archaeology." *Journal of Irish Archaeology* 19 (2010): 29–49.

McMann, Jean. "Forms of Power: Dimensions of an Irish Megalithic Landscapes." *Antiquity* 68 (1994): 525–44.

Mees, Kate. "From the Sublime to the Druidical: Changing Perceptions of Prehistoric Monuments in Southern Anglesey during the Post-Medieval Period." *Post-Medieval Archaeology* 47 (2013): 222–46.

Michell, John. *A Little History of Astro-Archaeology*. London: Thames & Hudson, 1989.

———. *Megalithomania: Artists and Antiquarians at the Old Stone Monuments*. Glastonbury, UK: Squeeze Press, 2007.

Midgley, Magdalena, S., ed. *Antiquarians at the Megaliths*. International Series 1956. Oxford: British Archaeological Reports, 2009.

———. "Monuments and Monumentality: The Cosmological Model of the World of the Megaliths." *Documenta Praehistorica* 37 (2010): 55–64.

Mohen, Jean-Pierre. *Standing Stones: Stonehenge, Carnac and the World of Megaliths*. London: Thames & Hudson, 1999.

Mohen, Jean-Pierre, and Christiane Eluère. *The Bronze Age in Europe: Gods, Heroes and Treasures*. London: Thames & Hudson, 2000.

Morner, Nils-Axel, and Bob G. Lind. "Stonehenge Has Got a Younger Sister—Ales Stones in Sweden Decoded." *International Journal of Astronomy and Astrophysics* 2 (2012): 23–27.

Munro, Robert. "Megalithic Monuments of Holland and Their Relation with Analogous Remains in Northern Europe." *Proceedings of the Society of Antiquaries of Scotland* 18 (1884): 19–35.

Murphy, Eileen M. "Children's Burial Grounds in Ireland (Cillini) and Parental Emotions toward Infant Death." *International Journal of Historical Archaeology* 15 (2011): 409–28.

Nash, George. "Light at the End of the Tunnel: The Way Megalithic Art Was Viewed and Experienced." *Documenta Praehistorica* 33 (2006): 209–27.

———. "The Symbolic Use of Fire: A Case for Its Use in the Late Neolithic Passage Grave Tradition in Wales." *Time and Mind* 1 (2008): 143–58.

Nash, George, and Adam Stanford. "New Megalithic Art within the Neolithic Passage Grave of Barclodiad y Gawres, Anglesey, North Wales." *Rock Art Research* 24 (2007): 257–60.

O'Connor, Blaze, Gabriel Cooney, and John Chapman, eds. *Materialitas: Working Stone, Carving Identity*. Prehistoric Society Research Paper 3. Oxford: Oxbow, 2010.

O'Kelly, M. J. "The Restoration of Newgrange." *Antiquity* 53 (1979): 205–10.

O'Sullivan, M. "Megalithic Tombs and Storied Landscapes in Neolithic Ireland." Paper of the European Megalithic Studies Group, August 23, 2010, 1–18.

Oliver, Neil. *A History of Ancient Britain*. London: Weidenfeld & Nicolson, 2011.

Pace, Anthony. *The Hal Saflieni Hypogeum, Paola*. Malta: Heritage Books, 2004.

———. *The Tarxien Temples, Tarxien*. Malta: Heritage Books, 2010.

Parker Pearson, Mike. *Bronze Age Britain*. London: Batsford, 1993.

Parker Pearson, Mike, Richard Bevins, Rob Ixer, Joshua Pollard, Colin Richards, Kate Welham, Ben Chan, Kevan Edingborough, Derek Hamilton, Richard Macphail, Duncan Schlee, Jean-Luc Schwenninger, Ellen Simmons, and Martin Smith. "Craig Rhos-y-felin: A Welsh Bluestone Megalithic Quarry for Stonehenge." *Antiquity* 89 (2015): 1331–52.

Parker Pearson, M., J. Pollard, C. Richards, D. Schlee, and K. Welham. "In Search of the Stonehenge Quarries." *British Archaeology* 146 (2016): 16–23.

Parker Pearson, Mike, and Ramilisonina. "Stonehenge for the Ancestors: The Stones Pass on the Message." *Antiquity* 72 (1998): 308–26.

Parker Pearson, Mike, Colin Richards, Kate Welham, Chris Caswell, Charles French, Duncan Schlee, Dave Shaw, Ellen Simmons, Adam Stanford, Richard Bevins, and Rob Ixer. "Megalith Quarries for Stonehenge's Bluestones." *Antiquity* 93 (2019): 45–62.

Paschou, Peristera, Petros Drineas, Evangelia Yannaki, Anna Razou, Katerina Kanaki, Fotis Tsetsos, Shanmukha Sampath Padmanabhuni, Manolis Michalodimitrakis, Maria C. Renda, Sonja Pavlovic, Achilles Anagnostopoulos, John A. Stamatoyannopoulos, Kenneth K. Kidd, and George Stamatoyannopoulos. "Maritime Route of Colonization of Europe." *Proceedings of the National Academy of Sciences* 111 (2014): 9211–16.

Patton, Mark. "Megalithic Transport and Territorial Markers: Evidence from the Channel Islands." *Antiquity* 66 (1992): 392–95.

———. "Neolithisation and Megalithic Origins in North-Western France: A Regional Interaction Model." *Oxford Journal of Archaeology* (1994): 279–93.

———. "On Entopic Images in Context: Art, Monuments and Society in Neolithic Brittany." *Current Anthropology* 31 (1990): 554–58.

———. *Statements in Stone: Monuments and Society in Neolithic Brittany*. New York: Routledge, 1993.

Paulsson, B. Schulz. "Radiocarbon Dates and Bayesian Modeling Support Maritime Diffusion Model for Megaliths in Europe." *Proceedings of the National Academy of Sciences of the United States of America* 116, no. 9 (2019): 3460–65. https://doi.org/10.1073/pnas.1813268116.

Piggott, Stuart. "A Saint in a Stone Circle." *Antiquity* (Notes & News) 47 (1973): 292–93.

———. "The Excavation of the West Kennet Long Barrow: 1955–56." *Antiquity* 32 (1958): 235–42.

Piggott, Stuart, and T. G. E. Powell. "The Excavation of Three Neolithic Chambered Cairns in Galloway, 1949." *Proceedings of the Society of Antiquaries of Scotland* 83(1949): 103–61.

Pili, P., E. Realini, D. Sampietro, M. P. Zedda, E. Franzoni, and G. Magli. "Topographical and Astronomical Analysis of the Neolithic 'Altar' of Monte d'Accodi in Sardinia." *Mediterranean Archaeology and Astronomy* 9 (2009): 61–69.

Pimenta, Fernando, and Luis Tirpicos. "The Orientations of Central Alentejo Megalithic Enclosures." *Archaeologia Baltica* 10: 239–40.

Pitts, Mike. *Hengeworld*. London: Arrow, 2001.

———. "Stonehenge without Borders." *British Archaeology* 160 (2018): 20–35.

Pollard, Joshua. *Neolithic Britain.* Princes Risborough, UK: Shire, 1997.

Powell, Andrew B. "Newgrange—Science or Symbolism." *Proceedings of the Prehistoric Society* 60 (1994): 85–96.

Powell, T. G. E. "The Chambered Cairn at Dyffryn Ardudwy." *Antiquity* 37 (1963): 19–24.

Powell, T. G. E., J. X. W. P. Corcoran, Frances Lynch, and J. G. Scott. *Megalithic Enquiries in the West of Britain.* Liverpool, UK: Liverpool University Press, 1969.

Prendergast, Frank. "The Loughcrew Hills and Passage Tomb Complex." In *Field Guide No. 29—North Meath,* edited by B. Stefanini and G. M. Glynn, 42–54. Dublin: Irish Quaternary Association, 2011.

Prendergast, Kate. "Knowth Passage-Grave in Ireland: An Instrument of Precision Astronomy?" *Journal of Lithic Studies* 4 (2017): 67–76.

Pyror, Francis. *Britain bc: Life in Britain and Ireland before the Romans.* London: HarperCollins, 2003.

Quinn, Colin P. "Returning and Reuse: Diachronic Perspectives on Multi-component Cemeteries and Mortuary Politics at Middle Neolithic and Early Bronze Age Tara, Ireland." *Journal of Anthropological Archaeology* 37 (2015): 1–18.

Ravillious, Kate. "Neolithic Europe's Remote Heart." *Archaeology* 66 (2013): 39–44.

Recchia, Giulia. "Burial Mounds and 'Specchie' in Apulia during the Bronze Age: Local Developments and Transadriatic Connections." In *Ancestral Landscapes: Burial Mounds in the Copper and Bronze Ages (Central and Eastern Europe–Balkans–Adriatic–Aegean, 4th–2nd millennium B.C.): Proceedings of the International Conference Held in Udine, May 15–18, 2008,* edited by Elisabetta Borgna, 475–84. Lyon: Maison de l'Orient de la Méditerranée Jean Pouilloux, 2012.

Reed, Robert. "Irish Court Tombs: A Minimal Colonisation Model." *Journal of Irish Archaeology* 4 (1987/1988): 1–6.

Renfrew, Colin. *Before Civilization: The Radiocarbon Revolution and Prehistoric Europe.* London: Pimilico, 1999.

———. "Colonialism and Megalithismus." *Antiquity* 41 (1967): 276–88.

———. "The Social Archaeology of Megalithic Monuments." *Scientific American* 249 (1983): 152–63.

Reynolds, Ffion, Seren Griffiths, Ben Edwards, and Adam Stanford. "Bryn Celli Ddu: Exploring a Hidden Ritual Landscape." *Current Archaeology* 310 (2016): 20–24.

Richards, Colin, ed. *Building the Great Stone Circles of the North.* Oxford: Windgather Press, 2013.

———. "The Great Stone Circles Project." *British Archaeology* 81 (2005): 16–21.

———. "Monuments as Landscape: Creating the Centre of the World in Late Neolithic Orkney." *World Archaeology* 28 (1996): 190–208.

Robb, John. "Island Identities: Ritual, Travel and the Creation of Difference in Neolithic Malta." *European Journal of Archaeology* 4 (2001): 175–202.

———. "People of Stone: Stelae, Personhood, and Society in Prehistoric Europe." *Journal of Archaeological Method and Theory* 16 (2009): 162–83.

Roberts, Jack. "The Brú Na Boinne: The Great Passage Cairns and Prehistoric Art of the Boyne Valley." *Adoranten* (2015): 44–65.

———. "The Sun Circles of Ireland." *Adoranten* (2014): 76–87.

Robin, G. "Art and Death in Late Neolithic Sardinia: The Role of Carvings and Paintings in Domus de Janas Rock-Cut Tombs." *Cambridge Archaeological Journal* 26 (2016): 429–69.

Robin, Guillaume. "Spatial Structures and Symbolic Systems in Irish and British Passage Tombs: The Organization of Architectural Elements, Parietal Carved Signs and Funerary Deposits." *Cambridge Archaeological Journal* 20 (2010): 373–418.

Rojo-Guerra, A., Rafael Garrido-Pena, and Iñigo García-Martínez de Lagran. "Tombs for the Dead, Monuments to Eternity: The Deliberate Destruction of Megalithic Graves by Fire in the Interior Highlands of Iberia (Soria Province, Spain)." *Oxford Journal of Archaeology* 29 (2010): 253–75.

Roslund, Curt, Yasmine Kristiansen, and Birgitta Hårdh. "Portuguese Passage Graves in the Light of the Easter Moon." *Fornvännen* 95 (2000): 1–12.

Scarre, Chris. "A Pattern of Islands: The Neolithic Monuments of North-West Brittany." *European Journal of Archaeology* 5 (2002): 24–41.

———. "Consolidation, Reconstruction and the Interpretation of Megalithic Monuments." *Arkeos* 16 (2006): 13–44.

———. "Contexts of Monumentalism: Regional Diversity at the Neolithic Transition in North-West France." *Oxford Journal of Archaeology* 21 (2002): 23–61.

———. "The Early Neolithic of Western France and Megalithic Origins in Atlantic Europe." *Oxford Journal of Archaeology* 11 (1992): 121–53.

———. *Landscapes of Neolithic Brittany.* Oxford Scholarship Online, Oxford University Press, 2015. doi:10.1093/acprof:osobl/9780/99281626.001.0001.

———. "Megaliths, Memory and the Power of Stones." In *Monumental Questions: Prehistoric Megaliths, Mounds and Enclosures*, edited by David Calado, 91–96. Oxford: Archaeopress, 2010.

———, ed. *Monuments and Landscape in Atlantic Europe: Perception and Society during the Neolithic and Early Bronze Age.* London: Routledge, 2002.

Scarre, Chris, Luc Laporte, and Roger Joussaume. "Long Mounds and Megalithic Origins in Western France: Recent Excavations at Prissé-la-Charrière." *Proceedings of the Prehistoric Society* 69 (2003): 235–51.

Scarre, Chris, Roy Switsur, and Jean-Pierre Mohen. "New Radiocarbon Dates from Bougon and the Chronology of French Passage Graves." *Antiquity* 67 (1993): 856–59.

Schulting, Rick J. "Antlers, Bone Pins and Flint Blades: The Mesolithic Cemeteries of Téviec and Hoëdic, Brittany." *Antiquity* 70 (1996): 335–50.

Schulting, Rick. J., Heather Sebire, and John E. Robb. "On the Road to Paradis: New Insights from AMS Dates and Stable Isotopes at Le Déhus, Guernsey, and the Channel Islands Middle Neolithic." *Oxford Journal of Archaeology* 29 (2010): 149–73.

Schulting, Rick, Alison Sheridan, Stephen Clarke, and Chris Bronk Ramsey. "Largantea and the Dating of Irish Wedge Tombs." *Journal of Irish Archaeology* 17 (2008): 1–17.

Schulting, Rick, Alison Sheridan, Rebecca Crozier, and Eileen Murphy. "Revisiting Quanterness: New AMS Dates and Stable Isotope Data from an Orcadian Neolithic Tomb." *Proceedings of the Society of Antiquaries of Scotland* 140 (2010): 1–50.

Schulting, Rick J., and Michael Wysocki. "'In This Chambered Tumulus Were Found Cleft Skulls . . .': An Assessment of the Evidence for Cranial Trauma in the British Neolithic." *Proceedings of the Prehistoric Society* 71 (2005): 107–38.

Service, Alastair, and Jean Bradbery. *A Guide to the Megaliths of Europe.* London: Granada, 1981.

Sharkey, John. *The Meeting of the Tracks: Rock Art in Ancient Wales.* Llanrwst, UK: Gwasg Carreg Gwalch, 2004.

Sharples, Niall. "Individual and Community: The Changing Role of Megaliths in the Orcadian Neolithic." *Proceedings of the Prehistoric Society* 51 (1985): 59–74.

Shee Twohig, Elizabeth, and Margaret Ronayne, eds. *Past Perceptions: The Prehistoric Archaeology of South-West Ireland.* Cork, IE: Cork University Press, 1993.

Sheridan, Alison. "Achnacreebeag and Its French Connections: Vive the 'Auld Alliance.'" In *The Prehistory and Early History of Atlantic Europe*, edited by J. C. Henderson, 1–15. British Archaeological Reports International Series 861. Oxford: Archaeopress, 2000.

———. "Megaliths and Megalomania: An Account and Interpretation of the Development of Passage Tombs in Ireland." *Journal of Irish Archaeology* 3 (1985/1986): 17–30.

———. "The Neolithization of Britain and Ireland: The 'Big Picture.'" In *Landscapes in Transition*, edited by Bill Finlayson and Graeme Warren, 89–105. Oxford: Oxbow, 2010.

Sherratt, Andrew. "The Genesis of Megaliths: Monumentality, Ethnicity and Social Complexity in Neolithic North-West Europe." *World Archaeology* 22 (1990): 147–67.

———. "Instruments of Conversion? The Role of Megaliths in the Mesolithic/Neolithic Transition in North-West Europe." *Oxford Journal of Archaeology* 14 (1995): 245–60.

Silva, Fabio. "A Tomb with a View: New Methods for Bridging the Gap between Landscape and Sky in Megalithic Archaeology." *Advances in Archaeological Practice* (2014): 24–37.

Sims, Lionel. "The Solarization of the Moon: Manipulated Knowledge at Stonehenge." *Cambridge Archaeological Journal* 16 (2006): 191–207.

Skeates, Robin. "Axe Aesthetics: Stone Axes and Visual Culture in Prehistoric Malta." *Oxford Journal of Archaeology* 21 (2002): 13–22.

———. "Making Sense of the Maltese Temple Period: An Archaeology of Sensory Perception." *Time and Mind* 1 (2008): 207–38.

Smith, George, Astrid E. Caseldine, Catherine J. Griffiths, Frances Lynch, and Genevieve Tellier. "The Bryn-Gwyn Stone Circle, Brynsiencyn, Anglesey." Gwynedd Archaeologica Trust Report No. 1174, July 2013, 1–19.

Souden, David. *Stonehenge: Mysteries of the Stones and Landscape.* London: Collins & Brown, 1997.

Sterling Saletta, Morgan. "The Arles-Fontvieille Megalithic Monuments: Astronomy and Cosmology in the European Neolithic." PhD dissertation, University of Melbourne, 2014.

Stoddart, Simon, Anthony Bonanno, Tancred Goulder, Caroline Malone, and David Trump. "Cult in an Island Society: Prehistoric Malta in the Tarxien Period." *Cambridge Archaeological Journal* 3 (1993): 35–56.

Sundstrom, Linea. "Mirror of Heaven: Cross-Cultural Transference of the Sacred Geography of the Black Hills." *World Archaeology* 28 (1996): 177–89.

Taçon, Paul S. C. "The Power of Stone: Symbolic Aspects of Stone Use and Tool Development in Arnhem Land, Australia." *Antiquity* 65 (1991): 192–207.

Tarabella, Natalia, Paolo Debertolis, Randa Romero, and Giovanni Feo. "Archaeoacoustic Analysis of Poggio Rota Stone Circle in Tuscany." In *Proceedings of the 21st International Conference and Assembly of the Experts of the Foundation Romualdo Del Bianco "HERITAGE FOR PLANET EARTH 2019—Heritage as a Builder of Peace," Florence, Italy, March 1–3, 2019.*

Taunt, Henry W. *The Rollright Stones of Oxfordshire.* Oxford: Henry W. Taunt, 1907.

Thomas, Julian. "Monuments from the Inside: The Case of the Irish Megalithic Tombs." *World Archaeology* 22 (1990): 168–78.

———. "The Social Significance of Cotswold-Severn Burial Practices." *Man* 23 (1998): 540–59.

Thomas, Julian, and Alasdair Whittle. "Anatomy of a Tomb—West Kennet Revisited." *Oxford Journal of Archaeology* 5 (1986): 129–56.

Thompson, Aaron, trans. *Geoffrey of Monmouth: History of the Kings of Britain*. Ontario: In Parentheses Publications, Medieval Latin Series, 1999.

Thorpe, Richard S., Olwen Williams-Thorpe, D. Graham-Jenkins, and J. S. Watson. "The Geological Sources and Transport of the Bluestones of Stonehenge, Wiltshire, UK." *Proceedings of the Prehistoric Society* 57 (1991): 103–57.

Tilley, Christopher. "The Power of Rocks: Topography and Monument Construction on Bodmin Moor." *World Archaeology* 28 (1996): 161–76.

Trevarthen, David. "Illuminating the Monuments: Observation and Speculation on the Structure and Function of the Cairns at Balnuaran of Clava." *Cambridge Archaeological Journal* 10 (2000): 295–315.

Trump, David H. *Malta: Prehistory and Temples*. Malta: Midsea, 2008.

Waddell, John. "The Irish Sea in Prehistory." *Journal of Irish Archaeology* 6 (1991): 29–40.

———. *The Prehistoric Archaeology of Ireland*. Bray, UK: Wordwell, 2000.

Waldren, W. H., J. A. Ensenyat, and R. C. Kennard, eds. *Ritual, Rites and Religion in Prehistory: IIIrd Deya International Conference of Prehistory*. Vols. 1 and 2. British Archaeological Reports, International Series 611. Oxford: Archaeopress, 1995.

Was, John, and Aaron Watson. "Neolithic Monuments: Sensory Technology." *Time and Mind* 10 (2017): 3–22.

Watson, Aaron. "Composing Avebury." *World Archaeology* 33 (2001): 296–314.

Wheatley, David W., Leonardo García Sanjuán, Patricia A. Murrieta Flores, and Joáquin Márquez Pérez. "Approaching the Landscape Dimension of the Megalithic Phenomenon in Southern Spain." *Oxford Journal of Archaeology* 29 (2010): 387–405.

Whitehouse, Ruth D. "The Megalithic Monuments of South-East Italy." *Man* 2 (1967): 342–65.

———. "The Rock-Cut Tombs of the Mediterranean." *Antiquity* 46 (1972): 275–81.

Whittle, Alasdair. "The Neolithic of the Avebury Area: Sequence, Environment, Settlement and Monuments." *Oxford Journal of Archaeology* 12 (1993): 29–53.

———. "Wayland's Smithy, Oxfordshire: Excavations at the Neolithic Tomb in 1962–1963 by R. J. C. Atkinson and S. Piggott." *Proceedings of the Prehistoric Society* 57, no. 2 (1991): 61–101.

———. *Europe in the Neolithic: The Creation of New Worlds*. Cambridge: Cambridge University Press, 1996.

———. *Sacred Mound Holy Rings: Silbury Hill and the West Kennet Palisade Enclosures: A Later Neolithic Complex in North Wiltshire*. Oxford: Oxbow, 2007.

Whittle, Alasdair, Alex Bayliss, and Michael Wysocki. "Once in a Lifetime: The Date of the Wayland's Smithy Long Barrow." *Cambridge Archaeological Journal* 17 (2007): 103–21.

Whittle, Alasdair, and Michael Wysocki. "Parc le Breos Cwm Transepted Long Cairn, Gower, West Glamorgan: Date, Contents, and Context." *Proceedings of the Prehistoric Society* 64 (1998): 139–82.

Woolner, Diane. "Graffiti of Ships at Tarxien, Malta." *Antiquity* 31 (1957): 60–67.

Wysocki, Michael, Seren Griffiths, Robert Hedges, Alex Bayliss, Tom Higham, Yolanda Fernandez-Jalvo, and Alasdair Whittle. "Dates, Diet, and Dismemberment: Evidence from the Coldrum Megalithic Monument, Kent." *Proceedings of the Prehistoric Society* 79 (2013): 61–90.

Zammit, T., T. Eric Peet, and R. N. Bradley. *The Small Objects and Human Skulls Found in the Hal-Saflieni Hypogeum at Casal Paula, Malta* (Second Report). Malta, 1912.

Index

Aboriginal peoples, Australia, 2, 54
Achnacreebeag passage grave, 177–78, 179
Achnacree passage grave, 179–80
Aldebaran, 53, 54
Ales Stenar megalithic ship setting, Sweden, 197–99, *198*
allée couvertes (gallery graves), 15, 26–27, 34, 35, 38–39, 43, 67, 68, 158, 196
Almendres Cromlech, 48–49, *49*, 51
Altar Wedge Tomb, Ireland, 159–61, *160*
Alto Alentejo region. *See* Évora district, Portugal
Anasazi people, American Southwest, 81, 213n12
Andalusia, Spain, 41, 45, 46
Anderson, Joseph, 173
Anglesey, Wales, 14, 90, 131, 139, 140
arc boutée, megalithic tombs, Brittany, 27
archaeoastronomy, 143
Arran, Isle of, Scotland, 175
arrowheads, 46, 47, 67, 103, 119, 122, 137, 141, 162, 192, 209n10
Arzon, Brittany, 30
Askeberga megalithic ship setting, Sweden, 221n7
Atkinson, Richard, 101, 119, 121, 122, 136
Aubrey, John, 104, 117–18, 121, 159, 215n4
Avebury circle henge, England, 10, 11, 83, 95, *96*, 96–103, *97*, *98*, *101*, 214n1, 215n4, 215n7; "barber-surgeon" of, 101–2; Beckhampton Avenue, 100, 214n2

Axel-Mörner, Nils, 199
axe motifs, 19, 30, 106
axe-plow motif, 24
axes: bronze, 106; copper, 46; stone, 18, 19, 20, 21, 22, 26, 30, 44, 50, 51, 67, 81–82, 85, 88, 92, 125, 158, 175, 176, 177, 189, 207n7, 213n15

Bach Wen dolmen, Wales, 133, *134*
Ballynoe stone circle, Ireland, 88
Balnuaran of Clava, Scotland, cairns of, 178–79, *179*
Barclodiad y Gawres passage grave, Wales, 139, 143–44, 218n14
Barnenez cairn, Brittany, 24, 26, 27
Barnhouse Stone, Orkney Islands, Scotland, 165, 219n3
Barry, George, 170
Bayer, John Otto, 57, 61
Beaker culture, 26, 36, 104, 117, 132, 184, 209n10
Bear Butte, America, 2
Bedd Arthur bluestone oval, Wales, 110, *110*
Belas Knap long barrow, England, 115, *116*
Beltaine Celtic festival, 88
Beltany Tops stone circle, Ireland, 87–88, *87*
Berg, Håkon, 192
Bisceglie gallery grave, Italy, 38–39
Blacket, W. S., 111
Black Mountains, Wales, 136, 137, 138
Blieskastler Mountain, Germany, 181

Boas, Franz, 2
Boehlau, Johannes, 186
Bøgo, Denmark, 6
Bohuslän, Sweden, 196
Bonnanaro culture, Sardinia, 68
Borger *hunebed*, Holland, 189–90, *190*
Boscawen-un stone circle, Cornwall,
    7, 106
Bougon necropolis, France, 31, *32*
Boyne Valley, Ireland, 139, 151
Brennan, Martin, 153
Bricklieve Mountains, Ireland, 155
Broceliande forest, Brittany, 14
Brochtorff, Charles, 61
Brochtorff Circle. *See* Xagħra Circle, Gozo
Brodgar. *See* Ring of Brodgar stone circle,
    Orkney Islands
Brongserma, Titia, 189, 190
Bronze Age, 4, 35, 39, 68, 75, 82, 89, 91, 93,
    100, 106, 137, 138, 149, 155, 161, 175,
    176, 181, 182, 199, 210n2, 212n4, 215n5,
    215n12, 221n7
Brownshill dolmen, Ireland, 219n15
Bruzelius, Magnus, 197
Bryn Cader Faner stone circle/cairn, Wales,
    91–92, *92*
Bryn Celli Ddu passage grave, Wales, 138–43,
    140, *142*
Bryn Gwyn stone circle, Wales, 90–91, *91*
Burenhult, Göran, 157
Burl, Aubrey, 93, 96, 138
Burren, Ireland, 161, 162, 163
Burrow, Steve, 143

Cairnholy I and II, Clyde-Carlingford
    cairns, Scotland, *174*, 174–75, *175*
Calderstones passage grave, Liverpool, 145
Callanish stone circle, Isle of Lewis,
    Scotland, 78–79, *79*
Camden, William, 10
Camster Long and Camster Round stalled
    cairns, Scotland, *172*, 173–74
Carnac alignments, Brittany, 17–19, 181
Carnbane Hills, Ireland, 155
Carn Goedog, Wales, 108, 109, 110
Carn Ingli, Wales, 135
Carn Meini ridge, Wales, 90

Carn Menyn, Wales, 107–8, *108*, 109–10,
    110, 111–12, *112*
Carreg Coetan dolmen, Wales, *132*
Carreg Lleidr standing stone, Wales, 14
Carreg Samson passage grave, Wales, 139
Carrowkeel passage tomb complex, Ireland,
    154, 155–56
Carrowmore passage tomb complex, Ireland,
    154, 156–57
Castlerigg stone circle, Lake District,
    England, 81–82, *82*
Câtel menhir, Guernsey, Channel Islands,
    128, *129*
Cauria I and IV statue menhirs, Corsica, 71
Cefn Coch, Wales, 92
Chaco Canyon, New Mexico, 213n12
Champ Dolent menhir, Brittany, 28, *28*
Childe, Vere Gordon, 170
Christians, destruction of megaliths, 4, 124
Chumash people, California, 2
cíllin/cíllini (children's burial grounds),
    Ireland, 158–59
circle henges, 95, 140
cist graves, 20, 35, 36–37
Clausen, Claus, 191
Clava cairns, Scotland, 178
Coddu Vecchiu giants' grave, Sardinia,
    68, *69*
Coldrum long barrow, England, 124
Comenda da Igreja passage grave, Portugal,
    50, 50–51
Constable, John, 11, *12*
Copper Age, 4
Cotswold-Severn long barrows, England
    and Wales, 115, 136–37, 138
Craig Rhos-y-felin, Wales, 109, 110
Creevykeel court tomb, Ireland, 158–59
crook motifs, 8, 24, 29, 48, 51, 107
Cuíl Ira peninsula, Ireland, 156
Cunnington, William, 138
cupmarks, 51, 80, 88, 89, 112, 126, 133, 139,
    145, 198

Dahl, Johan, Christian, 11
Daniel, Glyn, 143
Darvill, Timothy, 109, 110, 111–12
de Rais, Gille, 13

de Robien, Christophe-Paul, 11
Djursland peninsula, Denmark, 191, 194
Dolmen da Orca, Portugal, 53
Dolmens Angevin, France, 26
domus de janus rock-cut tombs, Sardinia,
  68–69
Dowth Hall passage grave, Ireland, 151,
  153–54
Drax, Colonel Edward, 100
Dromberg stone circle, Ireland, 89, *89*
Druids' Circle, Wales, 92–94, *93*
Dyffryn Ardudwy megalithic tomb, Wales,
  132, *133*

Easter Aquhorthies recumbent stone circle,
  Scotland, 80
East Kennet long barrow, England, 116
écusson motif, 26
El Romeral dolmen, Spain, 43–44, 45, *45*
Eogan, George, 152
Er Grah/Er Vingle Carnac mound,
  Brittany, 24
Er Lannic cromlechs, Brittany, 19, 23
Evans, Arthur, 86
Évora district, Portugal, 9, 47–48, 49, 50, 52

Fairies Rock. *See* La Roche-aux-Fées gallery
  grave, Brittany
Fajada Butte, New Mexico, 213n12
Falbygden region, Sweden, 196
Farrer, James, 167, 169
Filitosa statue menhirs, Corsica, 69–70, *70*
Finistère *départment*, Brittany, 24, 27
Fletcher, Alice C., 54
folklore, 13–15, 22, 28, 42, 44, 81, 82, 86, 94,
  112, 159, 169
Fontanaccia dolmen, Corsica, 69
Friedrich, Caspar David, 11, *12*
Funnel Beaker culture, 184, 220n1

Galles, Réne, 20
Gavrinis passage grave, Brittany, *23*, 23–24
Géant du Manio menhir, Brittany, 27
Geoffrey of Monmouth, 113
Geographical Information Software, 42
Geraldus Cambrensis ("Gerald of Wales"), 14
Gervasio, Michele, 39

Ġgantija temple complex, Gozo, *56*, 57, 58, 61
giants' tombs. *See tomba dei giganti*, Sardinia
Giot, Pierre-Roland, 24, 26
Giovinazzo gallery grave, Italy, 39
Gollenstein menhir, Germany, 181–82, *182*
Gors Fawr stone circle, Wales, 90
Gowland, William, 105
Grand Harbor, Malta, 60, 64
Grant, Walter, 171–72
Gray, Harold Saint George, 96
Great Dolmen of Zambujeiro, Portugal,
  51–52, *52*
Great Langdale, England, 82, 85
Grey Croft stone circle, England, 213n13
Grey Wethers Fyfield Down, Wiltshire, 98
Grey Wethers stone circle, Cornwall, 98
Griffiths, W. E., 93
Grimes, W. F., 135, 137
Grønhøj passage grave, Denmark, 192
Grønjaegers Høj, passage grave, Denmark,
  193–94
Grosjean, Roger, 69–71
Gyrn Goch, Wales, 133, *134*

Ħagar Quim temple complex, Malta, 59
Ħal Saflieni Hypogeum, Malta, 63–66, *65*, *66*
Harrison, Tom, 7
Hawkins, Gerald, 111
head-hunting, 217n13
Heapstown cairn, Ireland, 155
Hemp, W. J., 139, 141
Hencken, H. O'Neil, 158
Hilfeling, C. G. G., 11
Hjälteby passage grave, Sweden, 196
Hoedic Mesolithic cemetery, Brittany, 9–10,
  208n19
Hondsrug glacier, 187–88
Houel, Jean, 61
Hugboy, 169
Hulbjerg passage grave, Denmark,
  192–93, *193*
Hulehøj passage grave, Denmark, *6*
hunebedden megalithic tombs, Holland,
  187–90
hunter-gatherers, 8
hünengrabben megalithic tombs, Germany,
  184–86

Ille-et-Villaine, *départment* of, Brittany, 26
Imhotep (Egyptian god of medicine), 74
Inca civilization, 53
Iron Age, 10, 17, 23, 39, 41, 69, 88, 111, 129, 135, 161, 170, 182, 202, 214n2, 217n8
Isbister cairn, Orkney Islands, 176–77

jættestue graves, Denmark, 191
Jardin aux Moines megalithic enclosure, Brittany, 14
jewelry, 189, 208n8, 209n10
Joussaume, Roger, 33, 34, 48
Jutland, Denmark, 191, 192, 194

Karleby, Denmark, 196
Kåseberga, Sweden, 197
Kerlescan alignment, Brittany, 17–18
Kerloas menhir, Brittany, 27–28
Kermario alignment, Brittany, 17, *18*
Kernéléhen Peninsula, Brittany, 24
Kerzerho alignment, Brittany, 17
Kieller, Alexander, 99, 101–2, 215n7
King Eadred, 121
King's Men. *See* Rollright Stones stone circle, England
King Stone, 85–86
Kit's Coty House long barrow, England, 123, *123*
Kjærum, Poul, 195
Klekkende Høj passage grave, Denmark, 193, *194*
Knowth passage grave, Ireland, 151–53, *153*
Kodi district, island of Sumba, Indonesia, 7
Kong Asgers Høj passage grave, Denmark, 193
Kong Svends Høj passage grave, Denmark, 194

Labbacallee wedge tomb, Ireland, 159
La Chaussée Tirancourt gallery grave, France, 34–35
La Gran'mère du Chimquière. *See* Saint Martin menhir, Guernsey, Channel Islands
La Hogue Bie passage grave, Jersey, Channel Islands, *125*, 126
Lake Genève alignment, Switzerland, 35

Lake Neuchâtel alignment, Switzerland, 35–36
Lakota tribe, 2, 54, 121–22
langdysse dolmens, Denmark, 191, 193
Langeland, island of, Denmark, 192
La Pastora passage tomb, Andalusia, 46
La Peña de Los Enamorados, Andalusia, 42–43, *43*
Laporte, Luc, 33
La Roche-aux-Fées gallery grave, Brittany, 13, *15*, 26–27
La Table des Marchand passage grave, Brittany, 24, *25*, 29
La Tremblais menhir, Brittany, 14
LBK. *See* Linearbandkeramik culture
Leask, H. G., 159
Leclerc, Jean, 34, 35
Le Dèhus passage grave, Guernsey, Channel Islands, 126–28, *127*
Le Grand Menhir Brisé, Brittany, 28–29, *30*
Leisner, Georg and Vera, 49, 50
Le Manio long mound, Brittany, 18
Le Manio 2 long mound, Brittany, 18–19
Le Ménec alignment, Brittany, 17
Le Ménec cromlech, Brittany, 18
Le Petit-Chasseur necropolis, Switzerland, 35–38, *36*, *37*
Le Petit Mont passage grave, Brittany, 22–23
Le Roux, Charles-Tanguy, 23–24
Le Rouzic, Zachaire, 19, 20, 21, 209n5
Le Trepied passage grave, Guernsey, Channel Islands, 13
Li Muri Neolithic necropolis, Sardinia, 66–67
Lind, Bob G., 199
Lindeskov long dolmen, Denmark, 194
Linearbandkeramik culture (LBK), 34, 210n3
Listoghil megalithic tomb, Ireland, 156
Little Kit's Coty House long barrow, England, 123
Llŷn Peninsula, Wales, 133
Loanhead of Daviot recumbent stone circle, Scotland, 80
Loch Harray and Loch Stenness, Orkney Islands, 76, 165

Lockyer, Norman, 143
Lohra Steinkiste, Germany, 187
Long Meg and Her Daughters, stone circle, England, 80–81
Los Millares Copper Age settlement and passage graves, 45–46, *46*, 211n6
Lough Arrow, Ireland, 155
Loughcrew passage grave complex, Ireland, *154*, 154–55
Lubbock, John, 136
Lukis, Frederik Corbin, 128
Lynch, Ann, 162

Macalister, Robert Alexander Stewart, 155
Maeshowe passage grave, Orkney Islands, 165–69, *166*, *167*
Maeve's Heap. *See* Miosgán Meabha cairn, Ireland
Magri, Father Emmanuel, 64, 65
Mahón, Menorca, 73
Mané-er-Hröek Carnac mound, Brittany, 21–22
Masset, Claude, 34
Medinet Habu temple, Egypt, 71
Medway megalithic tombs, England, 122–24
megalithic art, 23, 26, 68, 107–8, 126–28, 139, 144, 148, 149, 152, 153, 155
megalithic "yard," 19, 209n3
Menai Strait, Wales, 139
Mên-an-Tol megalith, Cornwall, 14
Menga dolmen, Spain, 41–43, *42*
Mesolithic ("Middle Stone Age"), 4, 8, 9, 27, 48, 69, 140, 157, 208n19
Meux, Sir Henry, 97
Midhowe stalled cairn, island of Rousay, Scotland, *171*, 171–73
midsummer sunrise, 85, 104, 143, 179
midwinter sunrise, 27, 91, 97, 150–51, 185, 194, 195, 196
midwinter sunset, 81, 89, 91, 104, 153, 165, 179, 185, 194, 221n7
Milky Way, 54, *160*
Miosgán Meabha cairn, Ireland, 156, *156*
Mitjana, Rafael, 42
Mizen Peak, Ireland, 159, 161
Mnajdra temple complex, Malta, 55–56

Mondego Valley, Portugal, 53
Mont Beigua, Italy, 213n15
Monte dos Almendres, Portugal, 48
Montelirio passage grave, Spain, 46–47
Mont Viso, Italy, 213n15
Moore, Henry, 11
Mosso, Angelo, 39

Naseröd South round dolmen, Sweden, 196
Nash, Paul, 11
naveta monuments, Menorca, 71, *72*
Neolithic ("New Stone Age"), 4
Ness of Brodgar, Orkney Islands, 212n4
Newgrange passage tomb, Ireland, 147–51, *148*, *149*, *150*
Normanton Down Bronze Age barrow cemetery, England, 138
North Star, 54
nuraghi towers, Sardinia, 68, 73

O'Connor, Stanley, 7
Old Keig recumbent stone circle, Scotland, 79
Oliver, Neil, 75
Orkney-Cromarty megalithic tombs, 170, 173, 176
Orkneyinga Saga, 168, 219n6
Outer Hebrides, Scotland, 78

pagan, 4, 14, 81, 102, 126, 128
Paleolithic ("Old Stone Age"), 4
Parc le Breos Cwm Cotswold-Severn long barrow, Wales, 136–37
Parker Pearson, Mike, 109, 111
Pawnee people, 54
Pays de Loire region, France, 26
Penmaenmawr, Wales, 92
Pennant, Thomas, 141
Pentre Ifan portal dolmen, Wales, *5*, 131–36, *134*
Pemnwyrlod Cotswold-Severn long barrow, Wales, 138
Péquart, Marthe and Saint-Just, 208n19
Piccolo San Bernardo Cromlech, Italy, 39
Piggot, Stuart, 101, 119, 121, 175
Pina, Henrique Leonor, 48, 51
Plouarzel, Brittany, 27

Pogio Rota megaliths, Italy, 40
Poskaer Stenhus round dolmen, Sweden, 191–92, *192*
Poulnabrone portal dolmen, Ireland, 161–63, *162*
Po Valley, Italy, 210n8
Powell, Terence, 132, 143, 175
Preseli Hills, Wales, 107, 108, 109, 110, 112, 113
Price, L., 159
Prisé-le-Charrière long mound, France, xiii, *33*, 33–34

Quanterness passage grave, Orkney Islands, 169, 170
Quoyness passage grave, Orkney Islands, 169–70

Remedello culture, 37, 210n8
Renfrew, Colin, 8, 170
Rhuys Penisula, Brittany, 22
Ridgeway, England, 120
Ring of Brodgar stone circle, Orkney Islands, *76*, 76–77, 78, 165
Ritchie, Graham, 77, 78, 177
River Boyne, Ireland, 148
Roberts, Jack, 153
Rollright Stones stone circle, England, 84–86, *86*, 213n21
Rowlands, Henry, 90
rundysse dolmens, Denmark, 191

Sa Coveccada dolmen, Sardinia, *67*, 67–68
Saint Brynach, 135
Saint Geneviève, 13
Saint Martin de Corleans dolmens, Switzerland, 38
Saint Martin menhir, Guernsey, Channel Islands, 128–29
Saint Méen, 14
Salisbury Plain, England, 107, 108–9, 113, 215n12
Samarelli, Francesco, 39
Samhain Celtic festival, 161
Scarre, Chris, 33
Schimmer Es *hunebed*, Holland, 189, *189*

Schonhovious, Antonius, 188
Sea Peoples, 71
Seelenloch ("soul hole"), 187
Seelewey cairn, Ireland, 156
"Seine-Oise-Marne" culture, 34
Serra da Estrala ("mountain range of the star"), Portugal, 53
Silbury Hill, England, 100, *101*, 116
Simison, Ronnie, 176
Sioux tribe, 121–22
Siret, Henri and Luis, 45
Skara Brae Neolithic village, Orkney Islands, 78, 169, 213n6
Skinner, John, 141
Skogsdala long dolmen, Sweden, 198
Smyth, William Henry, 62
Société Jersiaise, 126
Söderberg, Bengst, 199
Somerville, Boyle, 89
Spellenstein menhir, Germany, 182, *183*
spina bifida, 119
Stanton Drew megalithic complex, England, 83–84, *84*
Stawell, Ralph, 103
Steinkisten tombs, Germany, 186–87
Stonehenge, England, 11, *12*, 103–13, *106*, 136, 138, 147, 181, 199, 214n1; Altar Stone, 105; Aubrey Holes, 104, 110; Bluestone Circle, 107; Bluestone Oval, 107; Great Trilithon, 104, 105; Heel Stone, 104; Sarsen Circle, 104, 105–6, 107; Sarsen Trilithon Horseshoe, 104, 107, 111
Stones of Stenness stone circle, Orkney Islands, 76, *77*, 77–78, 165
Strömberg, Märta, 197, 198
Stukeley, William, 10, 85, 95, 99, 100, 102, 104, 107, 118, 214n3, 215n12
Swinside stone circle, England, 85

Tabone, Joseph Attard, 62
Talatí de Dalt *taula* monument, Menorca, *73*, *73*
Talayotic period, Menorca, 71, 72
talayot towers, Menorca, 73
Talheim "death pit," Germany, 207n7
Taravo Valley, Corsica, 69

Tarxien temple complex, Malta, 58–61, *59*, *60*, 65

taula monuments, Menorca, 72–74

Taunt, Henry W., 85, 213n21

Tennison, Louisa, 156

tertre long mounds, Brittany, 18

Téviec Mesolithic cemetery, Brittany, 9–10, 208n19

tholos-type passage tombs, 43, 44, *45*, 46

Thom, Alexander, 19, 209n3

Thomas, Henry Herbert, 107–8

Thurnam, John, 116, 118

tomba dei giganti ("giants' tombs"), Sardinia, 68–69

Tomb of the Eagles. *See* Isbister cairn, Orkney Islands

Torajan Highlands, Indonesia, 7

Torrean people, 70, 71

torri towers, 70, 73

transepted passages, 116–17, 120

Trepuco *taula*, Menorca, 73

Troldkirken long mound, Denmark, 194

Tsimshian people, 2

Tumulus de Saint-Michel Carnac mound, Brittany, 20–22, *21*

Turner, J. M. W., 11

Tustrup megalithic cemetery, Denmark, 194–96, *195*

Ty-Isaf long cairn, Wales, 137, 138

Uenze, Otto, 187

Uffington Castle Iron Age hillfort, England, 217n8

Vale d'el Rei cromlech, Portugal, 48

Vale Maria do Meio cromlech, Portugal, 48

Valencina de la Concepción passage tombs, Andalusia, 46–47

Vales do Meio cromlech, Portugal, *9*

"Varna Chieftain," 208n8

Vatolahy standing stones, Madagascar, 111

Viera dolmen, Spain, 43, *44*

Visbek Brautwagen, 186

Visbeker Braut and Braütigaum monuments, Germany, 185, *186*

Vivian, Henry Hussey, 136

Wainwright, Geoffrey, 109, 110, 111–12

Wartberg culture, Germany, 186, 220n4

Wayland's Smithy long barrow, England, 115, *120*, 120–22, 217n8

West Kennet long barrow, England, 116–19, *117*

Whispering Knights megalithic tomb, England, 86

Wilde, William, 151

witches/witchcraft, 13, 81, 86, 159

Wordsworth, William, 81

Wyndham-Quin, Edwin, 136

Xagħra Circle, Gozo, 61–63; "Shaman's Cache," 62–63, *63*

Y Meni Hirion. *See* Druids' Circle, Wales

Ysbyty Cynfyn stone circle, Wales, 90

Zambujeiro, Great Dolmen of, Portugal, 51–52, *52*

Zammit, Themistocles "Temi," 58, 59–60, 64, 65

Züschen Steinkiste, Germany, 186–87, *187*

About the Author

Julian Heath was educated at the University of Liverpool, being awarded BA and MA degrees in archaeology. He has since gone on to lecture at the university and write several books, such as *Life in Copper Age Britain*, *Archaeology Hotspot Egypt*, and *Warfare in Neolithic Europe*, and he is particularly interested in the archaeology of prehistoric Europe and ancient Egypt. In addition to his writing, he has provided the illustrations for several archaeological publications and worked as an excavator and finds illustrator at various sites in Europe and Egypt. Heath has also worked with respected Egyptologist and author Joyce Tyldesley, providing the illustrations for her two children's books: *Stories from Ancient Egypt* and *Stories from Ancient Greece and Rome*. He now enjoys life in the Wirral Peninsula, Northwest England, an area noted for its Viking heritage and beautiful countryside, although he is proud to be a native "Scouser" of the famous city of Liverpool.